Daughters

of

Dissent

Elaine Kaye, Janet Lees and Kirsty Thorpe

with contributions from

Susan Durber, John Humphreys,
Marjorie Lewis and David Thompson

ISBN 0 85346 225 9
© The United Reformed Church, 2004

Published by The United Reformed Church
86 Tavistock Place, London WC1H 9RT

The
United
Reformed
Church

Produced by Communications and Editorial, Graphics Office

Printed by mcpgoldies limited, Units B2 & B3,
Hatton Square Business Centre, London EC1N 7RJ

Contents

Foreword

One of the joys of history is that it will never be fully told or completely understood, for human beings and human institutions are mysteriously made and perplexingly complex. History is always provisional. A newly discovered source document or an interpretation inspired by a different way of reading can change our understandings and challenge the way we view the familiar. The Daughters of Dissent project is important both because it has discovered new sources, and because it offers new ways of reading the familiar.

Dissenting history knows well how to offer subverting readings of a dominant myth, for Nonconformity in our three nations has been about an alternative way of being church. The 'hermeneutics of suspicion' come naturally to us. It is therefore all the more bracing to find a group of historians performing a neat deconstruction job on one of our favourite stories about ourselves – namely that we are pioneers in the ministry of women and can teach the rest of the Church Catholic a thing or two about equality. By God's grace we were pioneers; but now, thanks to Elaine Kaye, Janet Lees and Kirsty Thorpe, and to their many collaborators, we know the cost of that courage, and a due humility should mark our rhetoric.

The story of the church is the story of those who are 'in Christ', and it is a joy to discover the stories of such saints as Selina Hadland and Anna Lloyd, Margaret Bondfield and Jessie Spicer, Constance Coltman and Kathleen Hendry (of whom we already knew a little), Ella Gordon and Madge Saunders. In hearing their stories, we learn more of Christ's story. The project has allowed us to hear the voice of women. It has concentrated (not exclusively, but inevitably) on the story of the battle for ordination and therefore on ministers. Church history does that, almost by default. However, once it told the story as the story of ordained men. Thanks to Daughters of Dissent we have been liberated from that constraint. We have been shown a way towards a more inclusive telling of the church's story and we cannot but be richer for it. Maybe that might prompt us to venture on and discover not only the voice of the pulpit, but also the spirituality of the pew.

David Cornick

Acknowledgment

We are grateful to all the people who have helped us with this project over the last nine years.

First, we should like to thank all those who took part in the conference held at Mansfield College in September 1998, especially those whose contributions are included in this volume: Susan Durber, John Humphreys, Marjorie Lewis, and David Thompson.

The following were generous in sending comments and ideas, either in writing or during interviews: Hazel Barkham, Mary Barr Beryl Bennett, Gillian Bobbett, Gwynith Chalmers, Frances Chambers, Elizabeth Charles, Janet Chisholm, Ruth Clarke, Christine Collin, Kate Compston, Cheryl Dibeela, Joan Duncan, Susan Durber, Doreen English, Mary Evans, Selem Fagen, Elnora Ferguson, Christine Fowler, Rowena Francis, Rosalind Goodfellow, Dorothy Havergal Shaw, Kathleen Hendry, Margaret Laurie, Doris Leyshon, Janet Llewellyn, Arthur Macarthur, Catherine Middleton, Elizabeth Nash, Elisabeth Neale, Alice Platts, Tizeta Powell, Sheila Sanderson, Madge Saunders, May Segain, Jacqueline Smith, Gwen Smithies, Rachel Storr, Margaret Taylor, Sheila Thorpe, Tony Tucker, Janet Webber, Betty Williams, Janet Wootton, and Justine Wyatt.

Martin Smith has given valuable help with statistics.

We owe a great debt of gratitude to Sheila Maxey, and to Roger and Yvonne Tomes, who read through the manuscript and made valuable comments, and saved us from many mistakes (those that remain are our own).

Carol Rogers and Sara Foyle have been a great help during the process of production.

We should like to dedicate this volume to all the women, some named and others unnamed, whose dedication to the Gospel has inspired this work.

Introduction

The more things change, the more they stay the same, so the saying goes. There was a definite sense of the old and the new, side by side, when three British women gathered on 17 September 2002 in the Ukrainian (Catholic) Cathedral of the Holy Family in Exile, Binney Street, London. Elaine Kaye, Janet Lees and Kirsty Thorpe were in the building formerly known as the King's Weigh House Congregational Church to commemorate an event that might have seemed somewhat surprising to the present day worshippers. In that place 85 years earlier, a 'particularly interesting ceremony' [1] had occurred, as Constance Todd and her husband-to-be Claud Coltman were ordained to the Christian ministry.

The three collaborators, all members of the United Reformed Church, were shown around the church by Ukrainian priest Father Stephen Oracz. Together they had been exploring for nearly a decade the background, context and consequences of that historic ordination on 17 September 1917. Now they were standing in the place where London minister G Stanley Russell had told a large wartime congregation that the ordination of a woman meant a new era in relations between men and women was dawning. As Father Oracz invited them behind the magnificent painted icon screen to see the large wooden altar they were conscious of being welcomed into a holy place within a tradition where women's leadership has a very different face from that in British Nonconformity. The labelled coat peg of Dr Orchard, minister of the King's Weigh House Church at the time of the ordination, still survives in what is now the sacristy and forms another link with the building's past.

Elaine Kaye, Janet Lees and Kirsty Thorpe commemorated events 85 years earlier with their own 'interesting ceremony' and shared a prayer of penitence written in 1984 to mark the fortieth anniversary of the ordination of the first ever woman Anglican priest, Florence Tim Oi Li, in Singapore. As the subject matter they had been working on had often uncovered women's sense of wandering and restlessness, both in terms of ministry and of relations with men, it felt particularly appropriate that the King's Weigh House Church building should now be dedicated to the 'Holy Family in Exile'. This offered hope that people might hold work and relationships together well, even in a strange land, through the power of God's love. Equally propitious was the realisation that 17 September is also the feast day of Hildegard of Bingen, newly rediscovered giant of medieval mysticism, spirituality and prophecy.

These three women had been engaged with the project, which climaxed on 17 September 2002, since midway through the World Council of Churches Ecumenical Decade of Churches in Solidarity with Women (1988-1998). The United Reformed Church had set up an initiative, a network called Sharing People in Network (SPIN) for women and men, to further the aims of the Decade. At that time Janet Lees was one of its joint co-ordinators and proposed that SPIN should consider a project to recover the stories of women who had been active in promoting the ministry and contribution of women in the United Reformed Church and its predecessors. SPIN had already published the results of a Women's Research Project in 1992 when Keran Olm-Stoelting, a United Church of Christ minister on sabbatical leave from the United States, had interviewed a wide range of women from all over the country about their views of women's current contribution to the church.[2] However, SPIN was still struggling to involve more people in issues relating to the Decade, one aim of which was 'women's full participation in church and community life.'

Elaine Kaye had already written about Constance Coltman.[3] There were also many other stories emerging from women of all ages about their experiences of the Church, not all of which were positive. It seemed that there was a risk of losing some of these experiences as the storytellers got older (indeed, some of the earlier correspondents have died since this project started). Women's history was popular so why not church women's history? Elaine Kaye agreed to become a collaborator in a project which had little more than a name at that stage: 'Daughters of Dissent'. Many years previously, she had been a member of the King's Weigh House Church in London and had known both Constance and Claud Coltman. She had gradually become aware that in their quiet way they had been pioneers. Constance Coltman was the first woman to be ordained in Britain and had been in joint ministry with her husband for most of their lives. As Elaine Kaye says: 'At that time I regret to say that I failed to realise how significant an event that was and only on one occasion had I really talked to Constance about it, and that was very near the end of her life.' However, by the 1980s she had begun to appreciate more of its significance, and as 1987 approached it seemed important that the seventieth anniversary of this event should not go unnoticed. She then researched and published articles about Constance Coltman's life and her understanding of ministry.

About this time the question of the ordination of women was being debated in the Church of England. The experience of Congregationalists and other Nonconformists in this respect was largely ignored, which made the editors of this project even more determined to bring this story to a wider audience. Here was a worthwhile challenge. It coincided with the enormous growth of interest in women's history and new interpretations of that history, which also needed to be brought to bear on the history of Congregationalism. Such a task seemed appropriate for Elaine Kaye, who was teaching denominational church history at Mansfield College at the time. Through links with Mansfield she knew Kirsty Thorpe, then a United Reformed Church ordinand, who readily agreed to become a third collaborator. The three would make valuable and interesting collaborators.

Kirsty Thorpe immediately recognised the Daughters of Dissent project as something she had been waiting to do, and preparing for unwittingly over a period of years. In 1980, while studying journalism in Canada, she had discovered Christian feminism and through it a way into adult faith. It was in Canada that she had her first positive experiences of sisterhood. This was also the place where she first heard women ministers talking about hidden frustrations, where she had seen an Anglican Church start to come to terms with the reality of women priests, and where she had first become incensed at arrogant, rude responses against inclusive language. Coming back to Britain, after ten months in Canada, had been a shock. The Church in the UK was decades behind in the debate on women's participation. The United Reformed Church, her own tradition, seemed little changed at congregational level despite having then had 60 years' experience of ordained women's ministry. Small wonder that when SPIN emerged, as a response to the WCC Decade, developments were eagerly awaited. There were many questions to explore. Not least among these was why a long tradition of ordaining women had not brought about the longed-for transformation of the church community. Kirsty Thorpe also had lived in Wales for approaching 20 years at the start of the project. That had given her a helpful perspective on the way some cultures and languages can be marginalized and silenced.

The collaboration went ahead as the three women began to explore the issues around women's contribution to the life and ministry of the United Reformed Church. They learned something about the size of the task and the methods that would be appropriate to further exploration. They each had their own strengths and interests which shaped the project. To begin with they wrote to all those women listed in the *United Reformed Church Year Book* who had been ordained before union in 1972. Later they wove in some experiences of the women in the Churches of Christ[4] and the Congregational Union of Scotland[5] and of Congregational women who did not join the United Reformed Church.

They also began to collect stories from anyone who wanted to send something. It was surprising what people sent: pamphlets of local church history that highlighted the roles played by local women in leadership, stories of local people's experiences of women in ministry, eldership, Sunday School, articles from local newspapers and so on. The net was also cast wider through archives, networking with other scholars, previously published material, and the contributions of laywomen. It was clear that much of this material was dynamite: firstly because local people were getting involved in a SPIN project, something that had been difficult to initiate up until then, and secondly because it did not all support the party line or the official story of the United Reformed Church's record on women and ministry.

Meanwhile, Kirsty Thorpe was experiencing a 'recurring pattern' for women in ministry of having completed training but not being in pastoral charge. Taking matters into her own hands, she applied to do a PhD and began it in the Centre for Religion, Culture and Gender at the University of Manchester in 1997. Her thesis explores how

Congregationalism found itself in the position of pioneering women's ordained ministry. It draws together ideas and approaches from different forms of feminist theory and criticism. This research has fed into Daughters of Dissent. As she says: 'The model of the lone academic researcher is quite simply foreign to a collaborative, women's project like this one.'

After collecting much material over five or six years the collaborators decided to present some of the 'story so far' to a conference at Mansfield College, Oxford. This was the college where Constance Coltman had trained and the conference marked the eighty-first anniversary of the ordination. Thus in September 1998 about 40 people came to hear the three women present their work in progress and to listen to four other people responding to this material. The four respondents were David Thompson, Lecturer (now Reader) in Modern Church History and Director of the Centre for Advanced Religious and Theological Studies at Cambridge (a former Moderator of the United Reformed Church General Assembly); Susan Durber, United Reformed Church minister in Oxford (formerly Mona Powell Fellow at Northern College, Manchester); John Humphreys, then Moderator of the United Reformed Church National Synod of Wales; and Marjorie Lewis-Cooper (now Marjorie Lewis), ordained black woman from the United Church of Jamaica, then serving the United Reformed Church as Multi-racial, Multi-cultural Officer. The proceedings were chaired by Ruth Clarke (a former Moderator of the United Reformed Church General Assembly). All the responses to the project were valuable: many are included in this volume.

The book has twelve chapters which represent different aspects of the Daughters of Dissent project. It opens with a scene-setting chapter by Elaine Kaye in which the threads of the development of women's involvement in the traditions of the United Reformed Church are traced back into the nineteenth and early twentieth centuries, within the Church and the wider world. There follows a chapter by Janet Lees outlining some of the research and interpretative methods used in the Daughters of Dissent study.

In chapters three to eight a number of themes in ministry by women in the twentieth century are then taken up and explored further. Elaine Kaye examines the way in which structures and the forming of the United Reformed Church have worked for and against women's participation. She then looks at this same struggle in relation to theological education and preparation for ministry. Janet Lees and Kirsty Thorpe explore the history of preaching by women, including the experiences of some contemporary women preachers. In chapters six and seven Elaine Kaye examines the themes of Justice and Peace, and Ecumenism from the perspective of women participants. Janet Lees, a white woman, examines the United Reformed Church's record on the interactions between racism and sexism and Marjorie Lewis-Cooper, who is black, gives a response.

In chapter nine, Kirsty Thorpe and Janet Lees draw on further narratives and material collected from women themselves. Here women tell the stories of their own ministries. In chapters ten and eleven Kirsty Thorpe deploys feminist analytical tools to examine the history of women's ministry as it has been told both within the United Reformed Church and in the wider Church. Chapter eleven also includes evidence of recurring patterns in the way women's leadership has developed which come from outside the church. The challenge of the Daughters of Dissent project is how to respond to the recurring patterns and repeated stories that have been uncovered. Chapter twelve contains the responses of two male theologians, John Humphreys and David Thompson, who were invited to reflect on the project as 'work in progress' at the 1998 conference day. In the afterword Susan Durber, a minister in the United Reformed Church, sets the whole project in the wider context of rethinking gender issues not only for the Church but the whole of our culture.

The support felt by the authors as a result of the day conference at Mansfield College was a significant turning point in their confidence about the project. They take responsibility for the method by which various strands of recorded history, both traditional archival material and contemporary oral narratives, are woven together to illustrate themes in the lives of women and their contribution to the life of the United Reformed Church or its predecessors. They are grateful to all who have contributed, and for being able to include many diverse voices. This is only one milestone in the life of the Daughters of Dissent project. It is probably far from being the last word and all three women recognise their shared commitment to continue the pilgrimage as Daughters of Dissent.

Elaine Kaye   Oxford
Kirsty Thorpe   Northwich
Janet Lees   Sheffield

17 September 2002, being the Eighty-fifth Anniversary of the Ordination of Constance Coltman (née Todd) to the Christian Ministry.
Feast of St Hildegard of Bingen.

Chapter 1

Daughters of Dissent 1840-1919

> ... the great women of the Church of all generations have always had their due. It is for the ordinary woman church worker, whether professional or voluntary that recognition has had to be sought and won.[1]

This chapter will consider the role of women and the ideas of gender among the churches of the Congregational, Presbyterian and Churches of Christ traditions, that is, the traditions which have come together in the United Reformed Church in Britain.[2] There will also be some reference to the Baptist tradition (from which the Churches of Christ developed). These are all the heirs of Dissenting traditions which grew out of the religious conflicts of the seventeenth century in England and Wales.

During the turmoil of the conflicts of the mid-seventeenth century women found opportunities to take an active and significant part in religious life, including preaching.[3] Katherine Chidley, wife of a Shrewsbury tailor, was an outstanding radical Independent of the 1640s, whose significance was long overlooked. When official censorship collapsed she was able to publish *The Justification of the Independent Churches of Christ* in 1641 in answer to Thomas Edwards' attack, and was one of the leaders of the London separatists in that diocese.[4] Congregational polity, with its emphasis on the sovereignty of the church meeting, the gathered community of believers, men and women, might have been thought hospitable to the equal status of women, and indeed sometimes was in its earliest years. But the situation changed after 1660. The legislation of the 1660s, after the restoration of the monarchy, recognised the existence of 'Dissenters' as an identifiable group within society, but limited their civil rights. The Toleration Act of 1689 guaranteed their right to worship but did not extend their civil rights. Thus Dissent became institutionalised, with four main identifiable groups: Congregationalists (often called Independents), Presbyterians, Baptists and Quakers. Dissent now became more 'respectable', and its adherents were anxious to assert their loyalty to the Crown and to the laws of the country. As Dissenters adopted more of the culture of the rest of society, so women ceased to play any significant public role.

This lack of women in significant roles and their absence from most of the recorded history of the eighteenth and nineteenth centuries can be illustrated from two histories of Congregationalism in the mid-twentieth century. When Albert Peel published a book entitled *The Congregational Two Hundred 1530-1948* (London: Independent Press, 1948) he claimed to have done something to redress the masculine bias of his previous book entitled *A Hundred Eminent Congregationalists* (London: Independent Press, 1927), which included only one woman (Elizabeth Barrett Browning); but the result was the inclusion in his second volume of five women altogether, four of them American.[5] Fourteen years later, to mark the tercentenary of the ejection of Dissenting ministers in 1662, R Tudur Jones published a detailed and in many ways comprehensive history of Congregationalism in England since 1662, with over 1,325 biographical references. A study of the index reveals that of these references, 1,284 refer to men and 41 to women. Even David Cornick's *Under God's Good Hand* (London: United Reformed Church, 1998) has few references to women, though the author recognises the need to re-discover their history.

These authors wrote their histories using the sources accumulated since the seventeenth century, but without too much questioning of the accepted tradition in this respect. Yet all the evidence points to the fact that more women than men attended church during the nineteenth and early twentieth centuries, and that they frequently took an important role in church life. The growth of hymn singing helped to give women a more active role in worship. Clive Field's research has led him to the conclusion that among Congregationalists women on average made up two-thirds of congregations, and that they usually predominated in the membership.[6] Using an unusually rich collection of family papers, Marjorie Reeves has uncovered something of the astonishing extent and quality of the writing and correspondence of some gifted Nonconformist women (mostly Baptist) in the west of England in the eighteenth century. These women were steeped in the Bible, interested in theology and avid readers of devotional works.[7] Yet usually they had been very limited in their formal education. Clyde Binfield has discovered diaries and other papers relating to women and used them to provide a more inclusive history of Nonconformist life. One hopes that there are other such archives still waiting to be discovered.

The patriarchal ethos of the nineteenth century, reflected in the denominational structures and the restriction of the ordained ministry to men, meant that both official records and all but the most recent historical accounts give prominence to the achievements of men, but little to those of women. This chapter is an attempt to bring the contribution of women, and of those men who recognised the value of what they could offer, into the public arena, and therefore to go some way towards redressing the balance of received history. It also raises questions relating to the connection between Christianity and the feminist movement, and looks at the response of the churches of the particular traditions being considered here to the pressures from feminist reformers.

The modern feminist movement can be traced back to Mary Wollstonecraft's *Vindication of the Rights of Woman* (1792), a radical work inspired by the ideals of the French Revolution, one not much noticed in the author's lifetime, but deeply influential in subsequent years. Its author's unconventional lifestyle as well as her revolutionary opinions ensured that it would find little favour within ordinary church circles, though she had many friends among the 'rational Dissenters'. In the first half of the nineteenth century at least, the accepted views of the status of women were based on church teaching of the subordinationist position of women, linked to an identification of women with a particular ideal of feminine piety.[8]

It was only an exceptional woman like Selina, Countess of Huntingdon (1707-91),[9] a widowed peeress, who was able to use her legal right to appoint private chaplains and to act as patron of leading figures in the Evangelical Revival. Eventually the chapels under her patronage were registered as Dissenting Meeting Houses. Many of her followers became Congregationalists, while others remained in 'The Countess of Huntingdon's Connexion'.

The generally accepted views reflected to some extent the economic changes of the late eighteenth and early nineteenth centuries, which amongst the middle classes who predominated in the Nonconformist churches being considered here created a separation between the worlds of work and home detrimental to the position of women. Whereas the worlds of work and home were not distinct in earlier centuries and women were usually involved in both, they now became identified with domestic life, or at least with spheres outside the home which concerned women alone, while men were viewed as the sole inhabitants of the world of work. As cultural and intellectual activities became more professionalised, upper and middle class women were excluded from public pursuits such as medicine and the fine arts in which they had previously participated.[10] There developed the concept of 'separate spheres' for men and women, and there was a growing tendency to regard women as both weaker and purer than men, whose protection they therefore needed. It is not surprising that there was a revival of interest in the chivalric tradition during the nineteenth century.[11]

The more conventional view of the role of women can be found in the writings of two Congregationalists, one female and one male. Sarah Ellis (née Stickney, 1812-72) was the second wife of the Revd William Ellis (1794-1872), whose major life's work was as a missionary and then as secretary of the London Missionary Society; he also had pastoral charge of a Congregational church in Hertfordshire for a time. Sarah Ellis was brought up in the Society of Friends, but joined a Congregational church in 1837, the year of her marriage. She was a prolific writer who achieved considerable literary fame through the publication of several books on the theme of women's role: *The Women of England* (1839), *The Daughters of England* (1842), *The Wives of England* (1843) and *The Mothers of England* (1843). In the preface to *The Women of England* she stated that her books were addressed particularly to 'that estimable class of females who might be more specifically denominated *women*, and who yet enjoy the privilege of liberal education, with exemption from the pecuniary necessities of labour, but are almost wholly overlooked' rather than those who might be described as 'ladies'. Such women, she wrote, were important in 'upholding the moral worth of our country,' and their education should inculcate that 'disinterested kindness' which was the chief quality for which they were respected. While she expected that few women would find themselves called on to speak Latin, Italian or

French, all would be expected to visit the poor and the sick. Underlying her advice was the requirement to 'be content to be inferior in bodily strength'.[12] Presumably she inculcated these principles in the school for young ladies which she ran at Rawdon House.

Similar views could have been heard from the pulpit of Carrs Lane Congregational Church in Birmingham (a reasonably prosperous church whose members were largely middle-class), where John Angell James was minister. *Female Piety, or the Young Woman's Friend and Guide Through Life to Immortality* was originally a series of sermons especially addressed to young women. John Angell James was already very well known as the author of *The Anxious Inquirer* (London: 1834), a book which ran to six editions within the first year. His sermons to young women expressed the general assumptions of preachers and church leaders in all denominations of the period – that men and women had separate spheres of life and work. He quoted scripture (Ephesians 5 and I Corinthians 11, for example) in support of the view that woman is divinely appointed as subordinate to man:

> ... man shines as the primary planet, reflecting the glory of God, who is the
> orb of the moral universe; and woman shines as the satellite of man, deriving
> her splendour from the same source, and while equally obeying the law of the
> central luminary, is created for the primary dependent body, revolves in its
> attraction, follows in its course, and ministers to its comfort.[13]

At the same time, he recognised that Christianity had done much to elevate the position of women. Because of this women had a particular role and responsibility in spreading Christianity: '... the finishing stroke which Christianity gives in elevating the condition of women, is, by inviting and employing their energies and influence in promoting the spread of religion in the world.'[14] He recognised that a reading of Romans 16 demonstrates that the earliest age of Christianity was in advance of later ages 'in the respect thus paid to the female sex, by officially employing them in the services of the church, and in the wisdom which made use of such available and valuable resources.'[15] But this insight was then virtually ignored in his sermon on 'Woman's Mission', which extolled marriage and the home as the proper sphere of women's influence. Those who did not marry were also to think of the domestic sphere as their proper place, for the calling of woman was 'to advance the comfort of man in his private relations'. To those who were drawn to the ideas and policies of the emerging women's movement, John Angell James announced: 'Neither reason nor Christianity invites woman to the professor's chair, nor conducts her to the bar, nor makes her welcome to the pulpit, nor admits her to the place of ordinary magistracy. They claim not for her the right of suffrage.'[16] This view was supported by a majority of both men and women in the churches at the time, though a few were beginning to challenge it.

The accepted wisdom of Sarah Ellis and John Angell James did not mean that women had hitherto been inactive within churches and church life. Frank Prochaska, in *Women and Philanthropy in Nineteenth Century England* (Oxford: Oxford University

Press, 1980) has demonstrated how philanthropy, especially in evangelical circles, was an acceptable outlet for the time, energy and money of middle-class women. The Church was regarded as an appropriate social sphere for women. Bazaars were fashionable in the nineteenth century, and women developed their organisational and entrepreneurial skills in running them. Countless examples could be discovered. Some of the most ambitious among Congregationalists were those organised by supporters of the Lancashire Independent College in 1882 in both Liverpool and Manchester. The Liverpool bazaar was set in a mock Chinese city, while St James's Hall in Manchester was transformed into a late mediaeval German town for ten days in May 1882. As a result, the College's heavy debt was transformed into a healthy balance within a matter of days.[17]

Women were extensively involved in visiting, in temperance movements,[18] in raising money for missionary societies, in all kinds of fund raising and in Sunday School teaching. A good recorded illustration of this is the work of Martha Sherman, wife of the minister of the Surrey Chapel in south London, for James Sherman wrote an appreciative biography of his wife after her death, with a full account of her contribution to church life.[19] Martha Sherman instituted a monthly class for young women, a Maternal Association for mothers 'whose education, piety and station gave them influence in church and congregation', and another similar association for 'the poor mothers of the congregation'. In addition she organised a committee of 'ladies' to raise funds for a new school room. This pattern of activity was expected of women who married ministers, and most of them fulfilled this with energy and dedication, yet their lives and contributions were usually recorded in one or two sentences at the end of their husbands' obituaries.

From this tradition of voluntary charitable work there developed within the Church of England in the mid-nineteenth century several different opportunities for full-time church work by women, providing a sphere of fulfilment for some of the 'surplus' women of Victorian England.[20] The first Sisterhood, separate from the parish system, was founded at Park Village in London in 1845; this and succeeding communities gave women experience of organisation and the exercise of authority. The first Anglican deaconess was 'set apart' in 1862, to be followed by many others. The non-denominational Ranyard Bible Women and the Anglican Church Army provided further opportunities for training and service amongst women of lower social standing.[21] The Wesleyan Methodists established an order of deaconesses in 1890, and the Baptists began appointing deaconesses two years later.

The Congregationalists had no officially recognised deaconesses until after the First World War, although a few individual congregations did employ full-time workers outside any formal organisation. The desirability of appointing Presbyterian deaconesses was raised in a report to the General Council of the Presbyterian Alliance in 1888, together with confirmation, in the view of the committee concerned, that the New Testament evidence prohibited the ordination of women. Although the Church of Scotland followed up this idea, little was done in England until much later.

In 1842, the year in which Sarah Ellis published *The Daughters of England*, another more radical voice was heard within Congregationalism. The minister of Ebley Chapel,[22] near Stroud, Benjamin Parsons,[23] published a remarkable book entitled *The Mental and Moral Dignity of Woman* (London: John Snow, 1842), to be followed three years later by *Education, the Birthright of Every Human Being* (London: John Snow, 1845).[24] Parsons (1797-1855) was a Gloucestershire man who had grown up during the hard years of the Napoleonic wars. The fact that his father was ruined by his landlord just days before the boy's birth, his father's sudden death when he was only six, and his own lameness caused by damp living conditions, all combined to produce a passionate radical preacher who supported the temperance movement, the campaign against the Corn Laws and the demands of the Chartists as well as his major concern of education. His good fortune in early life was to have attracted the attention of the evangelical preacher Rowland Hill, who helped him to gain a place at Wotton-under-Edge Grammar School, and led ultimately (after several years of working for a tailor) to his entering the college of the Countess of Huntingdon's Connexion at Cheshunt in 1821. He began his ministry at Ebley in 1826 and remained there for the rest of his life. In Ebley he established two day schools, one attached to the chapel, the other in his own house. His ministry was to a village community, largely working class, in the centre of the woollen cloth industry.

His express purpose in writing *The Mental and Moral Dignity of Woman* was 'to prove satisfactorily that the minds of women are equal to those of man'. His thinking on the position of women was stimulated through preparing a series of sermons on both male and female biblical characters during the earlier years of his ministry, and later through preaching an anniversary sermon which drew the attention of parents to the importance of the education of their daughters. The response to these encouraged him to develop his arguments in a book. His thinking was given a further spur by reading a review article in the *Westminster Review* for January 1841 on 'Woman and her social position' and finding himself in agreement with the reviewer's sympathies.

He wrote partly from his own experience that girls learn as well as boys, sometimes better. In the main section of the book he argued from a detailed categorisation of nine operations of the mind or thought, that in each, women's powers were equal to those of men. Like all clerical writers on the subject he quoted scripture, but came to different conclusions. He used his knowledge of Hebrew to demonstrate that the word employed in the Authorized Version to translate the description of woman in Genesis 2:18, 'help meet' actually placed woman on an equality with man, but had been debased by the current attribution of inferiority to women; '... nothing has tended more to degrade women than those low and vulgar interpretations which have been given to the text in question.'[25] When he quoted from Paul, it was from Galatians 3:28 rather than from the usual passages in Corinthians admonishing women to be silent. 'We shall, perhaps, by and by discover that in natural mental power, as in Christianity, there is neither "male nor female, barbarian nor Scythian, bond nor free"'.

It is difficult to assess the influence of Parsons's book. It went through three editions (1842, 1849 and 1856) and was generally welcomed by the *Evangelical Magazine*, which recognised the book's originality. But one book was not sufficient to bring about a real change of attitude.

No better example of Parsons's argument could be found than a young woman then known as Marian Evans (later known to the world as George Eliot). She was brought up within an Anglican family, but had Nonconformist friends, including the Sibree family,[26] and it was a Congregational minister (Francis Watts, tutor at Spring Hill College, Birmingham) whom the Sibrees asked to talk to her during a period of intense religious questioning. By 1842 she was avidly reading the latest German theology, and two years later was invited to undertake the translation of D F Strauss's massive work *Das Leben Jesu*. It was published in 1846 as *The Life of Jesus, Critically Examined*, without any credit to her; her fee for the two years' work was £20.

Her novels reveal an interest in both religion and the social position of women, though despite being a close friend of supporters of women's rights such as Barbara Leigh Smith and Bessie Rayner Parkes, she herself was never a radical campaigner for them. However, when she left her family in 1851 to establish herself as an independent single woman journalist in London, her lifestyle symbolised the challenge which she and others were now prepared to make to conventional ideas about the position of women.[27]

The decade in which Marian Evans moved to London was the decade in which the women's movement began to gain momentum. Though we may now label it 'feminism' (while being careful to recognise that there were in fact many 'feminisms'), the actual word did not gain currency until the end of the nineteenth century. It was in the mid-1850s that Florence Nightingale challenged male bureaucracy and established an independent role for women as nurses. In 1855 George Eliot's friend Barbara Leigh Smith (a cousin of Florence Nightingale, later Madame Bodichon[28]) formed the first feminist committee, whose aim was to collect petitions in support of a parliamentary bill to secure the rights to property of married women.[29] Both she and another leading figure, Bessie Rayner Parkes, had been brought up as Unitarians.[30] It was from this group that there emerged the 'Langham Place Circle' of like-minded women, who were responsible for producing the *English Women's Journal* from 1857, and around whom several reforming groups gathered. A decade later the movement for women's suffrage began. It was in 1861 that John Stuart Mill, with the help of Harriet Taylor Mill, wrote his famous work on *The Subjection of Women* (though it was not published until 1869), in which he argued that the legal subordination of one sex to another was intrinsically wrong, and that 'it ought to be replaced by a principle of perfect equality, admitting no power or privilege on the one side, nor disability on the other'. The argument over women's status now shifted from church teaching to a utilitarian basis of 'equal rights', and the means to improve that status was perceived to be through political pressure.

A petition to extend the franchise to women was first presented to the House of Commons in August 1832, during the debates on the first Reform Bill, though no one believed that it would gain a hearing.[31]   When a second Reform Bill came before the Commons in 1867, John Stuart Mill proposed an amendment which would have substituted the word 'person' for 'man' thus extending the franchise, and the two leading Congregational MPs, George Hadfield and Edward Baines, were among the 80 MPs who supported him.

Education

The impetus for change was growing, and was bound to bring challenges to both church structures and theology. If women were to make the challenge effective, they needed education equal in intellectual depth to that of their brothers, and they needed male support.[32] Education was the key to change.

Commentators have tended to ignore the fact that Victorian Britain had a large surplus of unmarried women and widows, many of whom were left to eke out a paltry living, usually as a governess. It was in order to help the latter that Queen's College was founded by the Governesses' Benevolent Institution at the instigation of the Revd F D Maurice and his sister Mary Maurice in 1848, soon to be followed by Bedford College, London eighteen months later. The Maurices and their supporters were Anglican, while Mrs Reid and her supporters who founded Bedford were largely Unitarian.[33]

Thus began the move to provide higher education for women, not only as a means to provide better informed mothers for the next generation, but, as many argued, on the basis of equality of rights; girls had as much right as their brothers to access to higher education. Women were admitted to official lectures at University College, London in 1878. At Owens College in Manchester women were first admitted to classes in 1874. Girton College was founded in Hitchin in 1869 and moved to Cambridge four years later. When Newnham College opened two years later the first students included the daughters of wealthy Congregationalists. In 1878 the first colleges for women were opened in Oxford. Lady Margaret Hall was founded on a religious (Anglican) basis; Somerville Hall (later College) was non-sectarian and was soon supported by the staff of Mansfield College, opened in Oxford in 1886 for the training of Nonconformist, principally Congregational, ministers. Mansfield's first principal, A M Fairbairn, served on the Somerville Council and his wife took a particular interest in the students from Somerville who attended the Sunday services in Mansfield College Chapel. The Mansfield members of staff supported the (unsuccessful) movement to grant degrees to women in Oxford in the 1890s.[34]

There had long existed numerous small schools, many run by Nonconformists, providing an education strong in languages and artistic accomplishments for middle-class girls.[35] However it was not until after the Schools Inquiry Commission's reports in the 1860s had revealed to a more sympathetic public the great discrepancy in provision for girls and boys that enormous effort was directed into founding schools for girls which could offer an education comparable to that provided by grammar schools for boys. The Girls' Public Day School Company was founded on non-denominational lines in 1872, and its schools were established in London and several provincial cities. J B Paton, principal of the Nottingham Congregational Institute, took a leading part in the founding of the Company's school in Nottingham.

Schools such as Mill Hill in north London and Tettenhall in Wolverhampton had been founded earlier in the nineteenth century for the sons of Nonconformist families. The earliest similar school for girls was Walthamstow Hall, which opened in Marsh Street, Walthamstow in 1838, specifically for the daughters of missionaries. Though it was officially non-denominational, its management was largely in the hands of Congregationalists. It was founded due to the inspiration of Mrs Foulger, the wife of a Cape merchant who was also a Director of the London Missionary Society.[36] At first women members of staff played a subsidiary domestic role, while visiting masters did most of the 'serious' teaching. But after a move to Sevenoaks in 1878, the Lady Superintendent was soon styled as 'headmistress' and women took over most of the teaching roles.[37] One of the reasons was that teaching was now the main profession open to the growing number of women who had taken university courses.

In 1871 the Revd William Guest, a minister in Gravesend, opened a subscription list for the foundation of a school for the daughters of Congregational ministers. While producing an English edition of the life of Fidelia Fisk his attention had been drawn to Mount Holyoake 'Female Seminary' in Massachusetts;[38] this led to correspondence with the Seminary's president, Dr Kirk of Boston. 'The subject was thus frequently pondered of founding in England a school where the aim should be the thorough religious, literary and domestic culture of young ladies, and which, under the management of a Board and a Committee should secure public confidence, and become a permanent Institution for the same ends as the American one'.[39] The salaries of ministers, he explained, were insufficient to pay large school fees, and yet there were no bursaries for girls comparable to those available for their brothers.

'There is hardly a class who are sent into life under greater disadvantages than the daughters of poor professional men,' declared a notice in *The Christian World* on 3 March 1871, adding, 'It is singular that the ladies of Congregational families have not taken up an educational scheme on their behalf'. William Guest's published letter on 7 April in *The Christian World* declared 'that the greatest advance which we can make to remedy the ills of the world is the thorough Christian, intellectual, and domestic culture of woman'. On the whole the journal's correspondents supported his scheme.

With the aid of several prominent and often wealthy Congregationalists and a host of 'lady fund raisers' in local churches the scheme came to fruition in May 1873, when the doors opened to 109 (mostly boarding) pupils. The project was supported by leading members of the denomination; the Board of Management included many leading (male) Congregationalists – 16 ministers and 16 laymen. Emily Davies, founder of Girton College, and Frances Buss, headmistress of North London Collegiate School, were present at the inaugural meeting. The school was named after its location, Milton Mount, in Gravesend, and it was given the designation 'college' because it also included a department for training teachers.

The first principal was Selina Hadland (1838-1919),[40] chosen by a subcommittee of both men and women from 58 applicants. Together with Frances Buss and Dorothea Beale she was one of the founders of the Headmistresses' Association. Like other contemporary headmistresses, Miss Hadland had a difficult time in asserting her authority in educational matters; the male management committee felt it had a right to interfere freely, and assumed a superiority in educational as well as administrative wisdom. Selina Hadland was once described as 'a moral and spiritual dynamo' and there were some spectacular rows before her authority was fully established.[41] Milton Mount was one of the first girls' schools to have a gymnasium, to gain recognition as a school of art, and to require practical work in every scientific subject. The Management Committee told Selina Hadland in her letter of appointment that 'our desire is to prepare the pupils to be wives, mothers, teachers and missionaries'. She herself laid as much emphasis on the need to prepare her pupils to earn their own livelihoods, should it be necessary, in a somewhat wider range of careers.[42] After her resignation in 1889 she and her sister travelled a great deal in Europe, the Middle East and the United States, and she retained her interest in educational questions until her death. In 1892 she was one of two women (the other was Harriet Byles of Saltaire) appointed to the newly-constituted Congregational Council for Secondary Education, whose brief was to promote Nonconformist public schools and religious equality in public schools in general.[43] In 1895 she published *Education and Life in the United States*, reflections on an extended visit to the United States and Canada.

Another Congregational school opened in St Ives, Huntingdonshire in the same decade. A daughter of Benjamin Parsons, Anna Lloyd (1837-1912), was married to the minister of St Ives Free Church, Thomas Lloyd. She and her husband, fearful that a local girls' school would fall into the hands of Roman Catholics, persuaded Nonconformists in the area to contribute towards the purchase of Slepe Hall, then an Anglican school whose principal and owner was about to leave the district. The Lloyds moved into the Hall, and Anna Lloyd became principal of the school. It was both a day and a boarding school, and attracted the daughters of local Nonconformist families. It was less adventurous educationally than Milton Mount, but served the local clientele well for many years.[44]

In July 1872 Thomas Binney, leading senior statesman of English Congregationalism, spoke at the opening of the East Anglian Girls' School in Bishop's Stortford. He welcomed the provision of more advanced education for girls, even advocating a measure of co-education.[45] Thus Congregationalists did support the development of girls' education, but it was the Unitarians who were by far the most active religious group in this enterprise.[46]

Missionaries

The missionary societies (the London Missionary Society, largely supported by Congregationalists, and the Presbyterian Missionary Society) were pioneers in offering women an acceptable sphere of activity and responsibility during the years when they were beginning to seek more active participation towards the end of the century.[47] The first woman to go out in her own right was Maria Newell, who went to Malacca in 1827 to teach Chinese girls. Two years later she married Karl Gutzlaff, and together, before her premature death in 1831, they translated the Bible into Siamese. She was supported financially by Mary Aldersey of Chigwell, who, according to Cecil Northcott, 'constantly reminded the Society [LMS] that women were fit to be missionaries'.[48] However it was not until the 1860s that any more women went out as LMS missionaries.

The wives of missionaries had contributed from the beginning, but their service, like that of ministers' wives, was not only unpaid but frequently unrecognised. In his history of the London Missionary Society, published in 1948, Norman Goodall wrote in the opening chapter:

> ... there has always been rendered by missionaries' wives an immense volume of work in schools, dispensaries and cottage industries, in translation and literary work, in the training of women workers, and in experiments that bear the stamp of a creative originality. To have attempted a record of this work, or even to have named all the outstanding illustrations of it would have been too large an undertaking. With all its inadequacy this single salute to a company which included in many cases the real heroes of the story must be all that can be offered.[49]

One exception to the silence concerning the work of missionary wives was *The Lives of Robert and Mary Moffat* (London: T Fisher Unwin, 1885) by their son, John Smith Moffat, in which their partnership in missionary activity in Africa was recorded. Cecil Northcott gives more personal recognition to the work of missionary wives, and lists as examples eighteen outstanding women by name.[50] More recently Valentine Cunningham has discovered a tombstone in Calcutta to the memory of Mary Hill (1790-1847), wife of the Revd Micaiah Hill of the LMS. It records her 'missionary zeal, in establishing and superintending religious schools' and her untiring work for 'the spiritual and temporal welfare' of those among whom she lived over a period of 20 years. Cunningham was able to discover something of the hardships she and other missionaries' wives had to endure, although these tended to be glossed over in LMS Reports.[51] It is good to think that others are now attempting to recover the presence and contribution of missionary wives.

It was the Indian zenanas – high caste Hindu dwellings from which men outside the immediate family were excluded – which first gave women in any numbers an opportunity to establish an independent role connected with missionary societies. In 1854 Elizabeth Sale, wife of John Sale of the Baptist Missionary Society, was granted admission to a zenana in Jessore, and her example was soon followed by others. A number of women's missionary organisations were founded in the 1860s (by, for example, the Wesleyan Methodist Missionary Society, the Society for the Propagation of the Gospel, and the Baptist Missionary Society). It was in the 1860s that a few women went out to serve with the LMS in South Africa, Madagascar and China.[52] In 1863, for example, Miss E M H Sturrock went out to Peelton, Kaffirland, jointly sponsored by the LMS and the Society for the Promotion of Female Education in the East (founded 1834) and remained for more than 20 years.

Not until 1875 was a decision taken to recruit women candidates actively for the London Missionary Society, and a Ladies' Committee established 'to advise and assist the Board in the management and extension of this branch of missionary effort.' Fifteen women, all normally resident in London, met monthly as this committee. The president, from its establishment until 1893, was Anna Wardlaw, who had accompanied her husband to South India from 1841 until his death in 1859. The main task of this committee was to interview potential women candidates, and then to make recommendations to the Board. Unlike most other missionary societies (including the Presbyterian) the London Missionary Society did not organise the work of women missionaries separately. By the early 1890s there were more than 60 women in the field, supported by flourishing Ladies' Auxiliaries up and down the country. Applications had been received from 400 women of whom 214 were recommended. No woman was acceptable if she was married or engaged, and if she married after beginning her service she had to resign, though those who married missionaries often continued their service in an unpaid capacity.

The equanimity with which the missionary wives accepted this situation was illustrated in a report to the Presbyterian Missions Meeting in the Queen's Hall, reported in the *British Weekly* on 27 May 1909:

> Mrs [MacDonald] Smith amused the meeting by saying that she and the other missionaries' wives called themselves 'the little m's'. The reason is that on prayer cards and reports of certain missionary societies married missionaries have a small 'm' printed after their names.

The Edinburgh Missionary Conference of 1910 caused some re-thinking in the churches, for almost all the eight reports of the conference referred to the importance of work among and by women. Whereas a proposal to set up a training centre for women missionaries had been rejected by missionary societies on the grounds of cost in 1906, it was more readily welcomed in 1911, and led to the opening of the United Missionary Training Hostel (later renamed Carey Hall) in Selly Oak in 1912. Baptists, Congregationalists and Presbyterians all supported and used it.[53]

The London Missionary Society was the first major British missionary society to appoint women to its Board of Directors. In 1891 the Ladies' Committee was re-formed as the Ladies' Examination Committee (with responsibility solely for selection and training), and women were invited to join the Board of Directors of the Society. Out of a total membership of 295 in 1895, only 33 were women, and so it can be assumed that for some years the influence of women was not strong.[54]

The Churches of Christ did not begin overseas missionary work until 1892, when a Foreign Missionary Committee was formed. The first three missionaries to be appointed went to Burma, and the wives of two of them, A E Hudson and Robert Halliday, joined them a year later. It was soon accepted that married couples would work together, and single women were also soon appointed.[55]

The Women's Missionary Association (WMA) of the Presbyterian Church of England was founded in December 1878 by a group of women from London Presbyterian churches who shared a concern to develop the work among the women and girls of China which had been begun by the wives of some missionaries. They raised money to support their own missionaries, the first being Catherine Ricketts,[56] who went to China in 1878 and served until 1907. The first president was Mrs Hugh Matheson, wife of the Convener of the Presbyterian Foreign Missions Committee.[57] Within three years there were 74 branches, including some in every presbytery, and by 1888 the Association was supporting the work of at least 14 workers in China and India.[58] In 1892 the WMA joined the International Union of Presbyterian Women's Missionary Societies.[59] However, it was 14 years before the women members were allowed to conduct their own annual meeting themselves, and not until 1925 that the WMA and the Presbyterian Missionary Society were amalgamated as one institution.[60]

Participation in Public and Church Life

As women's groups became more active in fund raising, so their voices became more active in church affairs. For instance, in Crewe Congregational Church, the church deficit in 1900 had to be met by appropriating the Ladies' Sewing Meeting Fund. During the following decade the church was financially dependent on the efforts of women members in raising money through sales of work or bazaars. The church's historian (writing in 1947) noted: 'This increased dependence on the money-raising efforts of women members of the church may be one of the reasons for the increasing part they played in church affairs.' In 1901, for example, Congregational women members were appointed for the first time to Crewe and District Free Church Council.[61]

Some of the newly-educated Nonconformist women made an outstanding contribution to both church and secular life. Charlotte Scott, daughter of the principal of the Lancashire Independent College, was a wrangler at Cambridge and became an outstanding mathematician. She was a founding member of the faculty at Bryn Mawr College, Pennsylvania.[62] Ella Sophia Bulley (1841-1931), daughter of a noted Liverpool Congregational cottonbroker and grand-daughter of the famous Dr Thomas Raffles, minister of Great George Street Congregational Church, Liverpool, had vowed at an early age to overcome 'the accursed thraldom of womanhood'. At the age of 29 she was one of the first five students at Newnham College in Cambridge; among near contemporaries were her two sisters and her future sister-in-law, Annie Armitage. She was the College's first research student. In 1874 she married Elkanah Armitage, and while they lived in Manchester she taught history at Owens College. After her husband was appointed to the staff of Rotherham Independent College, she was the first woman to serve on the Rotherham School Board, and when she and her husband later moved to Bradford she was appointed as an assistant commissioner to the Royal Commission on Secondary Education. Within the church, she was active in promoting 'service in song' – she wrote several hymns herself [63] – and preached her first sermon in a Bradford church in 1891.[64] In the same year she founded a Women's Guild of Christian Service (a model which was soon followed in other counties) and instituted a Women's Conference of the Yorkshire Congregational Union. At the same time she continued her professional work, and achieved recognition as a distinguished mediaeval historian and archaeologist.[65]

With the advent of the settlement movement in the late nineteenth century, it was not long before separate women's settlements were established, offering middle class women (especially single women) new opportunities for philanthropic work.[66] Settlements were attempts to create communities in inner-city areas in which university graduates would live for a few years, attempting to bridge the differences between middle and working class values and lifestyles through educational and social activities. Mansfield House Settlement was opened in 1890 in Canning Town and maintained close links with the Oxford college after which it was named. Two years later an associated women's settlement was founded, with Rebecca Cheetham, an old girl of Walthamstow Hall, as Warden.[67] Another old girl of Walthamstow Hall, Dr Margaret Pearse (who later married Percy Alden, the Mansfield Settlement's first Warden) was medical superintendent for a time. By 1894 there were 14 residents and a variety of activities involving women. The girls of Milton Mount supported the settlement from an early date, and some of its old girls became residents for a time.[68] Soon the Congregational theological colleges in Manchester and Bradford established similar settlements, and each had a women's branch. The settlement movement was greatly inspired by an outstanding American woman Congregationalist, Jane Addams, Warden of Hull House, Chicago; she visited the Mansfield Settlement in 1896.

Alongside the suffrage movement and the gradual opening of local statutory committees (such as School Boards) to women came a growing demand for women to share in church government. It was not surprising that the movement for the higher education of women, which had on the whole been encouraged by the churches, produced a new generation of women who sought to use their trained gifts in the service of the church, and indeed to raise questions about their treatment by the church.

In the Canterbury Convocation of the Church of England in 1897 a move to delete the word 'male' from a clause defining the qualifications of elected representatives on parochial church councils was supported by a petition signed by 1,100 women but was defeated by two votes.[69] Continued pressure led to the rule being changed in 1914, and by 1919 women were eligible for election to the National Assembly of the Church of England. The Wesleyan Methodists had voted to admit women to their conference in 1910.

Before the end of the century it was usual for women to be allowed to vote in Congregational church meetings,[70] though a clause in the Trust Deed which debarred women from voting for a new minister was invoked at Carrs Lane Church, Birmingham in 1906.[71] Harriet Spicer was the first woman to be appointed as a delegate to the Congregational Union Assembly in 1892;[72] she apparently had great difficulty in persuading the police on duty that she had a right to sit among the delegates on the floor of the house. In his first address as Chairman of the Congregational Union in 1893 her brother Albert Spicer[73] issued a plea that 'our Churches should recognise the change [in the status of women] and withdraw the limitations that preclude women from being chosen as Church officers where they have the necessary qualifications'. He did not advocate quotas, but that 'those be chosen, whether male or female, who in the opinion of their fellow-members are best suited for the various positions'.[74] It was almost 20 years later before a few women – Lady Spicer among them – were appointed to the Council of the Union.

It was in the early 1890s that women began to hold separate meetings during the October Assembly meetings of the Congregational Union, following the example of the Yorkshire Women's conference. The first was held in Bradford in 1892 when Mrs Ella Armitage gave a talk on 'parental responsibility'. The following year, in London, Rebecca Cheetham of Canning Town spoke on 'East End Settlements'. A year later, in Liverpool. W S Caine MP read a paper written by his wife with the intriguing title, 'What a woman may do in a church, whether officially or otherwise'. Later these meetings were advertised as being open to both sexes. In 1899, in Highbury Chapel, Bristol, the Women's Conference was again addressed by Mrs Ella Armitage on 'The Second International Congregational Council in Boston, Mass', to which she had accompanied her husband, one of the delegates.[75]

Women now began to press for admission to the diaconate[76] of Congregational churches. The author of the anonymous pamphlet history of Trinity Congregational Church, Walthamstow claimed that Trinity was the first Congregational church to appoint women deacons, in 1895, not as a matter of principle, but for the purely practical reason that the very deaf treasurer needed his wife to interpret for him at deacons' meetings.[77] In 1913 Lady Spicer (Jessie Dykes Spicer) wrote that in most Congregational churches 'there is an attitude of superiority on the part of men, accepted and agreed on the part of women'. She reminded women that they often failed to recognise their responsibility to respond to new opportunities. She suggested that every Congregational church should appoint women deacons, and that representative women should serve on denominational committees.[78] At her church in Woodford Green a Ladies' Council was instituted in 1907, but a proposal to admit women as deacons was defeated by a two-thirds majority; they were finally admitted in 1929. In Summertown, Oxford, a proposal to appoint women deacons in 1906 was not finally agreed until 1918. The Presbyterians were rather more cautious in electing women as elders, and it was not until 1922 that the Assembly agreed in principle that women might serve as elders.[79]

The Churches of Christ were more conservative in their attitude to women than either the Congregationalists or Presbyterians. A series of Sisters' Conferences was inaugurated in 1880, and led to the formation of a Sisters' Committee, but this did not enjoy the same status as other committees in the denomination until 1937. The president from 1881 until 1894 was Louise King, a formidable person whose husband David King was an active leader in the denomination. In 1889 the Revd Sydney Black read a paper on 'The position and work of Sisters in evangelization' at the Annual Conference of the Churches of Christ, telling his fellow members that they were 'losing incalculable blessing and power by keeping our beloved sisters in such an unscriptural and senseless position'. But his stance was too radical for most members of the conference. Although women became eligible to sit on official committees from 1903, it was not until well into the next century that women were allowed to take anything like an equal role.[80]

Women had few opportunities for the formal study of theology, though many read widely. Sarah Ellis, as early as 1842, had suggested that it was not uncommon to find women who chose to learn Greek, Latin and Hebrew ('a wholesome exercise of the mind, provided there is nothing better to be done') though she thought a woman could use her time to better effect.[81] Frances Power Cobbe and Anna Swanwick had had to battle for permission to attend ethics lectures at the largely Unitarian Manchester New College in London in the 1870s.[82] The author of an article in the *Free Church Suffrage Times* (July 1913) reported that a woman took a Cambridge theology tripos in 1883, but that no one else had followed her example until 1913. The most remarkable early women biblical scholars were the Presbyterian twin sisters, Agnes Lewis (1843-1926) and Margaret Gibson (1843-1920), born Agnes and Margaret Smith in Irvine, Scotland.[83] Their mother died shortly after their birth, and they were brought up by their father, a lawyer. When he inherited a large sum from a distant relative, he was able to take his daughters on extended visits throughout Europe, experiences which first stimulated their enthusiasm for languages. After their father's death they moved to London to escape from the limited round of life of Irvine, and joined the Presbyterian Church in Clapham Road (later Kingston Presbyterian Church). They began to travel, and to study more languages, as the most interesting acceptable activities open to middle-class single women; visits to Egypt and Palestine in 1868 and to Greece in 1883 led to the publication of Agnes's books, *Eastern Pilgrims* and *Glimpses of Greek Life and Scenery*. But it was after each twin had had a happy but short-lived marriage, and after a move to Cambridge, that their most important travels began. In 1892, after an adventurous journey, they reached St Catherine's Monastery in Sinai, where they were received hospitably at the monastery and began work in the library.

Their knowledge of ancient and modern languages now proved invaluable. Agnes's alert eye noticed something unusual about the vellum fragment on which the butter was served; this led to the discovery of a very early Syriac MS of the Gospels, now known as the Lewis Syriac Gospel. On their return to Cambridge, they enlisted the help of semitic scholars in the university, notably F C Burkitt and Rendel Harris, who on a further visit in the following year, helped with the photographing and transcribing of the texts. Margaret's book, *How the Codex was Found*, based on Agnes's notes, was published in 1893, and Agnes's translation of the Codex was published a year later. Agnes's final definitive work, *The Old Syriac Gospels*, was published in 1910. Although Cambridge still excluded women from degrees, other universities were more ready to honour the work of both sisters. In 1904 they were the first women in the world to be awarded theology degrees, when the University of Heidelberg conferred doctorates of divinity on each of them. Trinity College, Dublin and the University of St Andrews later followed suit.[84]

The twins were great benefactors to the Presbyterian Church of England. They gave the land for the building of Westminster College in Cambridge (which was only accepted after long debates over the wisdom of moving the Presbyterian Church of England's college from London to Cambridge) together with a substantial endowment to the College, and their portraits now adorn the College dining hall. In addition they contributed towards the Presbyterian Chaplaincy in Oxford.

Congregational theological colleges had also benefited from benefactions from women, despite that fact that until the passing of the Married Women's Property Acts it was only widows or single women who were in a position to make donations in their own name. Elizabeth Mansfield and her widowed sister Mrs Sarah Glover shared in the foundation of Spring Hill College in Birmingham with their brother, George Mansfield, in 1838. When the college moved to Oxford it adopted the name of the original founders. Sarah Balme's gift to Airedale College enabled it to move to a new building on the outskirts of Bradford in 1831.

The name of Betty Hall (1832-1913), was little known outside Lancashire. She came from what would later be described as a one-parent family in Shaw, near Manchester, and began her working life in a factory, before discovering a talent for making money out of old clothes and bedding. Though she always lived very simply and never married, she accumulated large sums of money, much of which she gave in order to open a new Congregational church in the town. What was originally known as 'Betty Hall's chapel' developed into Shaw Congregational Church, in which she was content to work as a Sunday School teacher, though remaining indefatigable in fund raising and personal giving.[85] In another part of Manchester, Christ Church, Burnage owes its origin to Jane Watts (1838-1911), daughter of a prosperous Manchester retailer.[86] The Congregational Church which opened in Ewell in 1865 owed its origin to the efforts of Mary Wallis (1789-1879), a domestic servant who had earlier persuaded itinerant preachers to visit a small gathered community dissatisfied with local Anglican worship.[87]

Another outstanding benefactor was Mrs Louisa Martindale (1839-1914),[88] born the eldest of the ten children of James Spicer (and therefore sister of Albert and Harriet Spicer), member of one of the wealthiest Congregational families. Before her marriage to William Martindale she had become interested in the women's movement. When she was left a widow with three daughters she moved to Lewes and thence to Brighton, where she formed a group within the Women's Liberal Federation to work for women's suffrage in the 1880s. She was active in many public spheres, religious and secular - the London Missionary Society, the Women's Liberal Association, the National Union of Women's Suffrage Societies, the National Council of Women, and the Women's Co-operative Guild. She gave great encouragement to Margaret Bondfield, then a shop assistant in Brighton, who later became the first woman Cabinet minister. After a move to Horsted Keynes, and dissatisfaction with all local churches, she raised the funds to promote a remarkable new Congregational church (with the agreement of the Sussex Congregational Union); she stipulated that there should be equality of the sexes in both the conduct of services and the management of the attached Institute. The foundation stones were laid by a girl and a boy. Mrs Martindale invited Hatty Baker, who was already recognized as a gifted preacher, to lead the worship at least once a month, and gradually a pattern was established by which she alternated with students from Hackney College in the conduct of services.

Christina Sinclair Bremner wrote an article for *The Christian World* (15 April 1909) on 'Women in the Ministry' (a subject which had been brought before the Congregational Union Council) in which she recounted a visit to Horsted Keynes to hear Hatty Baker preach:

> She is a student, a woman of education, spiritually-minded, capable. Dressed in a black Geneva gown, cap and plain white collar, Miss Baker reverently conducted the devotions of the congregation. The sermon was thoughtful, carefully prepared, and left much that is practical and applicable to the conduct of life in the minds of her hearers. I was struck by the numbers of heads of families, who listened to those half-hour sermons with the closest attention. Miss Baker has baptised children, officiated at the communion table, and on the very day of my visit, heads of households, women as well as men, were signing a requisition to allow marriages to be solemnised in this beautiful little church.

Women preachers and evangelists were not unknown in Victorian England. Sometimes Congregationalists and Baptists had allowed their halls, though not their actual churches, to be used for revival meetings addressed by women in the wake of the Evangelical Revival of 1859-60. The Salvation Army gave remarkable freedom and scope to women, who were able to preach, conduct marriages and funerals, and exercise command over men, well before the end of the nineteenth century.[89]

By the end of the century lay women as well as men were beginning to act as 'pastors' to small Congregational churches, or as assistants in larger ones. Their names were included in the *Congregational Year Books* as 'Lay Evangelists and Lay Pastors'. By 1900 five such had been listed: Jeannie Rankin, Eliza Harris and Jane Brown in the Yorkshire Congregational Union, Laura Moffatt at Carrs Lane, Birmingham and Miss Coombs in Pontypridd.

Women and Ordained Ministry

The first woman to hold full pastoral charge in England was a Unitarian, Gertrud von Petzold (1876-1952). She was born in East Prussia, but received her higher education at the University of Edinburgh and Manchester College, Oxford. In 1904 she was called to pastoral charge at Narborough Road Free Church, Leicester, where she remained for four years. She spent time in the United States, but finally returned to Germany after the outbreak of the First World War. There she remained for the rest of her life, apart from occasional visits abroad.[90] Her example was soon followed by others, and in the 1920s and 1930s the Unitarians had more women ministers than any other denomination.

In *Women in the Ministry* (London: C W Daniel, 1911), an expanded version of a lecture to the City of London branch of the Liberal Christian League in 1911, Hatty Baker referred to the hostility she had met as a woman preacher, and to 'the unanimity with which all classes of people of somewhat narrow doctrines and antiquated views bombard me with St Paul'. One minister was doubly offensive in telling her that a woman in the pulpit 'is as incongruous and offensive to the public as a black man in the same position'.[91] But she also received many letters of support. By 1913 she was being styled 'the Reverend' Hatty Baker. In January 1917 *The Coming Day* reported her as being 'co-pastor in Plymouth where alternately man and woman preached Sunday by Sunday'. She had an answer to the charges against women preachers in a more thoughtful and informed study of the New Testament, and made a plea for 'a woman as well as a man to interpret the heart of our Mother-Father God', through ministerial teams of men and women together.

Hatty Baker was not only a preacher, but also the first honorary secretary of the Free Church League for Women's Suffrage, which advocated 'the enfranchisement of women on the same basis that men are, or shall be enfranchised, believing the present system of government by one sex only to be un-Christian in principle, unjust in practice, and indefensible from either an economic or religious standpoint'. The Free Church League for Women's Suffrage was launched in 1910, after a letter from Lilian Turquand appeared in *The Christian Commonwealth* (the newspaper of the Progressive League) on 13 July, urging the formation of a Free Church Suffrage League on the same lines as the Church League for Women's Suffrage, founded in the previous year. 'As it is we Nonconformists suffer the great disability of having no place, unless in an alien church, where we can bring our movement in touch with religion.' Two weeks later, Hatty Baker argued in a letter in the same journal that educated women would be alienated from the churches unless they found a religion which 'grew with the times', and gave them independent opportunities and status. The League gradually gathered support, and in 1913 began producing its own monthly journal, the *Free Church Suffrage Times*, undergoing a change of name to *The Coming Day* in 1917. Hatty Baker was one of the female vice-presidents of the League, alongside Lady Spicer, Mrs Philip Snowden and Mrs Sidney (Beatrice) Webb.

The Free Churches, as other churches, were divided over the issue of women's suffrage; many women as well as men were either opposed or indifferent. But there was a growing number of Congregational ministers as well as lay people who, with Hatty Baker, saw the issue as essentially a religious one. R F Horton, minister of Lyndhurst Road Congregational Church, Hampstead, spoke in 1913 of the 'sheer political justice' of votes for women, claiming that 'justice and just dealing are fundamental principles of religion itself.'[92] R J Campbell of the City Temple, who had caused a stir with his book, *The New Theology* (London: Chapman and Hall, 1907), was a firm supporter, as was Rhondda Williams, minister of Union Church, Brighton, and W E Orchard, Presbyterian minister of St Paul's, Enfield until he moved to the Congregational King's Weigh House in London in 1914.

After the outbreak of war in 1914, most of the contributors to the *Free Church Suffrage Times* shared three common concerns: the extension of the suffrage to women, non-violent ways of resolving conflict (for which they argued women had a special vocation), and the opening of the ordained ministry to women. The outstanding woman in articulating these concerns was Maude Royden (1876-1955),[93] who was later President of the Society for the Ministry of Women, but as an Anglican, could never be ordained. At the beginning of the First World War, she and Constance Todd (who was thirteen years her junior) began a life-long friendship and collaboration.

In the April/May 1917 edition of the *Free Church Suffrage Times*, Constance Todd wrote, 'It is imperative if the women's movement is ever to find its true spiritual level, that the spiritual oneness of man and woman should not only be recognised, but should receive full expression in the life and constitution of the Church of Christ.' It was Constance Todd, brought up in the Presbyterian Church of England, who a few months later became the first woman to be ordained to the Christian ministry in Britain.

Constance Todd was among the second generation of women to enjoy the opportunity of a full university education. Her mother, Emily Ellerman, was one of the earliest women medical students, though owing to an accident she never actually practised. Her father had studied at Oxford, and went on to become an Assistant Secretary in the Scottish Education Department. Constance was sent to the recently-opened St Felix School in Southwold before going up to Somerville College in Oxford to read history before the First World War. By the time she had finished her course, she was aware of a vocation to ministry, but was led to understand that the Presbyterian Church of

England, in which she had been brought up, would have no sympathy with such a proposal. She therefore went to see the principal of the Congregational Mansfield College in Oxford, W B Selbie, early in 1913. He was persuaded that her call was genuine and recognised that her intellectual ability at least equalled that of his male students. He did not deem it necessary to consult his College Council or any denominational council formally before making this decision to accept her. She entered the College in Michaelmas Term 1913, and was readily accepted by the other students. By the time she had completed the three-years course (with some distinction) she was already engaged to be married to a fellow student, Claud Coltman. Both were pacifists, and both supported the suffrage movement.

Constance Todd and Claud Coltman had been attracted by the preaching of the charismatic 'catholic' Presbyterian minister of the Congregational King's Weigh House, W E Orchard, and attended his church in the West End of London frequently. When the Weigh House made it known that they were looking for someone to take charge of their Darby Street Mission (sacrificial work, with a low salary) they both felt that this was a need to which they could respond. The church officially 'called' them as assistant ministers, with special responsibility for Darby Street. They were ordained on the evening of 17 September 1917, with Orchard, the future Roman Catholic priest, presiding alongside three other Congregational ministers, G E Darlaston (whose daughter, Mary Osborn, was later ordained), Stanley Russell and Leyton Richards. Among those present was Maude Royden, who had begun a preaching ministry at the City Temple (while remaining an Anglican) the previous day. Next day Constance Todd and Claud Coltman were married at the Weigh House. They were then actually inducted to the pastorate at Darby Street in December; on this occasion an official representative of the London Congregational Union, R J Evans, as well as W B Selbie, principal of Mansfield, took part in the service. There was as yet no clear agreed procedure for the conduct of ordinations, and it was only after the ordination that Constance Coltman's request for recognition as a Congregational minister had come to the London Congregational Union, who referred the matter to the General Purposes Committee of the Congregational Union.[94] The question of ordaining women had been raised eight years earlier, though the Council later equivocated.[95] When the issue was discussed again in 1917, reference was made to the earlier discussion (which most had forgotten), and the Committee and Council now accepted Constance Coltman's request. (See chapter 10 for a fuller discussion.)

Her request was granted without much public debate. The real struggle for the acceptance of women's ministry came in the following years, for it was not sufficient for a woman to be trained and recognised by the denomination; she then had to find a church willing to call her. The fact that Constance and Claud Coltman always had shared ministries meant that her path was smoother than many who came after.[96] Some others did not have the same advantages of education and family support that Constance Coltman had enjoyed.

Very soon after Constance Coltman's ordination the Baptist congregation of Little Tew, Oxfordshire, invited a woman (Edith Gates) to take pastoral charge, in 1918. She was followed by Maria Living-Taylor, wife of the Revd John Taylor, who like the Coltmans, held shared ministries. Baptist 'women pastors' were officially recognised in 1925, but it was not until much later (1957) that they were allowed the title, 'woman minister'.[97] Their numbers grew very slowly until the 1970s.

Thus by the end of the First World War Unitarians, Baptists and Congregationalists, as well as the Salvation Army, were just beginning the long and slow process of bringing women into the leadership of the Church.

Chapter 2

Statistics and Storytelling:
Reflections on Some of the Methodologies used in
the Daughters of Dissent Project

Introduction

This chapter is introduced by a conversation. The situation it depicts really happened in the early 1990s: only names and places and been changed to give some degree of anonymity. It provides an example of the type of material with which this chapter is primarily concerned. Three people are talking; Anne, an Anglican laywoman, chair of an ecumenical committee; Barry, an ordained minister of the United Reformed Church holding a national appointment and Catherine, an ordained minister of the denomination.

A: *So Barry, would you say that women experience equal opportunities in ordained ministry in the URC now?*

B: *Well, Anne, I think if you look at our statistics you'll see that we've come a long way. We have significant numbers of women in ministry and in training and we have an equal opportunities policy that is monitored by our equal opportunities committee.*

A: *Catherine, what would you say? What is your experience?*

C: *Well, Anne, as you know, I don't think it is one of equality of opportunity. I'm used to having the statistics quoted at me, and being told we've come a long way. I'm used to being told that there are no 'women's issues' in the URC. But that doesn't explain why I, and others I could add, can be trained and then find the denomination very inflexible about our deployment such that although the URC is reportedly short of ministers some women can spend several years without a job. It seems to me that statistics aren't everything and we have to find some way of understanding these experiences.*

Language and Silence

I am a speech and language therapist and an ordained minister of the United Reformed Church. These joint fields of interest provide me with two starting points for social research into issues of methodology in the study of ministry by women, which are the subjects of this chapter.[1] These are that 'language is a social process'[2] and that there are many layers of silence.

The first step in uncovering what is going on in the conversation is to analyse who is talking about what. Anne, as an outsider, breaks a silence about equality of opportunity in employment for women in the United Reformed Church by asking a direct question of Barry, a man familiar with the structures. Barry replies with one possible answer: there is a committee which deals with these things and statistics that cannot be argued with. What Anne does not know, amongst other things, is the remit of the committee and its experience of the matter, or the lack of statistics. If Anne accepts Barry's response she will have one answer to her questions and a lot of silence. As it is, Anne asks Catherine about her experience, which is different from Barry's. After all, Barry is not an ordained woman in the United Reformed Church, even if he knows some. Catherine is one and speaks from her experience, which is the starting point of feminist methodology. Catherine's answer refers to both the committee and the statistics. In other words, she acknowledges the official version but points to the silences. She goes on to allude briefly to her own story and the stories of other women. In itself this answer, as Catherine struggles to find her own voice, is also full of silences. We are not told how many women share these stories or what the details are. Catherine concludes by stating her position: statistics are not everything and we have to find a way of interpreting people's stories.

This chapter is about Catherine's position. Since I began training for the ordained ministry of the United Reformed Church in 1989, I have met many 'Catherines' and heard their stories. At my ordination I told my own story and drew attention to the layers of silence in my own experience. The telling of stories themselves, even though possibly therapeutic as a support mechanism, has not been taken seriously as a way of reporting evidence of unequal opportunity in the Church. It is not unusual to find that such stories are met with derision, doubt and eventual dismissal. They are only stories and 'telling stories' has a double meaning which includes the possible interpretation that what is heard is untrue. Thus such stories are overlooked, the statistics stay unchallenged and the silences remain.

Tools for interpretation

Whilst there are things about the ministry and contribution of women in the United Reformed Church that can be counted, and are amenable to statistical treatment, many aspects are not. It is not adequate to dismiss women's accounts of their own experience, a sizeable body of evidence in both texts and oral narratives, as of lesser value. Instead, we have to find ways to interpret texts and narratives, particularly personal narratives, which help us to penetrate the layers of silence about ministry by women. One method of doing this for texts, as opposed to conversations,[3] is discourse analysis. The data of discourse analysis is written narrative or text, in its many different forms. In itself the analysis of discourse, narrative or text, is not new. The Christian Church has been engaging in it for at least two millennia. However, there are some critical differences between the kind of discourse analysis used in the Daughters of Dissent project and the 'traditional' practice of dealing with narrative and texts in the church.

Traditionally the task of interpretation, called hermeneutics, is taught in academic institutions where the main text to be interpreted is the Bible. In this project we affirm that any text can be interpreted and that this procedure is not confined to academic activity. Widening the task of interpretation and the participant interpreters has some important effects. It opens up the opportunity for more voices to emerge from the interpreting process. Whereas 'silence is golden' might be said to summarise the traditional starting point for Christian spirituality, particularly as the proper holy response of Christian women, this project affirms that silence has many layers that need to be explored, particularly in respect of women and other marginalized groups.

Discourse analysis recognises that language has power and, furthermore, that some of this is hidden.[4] The power of language can be used to support or question the status quo. One analytical tool used in the Daughters of Dissent project is a *'hermeneutics of suspicion'*,[5] an interpretative method which reads 'against the grain' of the text to retrieve its hidden message. This chapter will also outline some other tools employed to analyse the narratives and texts studied in the project, both in terms of what they do say and do not say about ministry by women.

Since a woman was first ordained by a local congregation of the Congregational Union of England and Wales a number of reports have been produced concerning ministry by women. Daughters of Dissent, and the letters, narratives, conversations and oral material collected for this project, could be described as the latest of these. In the first stage of our research we wrote to all the women listed in the Congregational Year Book who were ordained prior to 1972, when the union of the Congregational Church in England and Wales and the Presbyterian Church of England took place. We invited them to confirm the accuracy of their Year Book entry and to give us any further reflections on their life in ministry, including any thoughts on the particular contribution that women had brought to ordained ministry. At the same time we wrote to *Reform*, the monthly magazine of the United Reformed Church, seeking material about ministry by women from women ministers themselves and the churches they had served. However, we did not confine ourselves to those ordained before 1972, and through personal contacts and the Women in Ministry Network[6] also received information both from and about other women during the course of the rest of the WCC Ecumenical Decade of Churches in Solidarity with Women.

We also contacted those identified as being amongst the first ordained women in the Presbyterian Church of England and Churches of Christ traditions. We then visited as many of these women as has been feasible in an un-funded project and conducted interviews with some of them. Further evidence came from the archives of the three traditions and other published material we collected. When, in 2000, the Congregational Union of Scotland augmented the Union further, we drew in some material from that strand too.

Statistics and ministry by women

Statistics are widely used to uphold or question the status quo in all walks of life. They are regarded as objective measures of performance, whereas the anecdotes people tell may be portrayed as merely subjective experiences that count for less. Statistics are useful if you want to know the characteristics of a group. Incomplete statistics are misleading. If we want to use statistics to support a particular view, then we need to be sure that appropriate and accurate statistics are readily available.

The conversation with which this chapter opened included a reference to statistics about ministry by women. During the conversation Barry states his view concerning the position of women ministers in the denomination by saying that there are statistics that suggest equality of opportunity. According to Barry such things are recorded, maybe alongside other statistics about ministry. Actually statistics about ministry by women are not recorded, or at least not formally. It was not until 1996 that statistics about all those ministers on the payroll of the United Reformed Church began to be kept centrally, for the purposes of longer term financial planning. These statistics do include male and female ministers but they are not collected primarily for the purpose of monitoring equal opportunities. If you want statistics about ministry by women, or black people[7] or any other group in the denomination you will have to collect them yourself. A few other statistics about membership and eldership are kept centrally. These data are in the Year Book, an annual register of all churches in the United Reformed Church and of ministers recognised by it. From this it is usually possible to determine the gender of ministers by their first names but not to determine race or disability for example.

By analysis of successive Year Books it is possible to compute the proportion of women in ordained ministry and any trend or change in numbers over the years, though this is rarely done. A 1993 report by the World Alliance of Reformed Churches on the ordination of women in its member churches included a table of those churches ordaining women. The table recorded the year in which each denomination first ordained a woman and the proportion of women then in ministry in that denomination expressed as either a percentage of total ordained ministers or a ratio of ordained women to men. Whilst the report noted that the United Reformed Church, from the Congregational tradition, had ordained women from 1917 neither the current percentage nor ratio of ordained women was given.[8]

The story Barry tells is the one commonly told by members of the United Reformed Church in ecumenical encounters, namely the story we like to tell of women's ministry. It is possible that Barry's position could be upheld with statistics but without an interview with Barry we cannot tell which particular statistics he might be thinking of. For some people, the increasing proportion of stipendiary women in active pastoral charge is the most significant statistic. For others what matters is that there are more women than ever before in the ranks of theological students, chaplains and retired ministers. Statistics can only be used to back up an argument in a meaningful way when we are clear about what the numbers mean and why we are using them.

The numbers game [9]

During the course of this project the relevance of using statistics about gender and ordained ministry has been raised in a number of ways. This has happened against the backdrop of the way in which statistics have become increasingly accepted as a valid historical tool in recent years. The introduction to a recent work on female spirituality among nineteenth century Nonconformists, based on the study of 240 obituaries, noted: 'Although the use of figures is more familiar in other fields such as economic history or electoral sociology, there is no reason why they cannot be drawn on for the study of spirituality'.[10]

In the same way an argument can be made for using statistics in a study of gender and ministry. There are, however, clear limits to their application. For one thing, there is no way of collecting some statistics that might be particularly relevant to this field. It will never be known how many ordained women have looked at the list of empty pastorates, over the years, and dismissed at the outset the idea of offering themselves to a 'big church'. Likewise, Moderators will not have records of pastorates that have consistently rejected women as prospective ministers, though they may be aware such patterns exist. Churches can always account for their resistance by saying they had theological or personality differences with a woman candidate, rather than acknowledging that her gender meant she never had a chance of impressing them.

Year Book statistics can never explore the silences which explain why a minister left a pastorate at a particular time, possibly because of congregational opposition and resistance to change. There are no statistics kept of time spent out of pastoral charge and very possibly without pay. Judging by the narratives Daughter of Dissent has examined this is a predicament that quite often affects women.

Where there are matters for which statistics can be collected this does not automatically mean the resulting figures deserve the sort of unthinking respect and recognition someone like Barry gave them in the conversation reported at the start of this chapter. Statistics can also notoriously be used to back up whatever case someone wants to make, as politicians and advertising copywriters know well.

One issue that this project has tried to explore statistically and through narratives is whether women are equally to be found serving as ministers in all parts of the church, 85 years after the first woman was ordained. The narratives of some contemporary ordained women suggest they encounter more than their fair share of struggling pastorates, with small numbers of people gathered in unsuitable buildings and very limited resources in terms of people and finance. Other voices declare women are present in every significant place in the church, with a profile on a par with that of men, and they point to women's ministerial leadership of 'big churches' to back this up.

In order to explore the statistical evidence for these two opposing positions a search of the 2001 Year Book was undertaken, and a database prepared of the 500 largest churches in the United Reformed Church in terms of membership and average congregation (taking account of ministerial vacancies and churches which are in a Local Ecumenical Partnership). A repeated discrepancy at once became evident between figures of stated church membership and those of actual average attendance at worship, so the decision was made to focus on attendance figures as providing a more realistic indication of the true strength of local congregational life. For instance, the largest church of all in terms of membership to be served by a woman had an average congregation of 100 fewer than the total membership.

The findings of the database reveal that the churches with the 14 largest average congregations in the United Reformed Church are all served by male ministers (100% men 0% women). Of the 30 largest average congregations only one has a woman minister (97% men 3% women). There are four women among the ministers serving the 50 largest churches (92% men 8% women) and the 100 largest churches in terms of congregation have 11 women ministers (89% men 11% women) among those serving them. Bearing in mind that roughly 24% of the stipendiary ministers in the United Reformed Church are women, these figures are a striking illustration of their absence from the ranks of ministers serving the denomination's largest churches. Statistically if there were real equality of opportunity one would expect to see 24 women among those serving the 100 largest churches in terms of congregational attendance. Instead of the one woman amongst those serving the 30 largest churches that would mean seven women ministers might be expected to be found.

Another way of looking at the statistics is to take groups of 50 churches, categorised in descending terms by average attendance, to see how many women ministers are serving there. The table below provides further evidence for the increasing presence of women ministers in churches with smaller congregations.

Group	Attendance	No. of women serving	% of women
1	145-310	4	8
2	110-140	8	16
3	90-110	10	20
4	75-90	10	20
5	69-75	10	20
6	54-69	14	28

Only in churches with average congregations below 70 people does the proportion of women ministers correspond with the overall average of women among stipendiary ministers as a whole. It does not take a mathematical genius to infer that to balance these figures out there must be many more women ministers serving churches with much smaller attendances.

Other figures could be collected from the Year Book about geographical representation of women among the different synods of the United Reformed Church. These might be used to explore the possibility of regional resistance to women's ministry. Anecdotal evidence suggests that the presence of a Synod Moderator who actively promotes women's ministry can make a significant difference to the number of women serving in a particular Synod. The Year Book could also be used to identify the gender profile of rural as distinct from urban ministry, and the pattern of how many churches ministers serve.

Narrative and ministry by women

This project is not primarily concerned with numbers or statistical patterns but with narrative ones. What narrative reveals about anything depends on the tools used in the analysis. Such tools can be briefly categorised into two approaches, either 'top down' or 'bottom up'. A 'top down' approach means deciding in advance the categories into which narrative responses can be sorted. A 'bottom up' approach has no predetermined categories but looks to the narratives themselves to see what themes arise. In the course of this chapter I shall refer to some strategies for interpreting narratives and texts that are 'top down' approaches. Then I shall briefly present what would be a 'bottom up' approach and show how these differ.

Hermeneutical strategies

The Roman Catholic feminist biblical scholar, Elisabeth Schüssler Fiorenza, has defined ten hermeneutical strategies that can be used with biblical texts and constitute examples of the 'top down' approach. They can be used in other settings and were the starting point in my own work on the ways of interpreting biblical texts with ordinary people, particularly people with communication disorders.[11] Reflecting on that work, and adopting the 'hermeneutics in society' approach[12], strategies like these could be used to interpret any texts or narratives about ministry by women. The fact there are ten strategies is an indication of the complexity of the task of interpretation.[13] Rather than give detailed examples of all of these strategies in this chapter, the following examples illustrate some of the different contributions that can be made to the analysis of narratives and texts. Furthermore they show how the different methods of the three collaborating editors have taken effect within the Daughters of Dissent project as a whole.

Example 1: A 'Grave' Incident

Using a 'revisionist' strategy, which seeks to reinstate the names of women omitted from so many of the previously published accounts of the history of these traditions, Elaine Kaye has identified around 100 Congregational women ordained between 1919-1972.[14] Whilst the names of these women could be gleaned from Year Books or other documents few of them are well known and most are long since forgotten. In chapter one Elaine Kaye has widened this to consider the social context from which the developments in women's ministry came about, a strategy of 'historical interpretation'.

As a church historian, Elaine Kaye has spent her adult life in the study of history, through teaching, research and writing. Her focus has been on Nonconformity, usually the history of Congregationalism, and especially of the nineteenth and early twentieth centuries. This has involved asking questions, seeking sources that might yield answers, and then ordering the findings in a coherent and interesting way. To discover the role of women in the United Reformed Church traditions has meant exploring some new territory, since so little has so far been written about it. Women have hardly figured at all in accounts of Congregational and Presbyterian history, partly because the record of both traditions has been conceived until recently as the history of ministers, synods, councils and committees where women had very little voice.

According to the British feminist theologian, Dorothea McEwan, history is 'what we remember, what we do not forget and what needs to be handed on to the next generations'.[15] A woman minister remembered for the Daughters of Dissent project was Sarah Eleanor Ffrench (called Sallie), the daughter of a Congregational minister.[16] She was introduced to the Dales Congregational Churches in 1953 at the age of 38 when, according to the minutes of the Congregational Union of England and Wales's (CUEW) Special Committee, 'owing to family responsibilities she has applied to LMS for indefinite leave of absence from the field' thus terminating her LMS service in June 1953. As she had already taken a three-year course at Carey Hall she was therefore admitted to List B after being called to the Dales.[17]

A report on 'Co-operation of Men and Women in the Church' submitted by the CUEW as part of a World Council of Churches (WCC) study in 1965 stated: 'One rector objected to the woman minister burying the dead in his churchyard'. In order to prepare a section of the report on women's ordination the group concerned had written to all women ministers, to the provincial moderators and to those churches that had received ministry from a woman since this became possible. The resulting answers were treated in confidence and used anonymously in the ensuing report, so the identity of the woman to whom the rector objected cannot be known for certain, but was almost certainly Sallie Ffrench.

That identification was borne out by one of the first people to respond to our request in *Reform* for information about ministry by women; Mr E Wightman who was church secretary at Newton in Bowland (1950-1969) and knew Sallie Ffrench well during her ministry there. He wrote us a letter recalling the graveyard incident. The funeral, her first, was that of Mr Wightman's father: 'We had prepared for difficulties with the local rector who was unhappy about having a woman minister conduct the funeral in "his graveyard"'.[18] The letter contained a number of other memories of Sallie Ffrench's ministry, including her first baptism, which was of Mr Wightman's daughter. Comparison of the texts of the Wightman letter and the report to the World Council of Churches shows that a 'text and translation' strategy has a contribution to make to our understanding of ministry by women, by helping us to analyse where original material about women gets omitted from later versions. We may need to seek out new texts in order to overcome the anonymity of women. This project includes an archive that contains new texts like the letter by E Wightman. One surviving piece of writing by Sallie Ffrench includes a story of her experience in South India:

> I was once returning from an evening service in an isolated Indian village, when the Biblewoman and I lost the path. We were walking in the dark with the possibility of scorpions and snakes in the undergrowth. Neither of us could relate our destination to the position of the glittering stars above. In our fear our thoughts turned higher. We stopped and prayed to God in our extremity. We set off again and suddenly saw the silhouette of a giant cactus flower, 10 feet high, against the starlit sky. Hours before we had noticed the rarity on our way to the village, so we knew we were on the right road and we thanked God for our deliverance.[19]

This passage suggests Sallie Ffrench might often have used such illustrations in her sermons, talks and writing. However, we have none of Sallie Ffrench's own words about the graveyard incident so we cannot use a 'women as authors and interpreters' strategy in order to understand how she interpreted the experience.

Example 2: From object to subject

One consequence of language as a social process is that it can be used to place people in a range of subject positions. There is a difference in the subject position of 'women' when we use the phrase 'ministry by women' as opposed to 'women's ministry'. Each type of discourse 'establishes a particular set of subject positions'.[20] This project has gathered a number of personal narratives and these allow people to construct their own subject positions rather than remain, as is often the case for women, the anonymous and peripheral objects of texts. A strategy of interpretation that has 'women as subjects' can be used to interpret these narratives. We can begin to explore how women see themselves as 'ministers', rather than how others see 'women ministers'. This strategy is important because for so much of our history the voice of women has been disregarded, ignored or silenced. One way to overcome that silence is to use the words women supply about themselves and their experiences.

Thus we can not only record that Beryl Bennett (née Russell) was the first woman admitted to train for ministry at the Yorkshire United Independent College in 1949, and that Janet Webber was the first admitted to trained for ministry at Cheshunt College, Cambridge in 1958, but we can also refer to their own narratives of their experiences. Narratives by women within the church are not new. Kathleen Hendry's autobiography of 60 years of ministry was published in 1991. [21] What is different about Daughters of Dissent is that it uses hermeneutical tools to analyse the narratives. The women do speak for themselves but the tools allow us to discern patterns and connections between narratives. These narratives feature in various chapters but particularly in chapter nine.

Example 3: The personal is political

Using a strategy of 'sociopolitical location' allows us to situate the Daughters of Dissent project within the worldwide women's movement. There we encounter the presence and contribution of black women and what many authors refer to as the 'double discrimination' of race and gender that has been experienced by black women in the United Kingdom over the last 50 years. In this way we make the links between women's experience in the Church, in the women's suffrage movement and in their struggle for the right to be political representatives, thus uncovering recurring patterns in narratives and the interpretation of narrative. We find that women in other Christian denominations and other faiths have begun to use similar strategies and methods to record their stories. In none of these strategies are narratives used to justify the way things are or have been. Rather narratives are used to challenge both former interpretations and the status quo in order to make better sense of them through the experiences of women. To return to the conversation with which this chapter began, Catherine's experiences, and those of others like her, are not recorded here in order to back up the statistics, or lack of them, about equality of opportunity for women in the United Reformed Church. Rather they are intended to challenge the way the story has been told, to raise awareness of the underside of history, and to change things that they may better reflect the whole range of experiences of ministry.

Interpreting history

Kirsty Thorpe's background included her training as an historian and her work as a journalist. When reporting on local government, health authorities and other public bodies, she had become aware of the difference between committee reports, minutes of meetings, and what was said 'on the record' or in a public debate, as contrasted with the behind the scenes politics and tensions known to exist. A reporter must write an intelligible, ordered news item, yet may still be trying to assimilate the confused and contradictory versions of events gained from different participants along the way. If this temptation to impose a structure on disordered reality was a potential trap of journalism, it might also apply to the reliability of the historical method. Kirsty Thorpe approached this project aware that historians also run the risk of portraying events as part of a planned progression, from the vantage point of hindsight, when in reality some 'advances' made by women were more a matter of chance and confusion, of two steps forward and one back.

Getting deeper into Christian feminism, Kirsty Thorpe had also come increasingly to question the 'story' of women in the Church that she had previously accepted at face value. Crucial to this was a lecture in 1981 in which she had heard the American scholar Phyllis Trible take to pieces the two creation myths in Genesis and reconstruct them. The message was clear – there was a need to frame a whole new set of questions when gathering stories about women in the Church, or assessing the accuracy of the oral or written tradition. We had to start looking for absence as well as presence, tuning in to silence as well as words, and to apply the technique of reading between the lines in a new way. The manner in which Kirsty Thorpe's work has subsequently developed includes a number of Schüssler Fiorenza's strategies, particularly the strategies of 'socio-cultural reconstruction' and of 'ideological interpretation'.

Exploring further layers of silence

A denomination that is proud of its record on the ministry of women still has to hear many contradicting voices. During my involvement with the SPIN network, more and more stories emerged from women about their experiences in the Church. Women would ring me up and tell me what had happened to them during the process of candidating for the ministry, or being introduced to a pastorate, or some other experience with church life or structures. They continue to do this. Often these were 'things they wanted to get off their chests', they felt no one in the church had listened to or heard them. Most of the time I had no idea what to suggest could be done about the situation, which often involved some unresolved injustice. But I did listen.

Later, when the Equal Opportunities Committee was formed, I used to discuss with its members some of these stories, the frustrations that lay behind them and what to do. I was once told by one of them that the Equal Opportunities Committee was 'the committee with the least teeth in the URC'. We were proud of being a denomination that had an Equal Opportunities Policy, in which women were paid the same as men in the ordained ministry at least, but we did not seem to know what to do with these stories of injustice. There was a feeling that these were 'only stories' and so did not need to be taken seriously, could even be rubbished, or the storytellers excused on grounds of insanity.

If issues of ministry by women were ever mentioned in ecumenical circles, women would often tell me how lucky we were in the United Reformed Church, but the weight of these stories did not always mean it felt as if we were lucky. I was used to working in the NHS, not necessarily always a fair place to be employed (speech therapists have been one of the lowest paid professions in the UK, interestingly a profession dominated by women) but I was used to equal opportunities interviewing and so forth. The United Reformed Church did not seem to have the first clue about these things.

While preparing for the ordained ministry and completing an MTh at the University of Natal, Pietermaritzburg, I began to make the links between the strategies of interpretation feminists use for scripture and strategies of interpretation which could be used for these personal narratives I had been hearing and reading. I have called myself a feminist all my adult life. I only began to explore Christian feminism in my mid 20s. It is not all that popular in the churches as a label and most people do not recognise what it is when they hear it from the pulpit. It sounds like another strand of dissent, which is of course exactly what it is. Like Jane Shaw, the Anglican theologian, I do not find feminism and Christianity incompatible. With her I wonder: 'not whether Christianity is viable for feminists, but whether Christianity is viable without feminists and the multiple voices, work and perspectives of other marginalised groups; whether the church can, in good conscience, fail to acknowledge that such work is indeed theology?'[22]

To analyse narrative in some of the 'top down' ways illustrated above is only one method. A 'bottom up' way would be to let the oral narratives 'speak for themselves'. This would mean analysing them without applying any predetermined categories. In this method conversations, letters and written narratives are used to see how participants themselves talk about a chosen subject, for example ministry. [23] By applying 'bottom up' analysis to some of the letters and documents we received for this project we have been interested to note two particular themes emerging about ministry. Firstly, there were a number of women who wrote about periods of ill health during their ministry.

> Leaving [ministry] at the end of 1987 because of ill health was one of the hardest things I've had to do, and I still miss the work (but not the committee meetings).[24]

Another woman wrote:

> I am suffering from ME and multiple allergies and I have not worked since I became ill in October 1990.[25]

Illness and ministry is still an area of silence for both women and men. A method that listens to the way ministers talk about their own experiences of illness may be a way of leading us out of this particular silence.

Secondly, there were a small number of women we contacted who did not want to take part in the project. One reason given for this was an understanding that they had been involved in 'ministry' and not 'women's ministry'. As noted earlier in this chapter, (example 2), the addition of the word 'women' to the word 'ministers' creates a whole new species in the minds of some people, and one that is of lesser value. It is not therefore surprising that, having experienced this, some women in ministry choose not to use the term. For example Frances Chambers wrote to say she did not think of herself as a 'woman minister' and therefore had avoided gatherings of women in ministry (see chapter nine for further discussion).

The isolation of women in a predominantly male occupation is something other correspondents referred to, but the down-playing of women's experience and contribution, and the marginalising of theology done by women have probably also played a part in causing some women to reject a perspective of ministry informed by their own experiences as women. Not all women regard themselves as feminists, even those who have in some sense been pioneers. Some see the term as 'anti-men' and therefore reject it. According to a survey of 80 years of former students of Girton College Cambridge[26] 'only after 1965 do those willing to call themselves feminists become the majority'. The relative isolation of women in ordained ministry and the conservative nature of the Church are two factors that could have delayed an adoption of this self-description by women in the United Reformed Church.

There were a few responses from women who chose not to share more of their experiences, perhaps because 'I don't think my ministry would be of interest' but also that 'I don't wish to recall the early battles with the denomination, or any of the battles in fact'.[27]

When we use narratives it is often easier to use the ones that support the point we want to make or have the preferred 'happy ending'. If we use narratives we must use them honestly, recording the positive and negatives stories, the ups and the downs of ministry and life in the Church. It may be harder to use difficult stories, especially if our audiences do not want to hear those, but if our method is to bear scrutiny then we need a balanced approach. We hope that this project will allow the voices of these women to come through as if in conversation with the reader: conversations in which 'one's voice is clear, honest, self-aware and respectful, and one's listening is attentive, respectful and inviting'.[28]

Conclusions

This chapter has presented a number of different methods that can be used to analyse different kinds of data about ministry, and particularly ministry by women. These methods are used in this volume, some more often than others. The methods could be used more extensively to understand past and contemporary patterns of ministry among women and men, black and white, homosexual and heterosexual, disabled and not-yet-disabled people. The Daughters of Dissent project is not only about historical patterns of ministry by women, but is also able to critique current patterns of ministry using appropriate tools. It is to be hoped that an appreciation of these interpretative strategies will equip women and men to understand ministry and mission in new ways. We need to collect and use appropriate statistics, uncover more contributions from forgotten people and listen to the words and silences offered about ministry by women and men.

At the end of this stage in the Daughters of Dissent project, and following the World Council of Churches Ecumenical Decade of Churches in Solidarity with Women 1988-98, much remains to be done. This is true even in the United Reformed Church, a denomination that claims a good track record in respect of ministry by women. Adrienne Rich has outlined in these terms what women in the churches still need:

> A reorganization of knowledge, perspectives, and analytical tools that can help us to know our foremothers, evaluate our present historical, political and personal situation and take ourselves seriously as agents in the creation of a more balanced culture.... We need access to the female past.[29]

Women and men need access to that past in order to understand history 'as a process of what shapes my today in order to shape my and your tomorrow'.[30] That process is not yet finished. The women of Zimbabwe, many of whom were active in that country's war of independence, have a saying: 'A woman's place is in the struggle'. It is my contention that the struggle as far as ministry by women in the United Reformed Church is concerned is not yet over, and we still have many silences to explore.

Chapter 3

Structures – Towards Co-operation

> It may be there will be a pause in the onward progress of organised Christianity
> until women are emancipated from the mere serving of tables and begin to
> take wide and long views of the Kingdom which Jesus so insistently preached,
> and of some of the implications of the Cross.

This was the vision of Harriet Byles, a woman already in her 70s, when she addressed
the annual meeting of the Yorkshire Congregational Union in 1926. Their first woman
chairman, she was a member of a prominent Yorkshire Congregational family. It
was an anaemic church, she said, which relegated the majority of its members to the
preparation of sales of work and serving teas. Like Lady Spicer, she looked forward
to the future church as one of 'men and women working in full co-operation,' while
recognising that in an interim phase women might have to develop their confidence in
separate organisations.[1]

The assumption that the main structures of the Church would be operated solely
by men had been challenged by a significant number of women and men since the 1890s.
The suffrage movement had stimulated eager discussion of the role of women, not least in
colleges and universities. The Student Christian Movement (SCM), which was of enormous
significance in the first half of the twentieth century in shaping the ideas and policies of
the future leaders of most Protestant denominations, and of the ecumenical movement, gave
women new opportunities for leadership. From the first, offices were open to women and
men equally, and a number of outstanding women emerged as leaders. In 1913 a group of
SCM members planned a book which appeared two years later, *Some Aspects of the Women's
Movement* (London, 1915), edited by Zoë Fairfield and published by SCM Press.[2] In it,
Cecilia M Ady, Vice-Principal of St Hugh's College, Oxford, argued that there was no evidence
that women's distinctive contribution could only be made in special directions, but rather
'the experience of history goes far to prove that they are capable of making it in any and every
department of life'. [p. 73]. At the same time, Zoë Fairfield pointed out that while 'the message
of Christianity' offered women new hope and freedom, churches themselves tended to be
conservative institutions and had not automatically proved to be supporters of the women's
movement. In churches as elsewhere, conservative and progressive forces clashed.

An appendix to the book set out the existing position of women in the Church of
England and the main Free Church denominations, each section the work of 'a responsible
member' (by implication, a woman) of each denomination. The most enlightened, as far
as women were concerned, were the Society of Friends and the Salvation Army, both of

which accepted in principle and practice the equality of men and women in ministry and discussion.[3] The Unitarians, also in advance of most other denominations, were not included in the survey. The Anglican position was avowedly 'complicated', but the account included reference to deaconesses, sisterhoods, licensed teachers, missionaries and the debate concerning the role of women in church councils. The Methodists (United and Primitive) and the Baptists allowed women to preach and take part in the councils of the church; the Wesleyan Methodists were more restrictive about women as preachers, but allowed them to act as class leaders.

The account of the position of Congregational women makes no reference to women preaching, but from other sources we know that this was already common in some areas. While noting that women had equal voting and speaking rights with men in church meeting, the anonymous author observed that it was only a small proportion of women members who actually attended church meetings; most married women assumed that their husbands would represent them. At the same time, there was a growing and encouraging tendency for a few women to be appointed to church committees.

The author of the account of Presbyterian theory and practice noted that the general Presbyterian attitude was that woman's place was in the home. However, there was a growing concern that women should be elected to church committees. As yet, there were no women elders (though women could at least vote for elders); yet, as this was 'a spiritual office', it was, the author suggested, surely a most appropriate role for women. The best hope for change was for women to prove their worth on committees; then 'their admission to the presbyterate [eldership] cannot long be deferred.'

This was the position as the First World War ended, and many looked forward to a new era in which women would play an increasingly significant role in the church and in society generally. Even before the start of the war the issue of women's ordination was stirring in the Church of England; the Archbishop of Canterbury set up a commission to consider the role of women in the church, especially as deaconesses. This led to a positive affirmation of the office of deaconess at the Lambeth Conference of 1920. The conference's reference to the need 'to trust ourselves to [the Holy Spirit's] inspiration in that present which is our time of opportunity, in order that He may lead us into whatsoever fresh truth of thought or of action is in accordance with the will of God,'[4] offered a ray of hope to advocates of women's ordination. But it was another 70 years before that particular hope was realised.

Congregational Churches

In the Congregational Union there was now a Committee for Women's Work, set up in 1915, to co-ordinate work already being done regionally, and to stimulate more ambitious activities. The chairman was A E Garvie, principal of New College in London, who was always regarded as an advocate of women's contribution. Among the organisations now affiliated to this Committee were the Yorkshire and Lancashire Guilds of Christian Service, founded in the 1890s and very active in social philanthropy; most influential of all was the Women's League of the London Congregational Union, dating from 1909. In 1920 the Committee sent a letter to all ministers, signed by A E Garvie as chairman and Richard J Wells as secretary, urging them to foster the desire of so many women to share in the wider work of the Church, and commending a proposed new Women's Training Institute in conjunction with New College and Claremont Mission:

> ... the new place women have won for themselves in society generally, and the new sense which is spreading among them of their wider function in society, is a summons to the churches not to quench this new spirit among them, but to give them fullest opportunity for the realization of their aspirations in the service of the Kingdom of God.[5]

It was a disappointment that very few women took up this particular opportunity.

Though the Congregational Union had been reluctant to provide any funds for administrative help at first, by 1921 the Council had agreed to fund the full-time appointment of a secretary. A former pupil of Milton Mount College, Lilian Pither, was engaged, but had to retire through ill health; she was succeeded by Mrs J G Stevenson. The Women's Guild, inaugurated on 4 October 1922, superseded the Committee, and within two years its quarterly News Sheet was circulating among the churches. In the 1920s and early 1930s there was an active network of women's organisations throughout the denomination, some of them linked to inter-denominational organisations. The increase in the number of women being appointed to the general committees of the denomination was slow; in 1925 only 12 out of 330 Council members were women.. In an article in *The Congregational Monthly* in 1925 Gertrude Gervan pointed out that this contrasted unfavourably with the number of Congregational women who held important positions in secular life; among her examples were Mrs C B Alderton, Mayor of Colchester (who was active in the Women's Guild),[6] Miss Colman, Lord Mayor of Norwich, Mrs Margaret Wintringham, recently MP for Louth,[7] and the Labour MP, Margaret Bondfield, who became the first woman Cabinet minister in 1929.[8]

In 1932 the Congregational Union appointed a commission to enquire into several aspects of the work of the denomination, and to consider whether, 100 years after its foundation, the Union needed a stronger structure. Its report on ministry, presented in 1934, led to the appointment of a further commission, specifically to consider the ministry (in a broad sense) of women. Eight men (including A E Garvie, who was elected chairman) and two women (Mrs L B Hall and Miss Ingleson) were appointed. After representations from the Women's Guild two additional women, Mrs S M Berry and Mrs J H Jowett, were invited to join.

Their report, which was presented to the May Assembly in 1936, was wide-ranging.[9] They were able to report on a multitude of women's activities in the traditional mode: work among young people, fund raising, social concern. They noted that 2,000 women were now serving as deacons (still an average of only one per congregation) and 200 women were acting as church secretaries. Slower progress was being made in the more traditionally public forms of ministry. Forty five women were lay preachers and 17 women had been ordained (13 of them currently in pastoral ministry); however they had to report with some disappointment on the reluctance of churches to consider a woman minister.

Their chief positive recommendation was for a properly constituted and trained Order of Deaconesses, similar to those in the Methodist, Presbyterian, Baptist and Anglican churches. There were a few deaconesses working in inner-city missions (at Claremont in Islington for example), but there were no proper facilities for training and there was no recognised order. This proposal was only partially followed up; the names of deaconesses serving in Congregational churches were listed in the next three *Congregational Year Books*, but no formal training was provided. When St Paul's House was founded a decade later to provide home missionaries (who exercised ministry of a similar kind), the denomination as a whole was equally lukewarm in its support, and a number of women who felt called to full-time service to the church (though not to ordained ministry) still had to remain outside the formal, recognized structures. Further discussion took place until the 1950s without leading to any specific action.

In 1939 the Women's Guild changed its name to the Federation of Congregational Women (FCW), with a more international dimension, since Congregational women's organisations in the Commonwealth were also included.[10] In practice, most of the church-based activity of women was still channelled through organisations for women alone, though there was no such official restriction. Those who belonged to the Federation found it a valuable support network, and it gave worthwhile experience in administration and leadership to numerous church members. The *Federation News* grew to a circulation of 7,500.

There was however a growing desire to achieve a closer link with other departments of the Congregational Union, a desire which finally reached fruition after the Second World War. In 1947 a new Life and Work Department was created, including representation of the Federation, through what was called the Women's Committee, signifying that it bore responsibility for all women's work in the denomination. At the same time Jean Lay, an experienced teacher with some theological training, was appointed secretary to the Federation. Marion Chaffey's account of these years[11] indicates that this was an unsatisfactory arrangement, with the new committee being given both a very general brief concerning women's work and also a very specific one for the autonomous Federation. Nevertheless a great deal was achieved during Jean Lay's secretaryship, particularly the promotion of study and discussion.

Meanwhile the number, and certainly the proportion, of women serving on national committees had actually declined. In 1950, of 291 elected members of the Congregational Council, only 19 were women; most counties sent only male representatives. Of 29 members of the General Purposes Committee, only two were women. Most committees included no women. In general, therefore, the decision-making processes of the denomination were still in practice in the hands of men. Whenever a committee was made smaller, women's representation suffered. There was one notable exception to this general situation, when the Revd Elsie Chamberlain,[12] then a member of the BBC Religious Department staff, was elected to the Chair of the Congregational Union for the year 1956-7. She had made a considerable impact on Christians of all denominations, as well as on others, through her regular broadcasting, and accustomed many listeners to the idea of a woman leading public worship and the role women might play in public ministry. She did not use her election to the Chair of the Congregational Union as an occasion for propaganda for the ministry of women. 'I believe that a minister is a minister regardless of whether that person is a he or a she. And it is as a minister that I shall be serving the Union'.[13]

Jean Lay resigned her secretaryship in 1956 on her marriage to the Revd Jack Andrews, and was succeeded by Edith Rawlings, a former missionary in China who had been interned in a Japanese camp during the war. She only had two years in post before her premature death, but during that short time she responded to the invitation from the Secretary of the Union to formulate a policy for the coming decade by presenting a strong challenge (fully supported by her committee) to the denomination to change its structure in order to reflect more adequately the church as 'a community of persons who must be in communication (communion) with the Head of the Church and in communication with each other.' Too frequently there was 'a split fellowship' of organisations serving members divided by sex or age. In addition there was an unhelpful division between the Federation and the LMS Women's Auxiliaries. This challenge remained at the forefront of the thinking of the Federation and the Women's Committee for the rest of its existence. It was a hopeful sign that suggestions were made in 1962 to work towards the integration of the work of home and overseas, that is, of the London Missionary Society and the Congregational Union.

When Edith Rawlings was no longer well enough to serve as Secretary of the Women's Committee, her work was taken over, at first on a temporary basis, by Dorothy Biggs. This became a permanent arrangement in June 1959 when she was appointed as one of the four Executive Secretaries of the Union with special responsibility for women's work. Dorothy Biggs had trained as a teacher at Westhill College, but had always taken a deep interest in the work of the London Missionary Society. Earlier in life she had been Youth and Education Secretary of the Society; more recently she had been Assistant Secretary of the International Congregational Council based at Memorial Hall in London. Her broad experience of Congregationalism, both national and international, as well as of the ecumenical movement, was widely welcomed. In tune with the thinking of the Federation of Congregational Women, she had a strong conviction that women's contribution should be fully integrated into the life of the church. In the 1960s Margaret Knee was secretary of the Commission which produced the Declaration of Faith for the Congregational Churches in England and Wales in 1967.

By 1960 there was a growing realisation at the international ecumenical level that church structures were obstructing the proper development of co-operation between women and men. In the United States the voices of women theologians were just beginning to be heard and feminist theology (which was not necessarily confined to women theologians) emerged as a new discipline.[14] In 1962 the department on the Co-operation of Men and Women in Church, Family and Society of the World Council of Churches sent member churches, including the Congregational Union, a copy of its report, and sought a response as to how far the principle of equal co-operation was carried out in practice. The Congregational General Purposes Committee appointed a group of four male ministers and two laywomen (Dorothy Biggs and Mrs J Rider Smith) to prepare a response. The chairman was the Revd Charles Haig. The Revd Florence Frost-Mee was subsequently added to the group.

Their response was largely based on the replies to questionnaires which were sent out to women ministers and churches which had already experienced the ministry of a woman, and to 200 churches concerning the role of women in church life generally, and to moderators and missionary societies. Most replied.

The major part of their response was devoted to reporting on ordained women. They referred to the ordination of '70 or 80' women since 1917, but noted that most of the women then in pastoral charge (35 out of a total of 1,275 ministers in pastoral charge altogether, ie 2.8%) had small churches; only 11 were serving in churches with over 100 members. In fact the *Congregational Year Book* for 1964-5 listed 59 women on the Roll of Ministers List A and six on List B (together with four who had the necessary qualifications but had not yet received a call) out of a total 1,774 ministers (ie 3.3%). When it is remembered that at the time the Presbyterians had one woman minister (Ella Gordon), the Methodists none,[15] and the Baptists three,[16] this was a comparatively good record, but fell far short of equality.

The women concerned often reported the difficulty of combining necessary domestic work with their ministry, and complained that some churches expected a woman minister to fulfil the traditional role of a minister's wife as well as her own. On the positive side they reported that younger ministers had found acceptance by a college and by a church easier than their older colleagues. More were being invited to serve on inter-denominational councils or committees. Four had been elected 'chairmen' of their County Union. Churches which had experienced the ministry of a woman declared themselves to have lost any earlier prejudice. 'Increasingly,' they reported, 'it is the individual personality and the ability to do a job of work, not the sex, by which a person is judged fit to be a minister.' Nevertheless, the progress from 'woman minister' to 'minister' was slow, and there were still instances of rejection by other clergy. Although not officially ordained, the home missionaries trained at St Paul's House (see chapter 4) were usually doing the work of a minister (including celebrating Communion) and the value of their work was commented on.

The record of the London Missionary Society was better (as it had been since the previous century). Of the 187 missionaries serving with the Society in 1963, 108 were men and 79 were women.[17] Salaries for single men and single women were equal. On three occasions a woman had served as Chairman of the LMS Board.[18]

As far as lay women were concerned, 'the typical Congregational church' had, according to the report, between one and six women deacons, who usually shared fully in the work of the church (except for taking the offertory). Not all were typical, and some churches restricted the election of women. The old patterns stubbornly remained, with a woman almost invariably acting as missionary secretary, and women taking the main lay responsibility for catering, sick visiting and children's work. In part, of course, this reflected the fact that the majority of middle-class married women were not in full-time employment, and were able to give considerable time to voluntary church work.

Overall the report had to admit that, whatever the principles affirmed, there was still prejudice (from women as well as men), and that family responsibilities frequently limited full sharing between men and women.

While this report was being prepared, significant changes were taking place in denominational structures. The first was the closer integration of overseas missionary work into the life of the denomination. After six years of discussion, the Congregational Council for World Mission was inaugurated in 1966, continuing and uniting the work of the London Missionary Society, the Colonial Missionary Society and six other related missionary bodies. The Congregational Church was given full representation on its Board, with 58 men and 16 women appointed in its first year.

The second change came in anticipation of the union of Congregationalists and Presbyterians, for which discussions had been continuing for two decades. The churches of the Congregational Union, originally formed on a federal model, were moving towards becoming a covenanting body, ' the Congregational Church of England and Wales', with a new structure. As a prelude to this, the Council and Assembly of the Union accepted a recommendation that in the new Church, future committees should always be made up of men and women serving together, and that the Women's Committee should be discontinued, enabling its work to be integrated into the new Church Life Department (though county women's committees would continue). The Federation of Congregational Women, after extensive consultation, recognised the advantage of such integration and accepted its own dissolution in 1965. The last President of the Federation, Mrs J Rider Smith (who had taken an active role on the Women's Committee) was one of the chief architects of these changes. The election of Mrs Gwen Hall as chairman of the Council of the Congregational Church and her effective steering of negotiations with the Presbyterians just before 1972 could have been seen as a vindication of this policy.

In place of the final issue of *News*, Marion Chaffey, who had a long record of service both to missionary work overseas and to women's work at home, produced an informative record of the service of the Women's Committee of the Congregational Union, *Towards Co-operation*. She and others had always kept alive the vision of equal co-operation with which the committee had begun 50 years previously.

The next task was to enter into serious negotiation with the leaders of women's work in the Presbyterian Church of England, as part of the discussions which were to lead to full union between the Congregational and Presbyterian churches in the United Reformed Church.

The Presbyterian Church of England

The Presbyterian Church of England (PCE) had always had a more structured organisation than the Congregational churches, and the decisions of its presbyteries and Synod were accepted as binding over individual congregations. Therefore the progress of women's participation in the councils of the Presbyterian Church was more dependent on decisions of Synod or Assembly[19] (which had to be approved by presbyteries) than in Congregationalism.

It has already been noted (chapter 1) that there was a strong Women's Missionary Association (WMA) among the English Presbyterian churches, affiliated to the International Union of Presbyterian Women's Missionary societies. This was a fund-raising Association which recruited and supported its own missionaries. By the 1920s there were 300 branches across the country, and its journal, *Our Sisters in Other Lands*, had a circulation of 12,000. Although the Association was amalgamated with the Foreign Missions Committee (with equal representation of men and women) in 1925, a separate Women's Missionary Association committee continued until 1947, after which time all missionaries were appointed by the same authority.

As the women's suffrage movement had gained momentum, and particularly after the extension of the franchise to many women in 1918, there was a growing awareness among Presbyterians as among others of the exclusion of women from the general service of the Church. As early as 1913 the Birmingham Presbytery had sent a formal 'overture' to Synod asking it to 'determine whether the time has not come to recognise the work of the Women Members of the Church, either by their admission to Offices already established in the Church or by the creation of other offices, such an Order of Deaconesses, or in such form as may seem advisable.'[20] This overture was withdrawn the following day without explanation. However, the subject was not to be ignored, and in May 1915 Synod appointed a special committee to consider the relation of women to the administrative work of the church. Its report was presented to Synod the following year and referred to local presbyteries. As a result, in May 1917 Synod agreed that women might be appointed to three specific national committees (foreign missions, Jewish missions, and instruction of youth), up to a proportion of one fifth. The following year, Synod agreed to promote the training of 'educated women' for the work of deaconesses and church sisters, and the Home Missions Committee was given authority to co-opt women members. In 1920 a subcommittee on the Training of Women reported that three candidates had been accepted for training, and that one (Marjorie Dundas Anderson Scott) was already at work in Islington. At the same time, the Committee noted that it was 'proceeding very cautiously' until it assessed what demand there was for their services.

In its report to Synod in that same year (1920) the Moderator's Committee referred to having given 'long and earnest consideration' to the question of women's role in the church: 'It feels that in the providential ordering of events there is an urgent call to us to face and settle this question'. The majority felt strongly that it was time for 'the barrier of sex' to be entirely removed from the organisation of the church; but in view of the far-reaching nature of such a change it was decided to postpone discussion until the following year.[21]

In 1921, therefore, the Moderator's Committee brought three recommendations to assembly. On two of these they were unanimous: that women should be ordained as elders and deacons on the same terms as men, and that 'women of gifts and consecration' should be authorised to give addresses in church. The majority also wished to affirm that there was no barrier in principle to the admission of women to the ordained ministry, but that a further report on the subject would be wise before bringing any more specific proposal to the Assembly. These recommendations were accepted by Assembly, and sent to presbyteries for further discussion.[22]

In the following year the opening of the eldership and diaconate to women, and the authorisation of women preachers, was affirmed in the light of the response from presbyteries. At the same Assembly, the Moderator's Committee presented its report on the admission of women to ministry. All members of the committee agreed that the New Testament provides evidence that women were active in the apostolic church, and that Paul's teaching on women's role is ambiguous, and all supported the work of women as evangelists and deaconesses. The view of the majority was 'that the church would be following not only the trend of our time but the direction of the liberating Spirit of God, if we opened our ministry to women'. A minority, on the other hand, believed that there were essential differences of function between men and women which excluded women from ordained ministry.[23] The report was sent to presbyteries for response to a specially appointed committee.

When this committee reported at the next Assembly in 1923 it was clear that opinion on the subject was still divided, and that the majority of presbyteries and sessions did not support the ordination of women.[24] Disappointingly for many, Assembly resolved 'that it is not the will of the Church that the question of admitting women to the regular Ministry of the Church should be further considered at the present time'.[25] Thus while there was strong support for women's ministry among many of the leaders of the Church, the more conservative view was predominant among the local presbyteries.

In 1924 Dorothy Wilson,[26] who had been Organising Secretary for Youth in the Presbyterian Church, was told that any application from her to prepare for ordained ministry by studying at Westminster College would be rejected, though she was offered part-time study without the prospect of ordination. She therefore, like Constance Todd, chose to study at Mansfield College instead, and was ordained to the Congregational ministry. It was to be another 30 years before the Assembly changed its mind.

There was slow progress towards the acceptance of both deaconesses (church sisters) and women elders. By 1924 there was only one official deaconess, Mrs MacLachlan,[27] a war widow. She served as deaconess for 29 years, from 1920 until 1949, and did much to develop the role of deaconess or church sister. She, like many who followed, trained at Carey Hall in Birmingham and at the Presbyterian Settlement, Poplar. Soon after she retired, however, there were 16 serving church sisters, and demand for them outstripped the supply. Yet it was not until 1956, after five years of discussion that it was finally agreed that church sisters should be ex officio members of Presbytery and Assembly, and therefore properly integrated into the denomination's structures.

There was no great rush to appoint women elders. A year after their acceptance by Assembly, there were only three, all in one congregation, and the numbers were slow to increase. By 1962 there were 533 women elders out of a total of 4,629, less than two per congregation, and many churches still had no women elders. However, a report prepared by the Church of Scotland (which was soon due to debate the issue) in 1965 provided the result of questioning 200 ministers, session clerks and women elders in the Presbyterian Church of England, and found almost entirely favourable, sometimes enthusiastic reports of the English experience.[28]

The question of the ordination of women as ministers was raised again in the early 1930s. An 'overture' on the subject presented to Assembly in 1931 was referred to the presbyteries; this time, eight out of 14 declared in favour. A committee was appointed to investigate the possibility. But it seems that the conservative forces in the denomination were able to stall the progress of the matter by highlighting the difficulties that Westminster College might face if women students were admitted: the alteration of the 'freedom and intimacy' in the social life of the college, and the likelihood that Cambridge University would withdraw its official recognition of the college as 'a house of residence' if women were admitted, thereby forcing Lewis-Gibson scholarship holders to move to another recognised hall, and thus removing them from the church's jurisdiction.

When the committee's report was finally discussed in 1935, these alleged 'insuperable difficulties' were accepted without question, though it was agreed that training for potential women ministers might be sought elsewhere. Assembly took the easier path, voted against setting up a committee to consider alternative means of training, and resolved instead 'to pass from the consideration of the subject at present'.[29]

The barrier was finally broken through the gentle perseverance of one woman, whom Arthur Macarthur has described as 'outstanding in ability, experience and grace of character'. Ella Gordon[30] had felt a call to ministry early in her life, but had been told that there was no place for a woman in the full-time ordained ministry. Instead she trained at St Colm's College in Edinburgh after taking a science degree at the University of Aberdeen, and went out to China in 1936 as a missionary of the Church of Scotland. She remained there until the Japanese invasion forced her home. She then took a theology degree, but, still frustrated about her call to ministry, taught science for two years in a Glasgow school. She was then persuaded by friends to become a church sister in the Presbyterian Church of England. She arrived in North Shields in 1952, as an assistant to Arthur Macarthur in the newly-united St Columba's Church. But the call to ordained ministry remained. Four years later she asked Arthur Macarthur whether he thought an application for ordination would be accepted. When he consulted the chairman of the presbytery (Alan Whigham Price), they both agreed that no male minister deserved to sit in judgement on her. Her application was supported by the Newcastle presbytery by 56 votes to one, with five abstentions. The climate of opinion generally had changed in the previous 20 years to the extent that when her application reached Assembly it was accepted by 253 votes to 25, though not without the attempt of an influential minority to re-open the debate on the principle at stake. The defeat of their amendment (by 229 to 123) owed much to Ella Gordon's personal qualities. As she already held three degrees from the University of Aberdeen, including a first class degree in theology, and had a wealth of pastoral experience, the question of further training did not arise. She was called to the ministry at Willington Quay and officially ordained in November 1956.[31] Arthur Macarthur later commented that 'she came to the ministry in spite of the prejudices of the time and raised it to new levels of respect by her vision of its meaning and the mature and often mischievous humour with which she met disappointments and frustrations.'[32]

The whole ordination issue was finally settled in 1959 when Assembly resolved to accept women candidates for ministry, and instructed Westminster College to make provision for their training. The residence issue was no longer a problem, because the University authorities in Cambridge were now prepared to recognise a mixed hall of residence. Thus what could have been an insuperable barrier to the union of Congregationalists and Presbyterians was finally overcome.

Meanwhile lay women in the Presbyterian Church continued to be active. The Women's Home Church Association (WHCA) had been founded in 1930 to promote women's service to the church, and in particular to support the work of church sisters. It was a large and influential organisation, and gave many women, ministers' wives especially, opportunities for speaking and for leadership. After the Second World War it began to work more closely in co-operation with the Woman's Missionary Association (WMA).[33] Women elders also began to serve on national committees. Mrs Nora Manson was prominent in this way, and was the only woman actually to chair a national committee (other than the women's committees) before 1972.[34]

After 1960, when union with the Congregationalists seemed a strong possibility, the representatives of the WHCA and the WMA met from time to time with representatives of the Congregational Union. By 1965 Congregationalists had already decided on a policy of co-operation between men and women in all the work of the church, rather than through the continuation of separate women's organisations. The Presbyterians were not as decisive on this point, and were reluctant to follow the Congregational example. But in 1972 the prelude to union with the Congregationalists was, legally, the dissolution of both the Congregational Church and the Presbyterian Church of England. Both the WMA and the WHMC sadly accepted their own death knell in the knowledge that there would be no formal separate women's organisations in the new United Reformed Church. Though this policy has been generally accepted, some have felt the lack of women's organisations keenly.

Churches of Christ[35]

The Association of Churches of Christ was a much smaller grouping of churches than either the Congregational Union or the Presbyterian Church of England, though it spanned Scotland and Northern Ireland as well as England and Wales. Its total membership peaked at 16,596 in 1930 and then began to decline.[36] The number of churches in the association never quite reached 200. It had a wider view of the term 'minister' than the Congregationalists and Presbyterians, and a strong emphasis on 'mutual ministry'. Elders and deacons as well as full-time ministers were ordained, and could, with the agreement of a particular congregation, both preach and celebrate communion (though the same person did not perform both functions at any one service). While full-time ministers were ordained at the Annual Conference and therefore had national recognition, elders and deacons were chosen and ordained at the local level and not subject to national regulation. Thus the role of women in any particular congregation depended on local decision.

Church sisters, however, were appointed by the Women's Committee and recognised at the Annual Conference. They had been active since the previous century under the aegis of a separate Sisters' Committee (which was given equal status with other committees in 1937); they worked particularly, often exclusively, among women. They were active in visiting, and usually took responsibility for a weekly afternoon women's meeting.[37]

By 1954 their numbers were reduced to two and while the need for them remained, funds to pay them were short. Women were also employed as Sunday School organisers, usually itinerant, moving to new areas every few months. Mary Francis (later Mary Barr) served in this capacity from 1949 until 1953, after training at Overdale, the college of the Churches of Christ in Selly Oak, Birmingham; during her four years of service, she worked in ten different areas.

It was not until after the outbreak of the Second World War that women collectively became more active, and that questions about women's public role began to be raised. The shortage of male deacons frequently led to their replacement by women, and when war ended their position was maintained. In 1947 the Annual Conference in Glasgow appointed a commission to report on the work and status of ministry; the commission included one woman, Mrs W W Short. Its report, which included reference to women's ministry, was accepted in 1953 and printed in the next Year Book.[38] While accepting the authority of the New Testament as holding 'supreme place as a standard of judgement on church belief and practice,' the Commission recognised that it could not give a complete answer to every question relating to the structure and form of the church. In an 'Additional Note on the Ministry of Women' the Commission accepted that the strictures of I Timothy 2: 8-11 against women's ministry may have had a special application in a particular situation, and therefore were not to be considered as binding on future generations. They referred to 'the wisdom of appointing women deacons', though they suggested that 'their functions may have special reference to the needs of the women members of the church and to duties for which women are naturally and specially fitted.'[39] They proposed that church sisters should be recognised as deaconesses and ordained at Annual Conference to serve the churches as a whole, rather than as previously solely in a local context. They concluded: 'There is no barrier in theology and tradition to the extension of the ministry of Deaconesses, even if the question of the ordination of women to the Presbyterate has to be left until a larger measure of agreement is reached.'[40] The whole report, with its recommendations, was accepted by the Conference.

In 1963, when the World Council of Churches was beginning its enquiries into the role of women, the annual Conference of the Churches of Christ asked for a new enquiry into the place of women in ministry. In some churches women were already being invited to preach. The question was eventually discussed at the Barnes Close Convention in 1965, when a group of ministers looked at the biblical and theological background to the issue and concluded by asking whether the time had not come 'when we can dispense with the primitive idea of the subjection and subordination of women and freely admit them to any ministry in the church, to which they are called?'[41] This report formed the basis for a more official study report, 'Women in the Church's Ministry' (*Churches of Christ Occasional Papers* 6, 1973), which asked the churches 'to consider whether the time is not overdue for a wholehearted acceptance of women into our ministries, both local and national'. That year marked a watershed, for not only had some women been ordained as elders (and therefore to the ministry of Word and Sacrament) in the previous decade, but Annual Conference had its first woman president, Mrs Winifred Clark.[42] It was now agreed at last that women might be accepted for training for full-time ministry. Rowena Gates (later Francis) began her training in 1976 (see chapter 4).

While the contribution of church sisters inevitably declined, the work of the Christian Women's Fellowship (CWF), founded in 1953, flourished. The CWF which took over much of the work previously done by the Sisters' Fellowships and the Young Women's Conventions (residential weekends for study, fellowship and worship, started in the late 1920s). Every woman who joined the Churches of Christ was automatically considered to be a member of the CWF, and was encouraged to take part in its life. It was a very active body, which stimulated study and discussion as well as pastoral work. Every year a study programme was circulated to each group, with specific suggestions for worship, study and service. The appointment of May Segain[43] as its organising secretary in 1956 strengthened its influence, and its affiliation with the World CWF gave it a welcome international dimension. Its annual conventions at Swanwick and in Scotland played an important role in the lives of many women members of the Churches of Christ, such that it has continued, since union, within the United Reformed Church.

In 1981 the Re-formed Association of the Churches of Christ[44] united with the United Reformed Church to become the United Reformed Church in the United Kingdom, and many of the elders of the former Churches of Christ were now ordained as auxiliary ministers of the United Reformed Church, including some women. They brought to the new Church a strong tradition of women's service and fellowship.

Continuing Congregationalists

A significant minority of Congregationalists remained outside the United Reformed Church; most of them formed the body which came to be known as the Congregational Federation. Among them were Elsie Chamberlain (president 1973-5) and the Federation's first president, Margaret Stansgate. Elsie Chamberlain had left the BBC in 1967 in protest against changes in religious broadcasting. For a short spell she was an assistant minister at the City Temple, but became increasingly unhappy at the prospect of joining with the Presbyterians in the United Reformed Church. Finally she decided to remain a Congregationalist, and was a dominant figure in the Congregational Federation in its early years. She continued to preach almost until the end of her life. Lady Stansgate became a Congregationalist in 1948 after attending the first meeting of the World Council of Churches in Amsterdam as an Anglican member of one of the Study Commissions. She had discovered that the Archbishop of Canterbury had written to the General Secretary of the Council warning him that her (positive) views on the ordination of women were not those of the Church of England.[45] Her strong Congregational convictions led her to join the Congregational Federation rather than the United Reformed Church in 1972.

An outstanding woman minister of the Federation is Janet Wootton, minister of Union Chapel, Islington since 1986 (she has subsequently moved to Nottingham). She was President of the Federation in 1990, and has served as both President and Chair of the National Free Church Women's Council. Only four women altogether have been Federation Presidents since 1972, and by far the majority of committee chairs and council members are male. However, since the formation of the APT (All People Together) Board in 1993 efforts have been made to facilitate the attendance of a greater number of women, and other changes to meeting times and places are under discussion.

In 2002 Janet Wootton was appointed Moderator of the International Congregational Fellowship for the next four-year term.

United Reformed Church in the United Kingdom 1972-2000

At the first General Assembly of the new United Reformed Church in October 1972, the agreed rules of procedure included the following:

> It is important to ensure adequate representation (eg ministerial and lay, men and women) at all levels (Assembly, Provincial and District). The Nominations Committee shall ensure that normally in any committee not less than one quarter of the total membership (excluding ex officio members) shall be men and not less than one quarter shall be women. A similar proviso shall apply in regard to ministerial and lay representation.[46]

A serious effort was made to ensure that this was put into practice. Yet the fact that by 1976 no national department or committee was chaired by a woman showed that real equality was still in the future.

Another step forward was made in 1981 when Rosalind Goodfellow was elected Moderator of General Assembly for 1982.[47] She therefore represented the United Reformed Church at the service which Pope John Paul II attended in Canterbury Cathedral during his visit to Britain in 1982. Five years later the situation had greatly improved; eight committees were now chaired by women, and in order to avoid difficulties over nomenclature, the word 'chairman' was now replaced by 'convener'. However, in 1989 the Faith and Life department still had to report on the need to do more to provide equal treatment for men and women.

These changes had much to do with the British Council of Churches Report on the Community of Women and Men in the Church, issued in February 1984. As a direct result of the recommendations in that report, the Church Life Department of the United Reformed Church brought to Assembly in 1984 a resolution asking all United Reformed Church departments and committees to ensure that their publications used inclusive language. For many who spoke in the ensuing debate, the subject was 'a red herring', and the resolution was only passed by a narrow margin of 226 to 205 votes.[48] Though some continued to regard this as a minor issue, the guideline was on the whole observed, and the reason for it has been more widely accepted.[49] Another resolution that the Assembly should express 'its ecumenical solidarity by recognising the contribution of feminist theology' was passed 212 votes to 165.

This was to have an influence on the work of the Doctrine, Prayer and Worship committee, for feminist theologians had gone further than asking for inclusive language in relation to humanity by challenging the use of masculine language about the deity. In the mid-1990s the committee produced a Statement of Faith in inclusive language, to be available alongside the existing Statement for those who wished. This provoked a lengthy and emotive debate at the 1996 Assembly, but ultimately it was accepted. Though it remains controversial, it may be regarded in the future as a pioneering attempt to meet the feminist critique of Christianity.

In the 1970s there had been a marked growth in the number of women who applied for acceptance for ordination training. Since 1977 there have been years in which the students in one of the theological colleges have been equally balanced between men and women. As part of the proposals for union with the Churches of Christ,[50] Assembly authorised the Ministerial Training Committee to prepare plans for Auxiliary Ministry (unpaid, part-time ministry), intended to be similar to the kind of ministry being undertaken by many elders in the Churches of Christ. This proved to be a route by which all the remaining former Presbyterian deaconesses (except one, who chose to remain a deaconess) could be ordained to the ministry of Word and Sacrament (a ministry they were in practice already exercising). It also proved a route into ministry for women with domestic commitments which precluded full-time training and service. In 1990 the term 'auxiliary ministry' was replaced by 'non-stipendiary ministry', in order to allay fears, not altogether successfully, that there were two levels of ministry.

In 1985 Helen Ashton, a retired minister, prepared a questionnaire which was sent to all the provincial moderators and to a selected group of churches and women ministers, on the subject of women's ministry. The questionnaire was carefully constructed and analysed. The results were published in an article entitled 'Women's Ministry in the United Reformed Church' in *The Modern Churchman* XXXII/3, 1990, pp. 1-31. Helen Ashton believed that the responses revealed that younger women had had fewer problems than their older colleagues, but that women were still very rarely introduced to, and even more rarely called to, larger churches, where tradition tended to be stronger. She concluded that 'the ministry of women revealed through these questionnaires is shown to be one still in the making'. The problems revealed, she felt, arose from a lack of awareness of the differences between women and men in ministry. With greater awareness, many problems could be solved.

New important steps forward were taken in the 1990s. The whole climate changed in 1991 when the Church of England decided to ordain women priests – though it was disappointing that so little notice was taken in the media of the fact that other churches had decades of experience of women's ministry. In 1990 Janet Sowerbutts, then tutor in pastoral theology at Westminster College, was appointed as the Moderator for Thames North Province – the first woman to hold such a post. Between 1996 and 1998 three further women, Elizabeth Welch, Elizabeth Caswell and Roberta Rominger were also appointed as Synod Moderators. General Assembly had two more women as Moderators, Ruth Clarke[51] in 1992 and Wilma Frew in 1998, as Moderators.

In 1988 the World Council of Churches declared its Ecumenical Decade of Churches in Solidarity with Women. In response, the Faith and Life Department of the United Reformed Church, prompted by a gathering at the Windermere Centre convened by Ruth Clarke, set up a network for the community of women and men in the church – 'Sharing People in Network' (SPIN) in 1990. Each province was asked to appoint a consultant, and each district a correspondent, to monitor progress. SPIN established links with the Ecumenical Forum of European Christian Women and with the Women's Inter-Church Consultative Committee (WICCC). In the same year the United Reformed Church officially adopted an equal opportunities policy, with particular reference to women and black people – disabled people were added later. This was to be monitored by an Equal Opportunities Committee. The very existence of this committee and the concerns which had led to its formation revealed the continuing existence of prejudice, often unexamined and unrealised.

SPIN was not regarded favourably by everyone; it was dogged by doubts as to whether or not it was to be considered as a separate women's organization, and it was regarded as a 'feminist' organisation by some women with a more traditional outlook. Some felt that the church had dealt with this problem and needed to move on to other 'more important' issues. But the last point is not the reported experience of many women. When SPIN joined with the Faith and Life Department and two provinces in sponsoring a research project on the position of women in the church,[52] all the respondents believed that the United Reformed Church was ahead of other denominations in including women in all aspects of church life. But the majority also reported and confirmed the continuing need for women's groups for support, fellowship and inspiration.

The United Reformed Church 2000-

On 1 April 2000 the United Reformed Church in the United Kingdom joined with the Congregational Union of Scotland[53] to form a new church – the United Reformed Church. The former Congregational Union of Scotland (which became the Scottish Congregational Church in 1993) had a long tradition of women in ministry and in its presidency, and has retained a strong Women's Union. The first woman to be ordained to a church of the

Congregational Union of Scotland was Vera Kenmure (née Findlay) in 1928.[54] She was elected President of the Union for the year 1951-2. Since that time another five women have served as President, four laywomen and one minister.[55]

The Women's Union dates back to 1893 and is a very active body, involved in many aspects of community service and pastoral care, with branches in almost every congregation and strong links with the Scottish Christian Women's Fellowship. The present president is Mrs Sheena Paul, who was secretary for 25 years until 1998. It has now become the Women's Union of the Scottish Synod of the United Reformed Church. At the Unifying Assembly the great service to the church of the Women's Union was acknowledged, and Mission Council was asked to consider 'whether there are implications for the central organisation of the church in the context of current ecumenical thinking'.

In July 2000 the General Assembly of the new Church elected for the first time an ordained woman minister, Elizabeth Welch, as its Moderator for the year 2001-2, and in 2003 elected the Revd Sheila Maxey as Moderator for 2004-5. The most important question to ask now may be whether women's participation in the councils of the church is challenging the actual structures themselves, and whether women are responding creatively to new opportunities.

Chapter 4

Ministry and Theological Education

The Dissenting tradition has generally valued 'a learned ministry', and expected church members to be informed and articulate about their faith, yet the public role expected of women church members was, until the twentieth century, a subordinate and practical one. That did not prevent some women from reading theology or learning biblical languages, and hymns, prayers and devotional works written by women were acceptable and often popular.

It was inevitable that the growth of higher education for women would eventually lead to an interest in studying theology at university level. One of the great changes in the study of theology in the twentieth century has been the number of women now choosing to study it at university, and time has shown that women can make a significant contribution to its development, not only through the new discipline of feminist theology, but through a different understanding of the whole field. Feminist theology is not simply an extra option added on to the existing curriculum; it is a challenge to the nature of the whole subject.

Carey Hall had already opened in 1912 as a training college for women missionaries (mostly from Nonconformist traditions), and it continued for this purpose in Selly Oak, Birmingham until its amalgamation with St Andrew's Hall in the 1960s. At Carey Hall women could take a three-year course which included biblical studies, sociology, education and applied theology, in preparation for service with the London Missionary Society, the Baptist Missionary Society or the Presbyterian Church of England Overseas Missions. The Hall had a series of distinguished principals, Presbyterian and Baptist.[1]

At the beginning of the twentieth century, university degree courses in theology were regarded primarily as preparation for ordination, usually in the Anglican Church, and therefore in practice taken almost exclusively by men.[2] For Nonconformists this was often a second degree, especially in cases where ministerial students were expected to have an arts degree before beginning concentrated study of theology.

Congregationalists

Constance Todd (later Coltman) had already taken a degree course in history at Oxford (not a degree, as women were still excluded from degrees at Oxford and Cambridge despite having taken all the necessary examinations) before she approached Principal Selbie at Mansfield College in 1913. She was admitted in the October of that year and took the standard course. She achieved some distinction, winning the Fairbairn Memorial Essay Prize and showing a particular aptitude for Hebrew.[3] As London University already granted degrees to women, she took the London BD degree.

Mansfield was not at that stage a residential college, and so the problems of residence which worried the staff and councils of certain other colleges did not arise. Mansfield was not yet a part of the University of Oxford (though all staff and students were individually matriculated members) and so was not subject to the rules of residence and common room life which complicated the college's situation after 1955 (when it became a Permanent Private Hall). The members of the Junior Common Room (JCR) seem to have been comparatively enlightened for the time, for on 17 October 1913, after 'prolonged discussion' they 'invited Miss Todd to make use of the JCR at any time (except during House meetings) and to attend conferences'. Somewhat patronisingly they also informed the principal that they had no objection to Miss Todd's attendance at sermon classes. Principal Selbie proved to be a firm supporter of women's ordination and was later a Vice-President of the Society for the Ministry for Women. One of his early students wrote at the time of his retirement that 'to his women students he was so kind and fair and wise; never hiding from them the fact that life for a woman minister is as yet bound to be difficult, but also making clear his conviction that God can speak through a woman as well as through a man ...'.[4]

It seems that Constance Todd took an active part in JCR life. For example, in 1915 she was responsible for inviting Maude Royden to address one of the regular college conferences, which she herself chaired. During her course she became engaged to a fellow student, Claud Coltman. They were both ordained on the eve of their marriage, and throughout their ministerial life enjoyed joint pastorates.[5] They divided the work between them by agreement with the church concerned; in practice Claud did most of the preaching and chairing of meetings, Constance did most of the baptisms and weddings, and was particularly active in visiting mothers and children.

One of the greatest influences on Constance Coltman's life was the minister of the King's Weigh House, W E Orchard. She and her husband-to-be had started attending his church during vacations from the Mansfield course, and were deeply influenced both by his pacifism and by his sacramental theology. It was Orchard who presided at their ordination; despite his eventual conversion to Roman Catholicism and his subsequent ordination to the Catholic priesthood, he was a lifelong supporter of women's political and religious equality. In 1920 he was one of the leaders of a movement known as the Society of Free Catholics, and a frequent contributor to its journal, *The Free Catholic*. The Coltmans too were sympathetic to this movement and in October 1920 Constance Coltman contributed an article on 'Women and the Priesthood' in response to the pronouncements of the recent Lambeth Conference, which had rejected a recommendation that ordained deaconesses should be able to administer the sacrament to the sick. 'Whence comes the widespread shrinking among men and women alike from a woman having aught to do with the Blessed Sacrament?'

She continued to contribute to the ecumenical debate concerning the ministry of women. In an article in the following year she wrote on 'The need for women confessors', arguing that many women preferred to consult a member of their own sex about pastoral problems; it was 'even possible' that some men might prefer a woman confessor about pastoral problems. Yet in churches which offered formal confession, this possibility was being denied. The Lambeth Conference had just specifically rejected such a role for deaconesses.

In later sermons and addresses Constance Coltman proposed that women would in the future have a particular contribution to make both to the understanding of ministry and to the understanding of God's relation to humanity. She and other pioneers of her generation 'had perforce to be trained at exclusively masculine theological colleges and our minds were moulded by a masculine curriculum, imparted by men professors'. But that phase would pass (though it probably took longer than she envisaged). She believed that women were peculiarly qualified to interpret the Passion as 'the gateway through which life and immortality were brought to light'.[6] She predicted correctly that in the future there would be more ministerial teams, and hoped that they would always include both men and women.

Constance Coltman was a close friend of Maude Royden (who remained an Anglican until her death in 1955, and was therefore never ordained). When Maude Royden wrote a book entitled *The Church and Woman* in 1924 she invited Constance Coltman to contribute a chapter on the Free Churches. Later the two of them were among the most active members of the inter-denominational Society for the Ministry of Women, which arose out of a conference of women ministers in 1926.

There was no great rush of women seeking admission to Mansfield College; only a handful of women took the full ministerial course in the 1920s and 1930s, though a few came for shorter courses in preparation for other forms of church service. One of the most able was Dorothy Wilson (1893-1956). Like Constance Todd she was brought up in the Presbyterian Church of England, and served her denomination as Young People's secretary from 1914 until 1918. In 1924 the Presbyterian Assembly was entirely unsympathetic to her application to train for ordination, but she readily found acceptance at Mansfield. Had she not had to wage a constant battle against ill-health almost all her life she would have made an outstanding contribution to Congregational life. As it was she had a series of short ministries, and was able to publish a number of works on religious education. Mary Darlaston (later Osborn),[7] who entered the college in 1934, was the daughter of one of the ministers who had officiated at the ordination of Constance Todd at the King's Weigh House in 1917. She married a fellow student, Reginald Osborn (who later became an Anglican) and assisted her husband at Abney Park Congregational Church.

Meanwhile other colleges had to decide on a response to potential women applicants. Attitudes towards women and their social and political aspirations were undergoing a change after 1914. Highly-educated women with determination and the advantage of some private means now had new opportunities. The vote was extended to women (provided they were over 30 and householders) in 1918, and in 1920 the University of Oxford finally opened its degrees to women. In April 1918 the Colleges Board of the Congregational Union had already suggested that women should be admitted to the theological colleges on the same terms as men.

In November 1918, just after the Armistice, Dr F J Powicke's proposal to the Committee of the Lancashire Independent College that they should be prepared to accept women students was agreed, though it was not put to the test until six years later, when an application was received from Margaret Hardy. Margaret Hardy (later Margaret Fullerton, 1890-1980) was 33 when she applied to the College in 1924. At school in Bournemouth she had come under the influence of the minister of Richmond Hill Congregational Church, J D Jones. Later as a journalist in London she was much influenced by Maude Royden, then assistant minister at the City Temple. More recently she had spent 18 months in pastoral charge of Milton Congregational Church, Hanley, and was currently full-time assistant to the minister of Hanley Tabernacle. She greatly impressed the interviewing committee as 'an able and consecrated woman', and was accepted unanimously. A year later, two younger women, Constance Clark (1902-69) and Kathleen Hall (later Kathleen Hendry, 1906-) were also accepted. Kathleen Hendry has written an account of those early years in *Don't Ask Me Why: Sixty Years a Woman Minister* (London: United Reformed Church, 1991). She relates how as a Methodist (her father was a Methodist minister) in north Manchester she met Margaret Hardy and heard about the opportunity for a woman to train for the Congregational ministry. A meeting with Dr Alexander Grieve, the principal of the Lancashire Independent College, was encouraging, and she was readily accepted by the interviewing committee. Constance Clark had spent her early life in Fleetwood and Southport, where she was encouraged in her wish to seek a form of full-time service to the church by the minister of Birkdale Congregational Church, Norman Popplewell. When she was accepted by the college, he coached her in Latin before the term began.

Unlike Mansfield College, the Lancashire Independent College was a residential college. The College Committee could not contemplate the idea of mixed residence, so the three female students had to live out. They were not allowed to become members of the common room, but were able to attend the weekly meetings of the Literary and Debating Society. The Assembly Hall had been adapted so that it could also be used as a badminton court, leading one wag to write in the College Newsletter (April 1925) that 'the flutter of the shuttlecock mingles sweetly with the flutter of the petticoats, and all is joyance within'.

These three women students achieved considerable academic distinction. Kathleen Hall, like Constance Todd, particularly enjoyed Hebrew, and won prizes not only in Hebrew but also in Greek, and was only the second woman to gain the Manchester BD degree. Although Kathleen Hall may have benefited from the fact that her father was a well-known local Methodist minister, it was remarkable that all three were called to pastorates immediately at the end of their training – a tribute both to them and to the churches concerned at a time when there was plenty of prejudice against the idea of women ministers in practice.

In 1938 Kathleen Hall married James Hendry, a doctor. At this time middle class professional women, however valuable their skills, were expected to resign upon marriage. The Congregational Union's Commission on the Ministry of Women had upheld this view when it reported in 1936, stating that 'it does not seem desirable for a woman to continue in a pastorate after marriage'.[8] After the death of her husband she returned to pastoral charge, and continued to preach regularly until she was in her eighties. Margaret Hardy spent all her ministerial life in Leeds, as did Constance Clark, and they exercised a notable joint ministry there at Marshall Street Congregational Church from 1930 until 1937. When Margaret Hardy married Andrew Fullerton she gave up pastoral ministry for hospital chaplaincy and Constance Clark continued alone. Both took a full part in wider church life, national and international; Constance Clark was only the second woman to be elected chairman of the Yorkshire Congregational Union,[9] and made a deep impression on the life of the city of Leeds.

Another woman admitted to the Lancashire college in the 1920s was Eva Gibbons (1902-75, later Eva Lazenby, always known as Mrs Walter Lazenby). Like Kathleen Hall she began life as a Methodist, and had originally planned a career in music. In order to support herself during training she acted as secretary to Dr Grieve, the principal. She was ordained in 1931 to the pastorate at Irwell Bank, Kearsley, but after her marriage to Walter Lazenby, another former Lancashire student, she continued her ministry in unofficial ways.

The Lancashire college committee of the 1920s displayed a more sympathetic attitude towards women students than most other college committees, and was probably helped by the presence of the first woman committee member, Constance Pilkington, elected in 1925. But by 1930 the college was adopting a more conservative attitude, and the admission of women was suspended from 1931 on three grounds: the small number of churches thought to be willing to call a woman minister, the alleged need for 'specialised training' for which there was as yet no provision, and the perceived unsuitability of the college's traditions and accommodation for co-education. There had not been a sufficient number of women students to cause any serious impulse for change – the women had to conform to the male norm. The Lancashire Independent College took no more women students in the next 20 years.

Meanwhile the Western College in Bristol admitted its first woman student in 1927. Ellen (Nellie) Leaton (1888-1964) was 39; she had already worked as a deaconess in the United Methodist Church for some time. She took the full course of five years and then had 24 years in pastoral ministry in different parts of the country. But a year after she left, the college committee voted to discontinue receiving applications from women students on the grounds that 'this College has not the facilities for the training of women students.' No more women studied at Western until the late 1940s. It is not clear what lay behind this. The principal at the time, R S Franks, was certainly a supporter of women's education in general. But it was to be his successor, H Lovell Cocks, who was positively welcoming again to women students. In 1949 he told the subscribers that 'our women students are among our best preachers, as they are among our best in the examination lists.' He advised the churches that they should overcome prejudice against women 'in their own highest interest'; 'it will be a happy day for the churches when they recognise it.'

The only other Congregational theological college to accept women students before the Second World War was New College, London. Mary Collins (1874-1945) was accepted in 1919, when she was 45. Until the previous year she had been an Anglican. She had considerable experience in journalism, having worked for the *British Weekly* since 1895, latterly as editor of the 'News of the Churches' section. After finishing her course she had a ministry of ten years in North Bow in the east end of London, struggling to reduce the church's mortgage and to keep the congregation alive to the needs of the neighbourhood. Evelyn Maitland entered the college a few years later, and was ordained in 1933 at the conclusion of her course for service with the London Missionary Society in China. There was also a short-lived attempt to offer a part-time training course for home missionaries and deaconesses in the 1920s. But the college then became almost as nervous as the Lancashire and Western colleges, and in 1939 laid down that no woman would in future be accepted unless she was at least 28 and was already a graduate or had private means; in other words, if she could support herself should she not receive a call to a church. Earlier in the decade Elsie Chamberlain had been discouraged from applying to New College by the principal, Sydney Cave, on the grounds that he was unable to reprimand women in the ways that students sometimes needed. Her response to this is not recorded. In the end she got round this by taking a theology degree at King's College, London and then persuading the denomination to accept her period of assisting Muriel Paulden in Liverpool in lieu of attendance at a theological college.

All this reflects the fact that most churches were unwilling even to consider a woman candidate for ministry, unless the salary they were able to offer was too small to support a man with family responsibilities. This was the finding of the commission on the ministry of women which the Congregational Union appointed in 1934. While they affirmed their support for women's ordained ministry in their report of 1936, they also reported 'a widespread and strong unwillingness among the churches to consider a woman as candidate in a vacancy,' and there is a clear implication in their report that women were being offered smaller salaries than their male counterparts. It noted that 17 women had been ordained since 1917, 13 of them currently in pastoral charge, adding that 'it is only as women are able to prove their distinctive worth that any change of attitude and action by the church can be expected.'[10] An illustration of this point is the fact that when the minister of Stanley Congregational Church in Liverpool, died in 1924 his widow, Edith Pickles, already a graduate and well known as a preacher in the area, was called to be his successor. The same thing happened in 1941, when Eleanor Shakeshaft was called to succeed her husband at Herne Bay Congregational Church. She then proceeded to take the required training by correspondence and private tuition in order to gain acceptance on the roll of ministers.

This route, which by-passed college training, usually led first to admission to 'List B' (a list of 'evangelists' authorised by the Congregational Union, a category which had been abolished by 1968), but could lead eventually, via a Congregational Union examination, to acceptance onto 'List A'. A considerable proportion of early women ministers entered ministry by this route. Later it was replaced by the Roll of Ministers (ROM) examination.

By the beginning of the Second World War women had made only slow progress in being actually accepted by the churches of the Congregational denomination. Constance Coltman had pointed out the peculiar difficulty faced by women in the Free Churches when she spoke to the Society for the Ministry of Women's conference in January 1939: 'Our democratic constitution makes it easy for a very small minority to thwart the desire, even of a majority of the congregation, to call a woman to their pulpit. This system of choosing a minister bears hardly upon the woman pioneer.'[11] It has to be said that this situation is still not entirely a thing of the past.

The Second World War was a further catalyst in opening new opportunities for women. The Yorkshire United Independent College in Bradford accepted its first woman student, Daisy Beryl Russell in 1943; 'apparently no one thought they would accept me. I had had no doubt that they would,' she later recalled. Originally she planned to be a missionary, but instead she married a fellow student, Harold Bennett. Subsequently she recalled discrimination: 'no one seemed able to grasp that a minister's wife could also be a minister in her own right and should be treated as such'.[12] Doreen Speck followed Beryl Russell in 1946 and Cynthia Brook in 1947.[13] But here as elsewhere, the college was cautious, and in 1947 resolved that women should only be admitted 'for strong reasons and under proper safeguards' (these were not elaborated). No further female students were admitted before the college closed in 1958.

Florence Frost-Mee, then a widow of 30, achieved a breakthrough at New College towards the end of the war. Her application was initially refused on the grounds that her certificate from the Brighton Diocesan Training College was not a degree, and therefore the college's rules made her ineligible. A person of great determination and spirit, she wrote to the chairman of the governors and asked for an interview with the principal. She reports that it took one hour and forty minutes of furious argument before he finally agreed to accept her. The rules were then changed. At the end of her course she was called to Charlton Congregational Church in south London, and saw its membership grow from 20 to 130 during the course of her 16-year ministry. She was the first woman to be appointed as a governor of the College.[14]

Janet Webber was the first woman student to be accepted by Cheshunt College in Cambridge, and the youngest to be accepted for ministerial training after the war. She was just 22 when she moved to Cambridge in 1954. She later reflected that the male students felt threatened by having a woman student on the same terms as themselves. 'The older women who came could be seen as mother figures, they were different, but I was one of the gang, and yet I wasn't. I had problems with this because I wasn't perceiving myself as a woman, I was perceiving myself as a student in training for the ministry'.[15]

The first woman to be ordained in Wales was Susannah Ellis (1897-1989), the daughter of a Welsh platelayer on the Great Western Railway. Through determination and private study she managed to win a bursary to study at Bangor University College, becoming the first woman to take the Welsh BD. She was ordained in 1925 at her home church, Pendref Chapel, Llanfyllin for service in Papua with the London Missionary Society. After six years she married Robert Rankin, and together they worked at the Chalmers Theological College in Papua; her husband was principal while she was a professor. She was a skilled linguist and published grammar books and story books in Papuan languages. Her experience as a child in Wales being taught in English gave had given her an understanding of the problems of learning in more than one language. After her husband's death in 1960 she herself became principal for the next four years. She retired to Australia where she worked on translations of the Bible. In 1972 she was awarded the MBE. She paid a visit to Wales in 1973 to receive an honorary degree from the University of Wales, but returned to Australia, where she died in 1989.[16]

It was not until much later, in 1954, that Jean Wilkinson was the first woman to enter Brecon Memorial College in Wales. She became the first woman Congregational minister in Wales when she was ordained at Providence, Mountain Ash in 1957. She continued in pastoral ministry, mostly in Essex, until her retirement in 1993.

In the 1950s and 1960s the numbers of women in ministerial training remained small.[17] At Mansfield College their position even deteriorated for a time after 1955, when the College became a Permanent Private Hall and began taking undergraduates; it was then subject to the rules of the University, whose colleges were all single-sex. Women students were excluded from dining rights, though a concession was made in allowing them to dine on their own in the Senior Common Room on occasions when evening events were held. George Caird, who became principal in 1970, was particularly sympathetic to women students, and encouraged Kate Chegwin (later Compston) to move from St Hugh's to Mansfield in 1971 after Mansfield had won the right to present its own ordination candidates for graduation. When Oxford, in its own cautious way, allowed a restricted number of undergraduate colleges to become co-educational in 1974, the situation improved greatly. Meanwhile New College made it possible in the 1960s for women to be resident (in part of a corridor re-named 'The Nunnery') and thus share more fully in college social life. Northern College also had a 'Nunnery' above the principal's lodgings.

St Paul's House

During these years there was a significant but comparatively short-lived experiment in training women for work as home missionaries. It was to be something of a parallel to Carey Hall, which had been training women missionaries for most of the century. St Paul's House was the vision and inspiration of one woman, Muriel Paulden (1892-1975).[18] Muriel Paulden had gone to Carey Hall in 1915, hoping to train as an overseas missionary. Here she benefited from hearing outside lecturers not only from the Quaker Woodbrooke College, but also from the Presbyterian Westminster College which was evacuated to Selly Oak from Cambridge. At the end of her course she was declared unfit for overseas service and so moved to Merseyside, where she took charge of the Berkley Street Training Centre for Sunday School teachers and youth leaders, a new initiative sponsored by the Merseyside Congregational Council. When the local church was re-established in 1922, Muriel Paulden was called to be minister; this call and its acceptance were generally understood to constitute ordination. The church flourished in the inter-war years, but had to be closed during the war because of bomb damage.

In 1945, Muriel Paulden, then chairman of the Lancashire Congregational Union, recognised the need for the church to be involved in the re-building of society after the war, and conceived the idea of a scheme for training women home missionaries. She wrote a letter to *The Christian World* in 1945 outlining her scheme:

> It is intended for women who want to devote their lives to the building up of the home Church as our missionaries give themselves to the Church abroad. ... After training they will be at the service of the Congregational Churches as they may be needed – to open up new work in a district – to initiate or develop some special piece of work in a church – to take charge of small country churches.

Potential candidates were to be between 20 and 40, and 'ready to take all the risks which a pioneering movement entails'. The example of Paul and the very first missionaries led to the enterprise being named 'St Paul's House'.[19]

A house which had been occupied by the army was rented in Sunnyside, Liverpool 8, and the first two students took up residence in October 1945, undeterred by the dry rot and decay then prevalent in the house. Within six months improvements were sufficient to hold an official opening. Local ministers were enrolled as tutors alongside Muriel Paulden, who was Warden, and the principal of Lancashire Independent College acted as chairman.

Admission to St Paul's involved becoming a member of a community as well as undertaking a two or three year training course. The course itself was divided equally between academic work and practical experience, and there was the opportunity to take a certificate, diploma or degree in theology. When a student had finished her course she was commissioned as a home missionary in an area of need, usually for about three years; she was given full pastoral charge, including the administration of the sacraments. During this time she was kept in close touch with the House and paid regular visits. At the end of three years she returned to St Paul's to await a new call, often to be succeeded by a full-time stipendiary minister with a much larger salary. Reflecting in 1995 on her experience as a member of St Paul's, Margaret Laurie wrote: 'There was an unwritten rule at St Paul's House about marriage. It almost went on the lines that marriage is a waste of a woman's training and against the vocation to serve as a home missionary'. Such an idea was commonly held at the time.

Muriel Paulden retired in 1957 and her place as Warden was taken Alice Platts, one of the first two students. Those trained at St Paul's during the years 1945-65 gave sacrificial service in difficult areas throughout the country.[20] But the enterprise was never wholeheartedly supported by the denomination (though there was much support from Merseyside), and by 1965 there was a feeling that as women could more readily find acceptance at the traditional theological colleges, that was where they should go. Many felt that the work of St Paul's was now done, though there was much sadness, for the House had been an inspiration to its students, many of whom would never have contemplated applying to a college. Mary Evans, a student at St Paul's 1954-7, later reflected that 'because of my background, I would never have considered applying to Brecon College through the usual channels of that time. ... I found it all very exciting and the three years went very quickly'. The house was closed, but the fellowship continued, and many of the former students were subsequently 'properly' ordained as ministers and continued to serve the church with more adequate recognition.

Presbyterians

So far this account has referred only to Congregationalists. Presbyterians were much more cautious in accepting any woman candidates into theological colleges and for ordination, despite the fact that the General Assembly of the Presbyterian Church of England had passed a resolution in 1921 affirming that there was no barrier in principle to the admission of women to the ordained ministry. However the Presbyterians had instituted the office of church sister (later deaconess) after the first world war, and training for this office included one year's study at Carey Hall, and one year's practical experience at the Presbyterian Settlement in Poplar. In 1934 a question was raised as to the effect the admission of women students would have on the status of Westminster College; the Senatus found 'insuperable difficulties' in the idea.[21] The first woman to be ordained by the Presbyterian Church of England was Ella Gordon (see chapter three), in 1956, but as she already had much experience and a degree in theology, the question of training did not arise. Once that barrier had been broken, it was less difficult to persuade Westminster

College (which, unlike Congregational theological colleges, belonged to the denomination) to accept a woman student. Margaret Taylor was accepted for training in 1959/1960, and recalls that she was readily accepted by the other students. She won the doctrine prize, and felt welcomed by local churches as a student preacher. At the end of her course she was called to pastoral ministry in Nunthorpe. She was followed by Doris Nix[22] in 1964 and then by Elizabeth Erlebach in 1967. The latter became Elizabeth Nash the following year after marrying a fellow student. However, by the time of the union of Presbyterians and Congregationalists in the United Reformed Church in 1972, there were still only four women Presbyterian ministers.[23]

Churches of Christ

The Churches of Christ had only just begun to ordain women to the full-time stipendiary ministry when their union with the United Reformed Church took place in 1981. It has to be remembered, however, that according to the Churches of Christ's tradition, elders could also preside at Communion, and women had been appointed as elders in the 1970s. In 1973 the Annual Conference agreed to accept the full-time ministry of women. Three years later Rowena Gates was the first woman candidate to be accepted for training for the stipendiary ministry in the Churches of Christ. Overdale College, Selly Oak (which since its foundation in 1920 had always taken women students preparing for missionary service or community work) was about to close, but its principal, John Francis, became a tutor at the Northern College in Manchester, with special responsibility for any Churches of Christ students. Rowena Gates therefore studied at the Congregational College, Manchester, and was followed the next year by Daphne Garrow. They took the course alongside United Reformed Church students. It was actually Daphne Garrow, later Daphne Jones (she married the Revd Dafydd Jones in 1978) who was the first woman to be ordained at the Annual Conference of the Churches of Christ at Swanwick in 1980. Both Daphne Jones and Rowena Gates (later Francis) became United Reformed Church ministers. Daphne Jones was tragically killed in 1984 in a car accident with her young daughter.

United Reformed Church

Since 1972 four colleges have provided training for ministry for the United Reformed Church, (and in some cases for Congregational ministry) – Northern College, Manchester (in effect an amalgamation of the Lancashire and Yorkshire colleges, the Western College and Paton College), Westminster College, Cambridge, Mansfield College, Oxford and the ecumenical Queen's College in Birmingham. All these colleges became more hospitable to women in the 1970s, and the Sex Discrimination Act of 1975 reflected a change of attitude in society as a whole (though churches were actually exempt from its requirements). At the same time the proportion of women candidates rapidly increased, sometimes forming half of the student body. Another development has been the proliferation of ecumenical part-time courses, particularly for non-stipendiary ministry, and many women with family responsibilities have found this a more feasible method of training.

It was another big step forward when Justine Wyatt was appointed assistant chaplain, with teaching responsibilities, at Mansfield College, Oxford in 1980. She combined this work with part-time ministry for the following 11 years. Yvonne Workman's tutorship at Mansfield a few years later was tragically cut short by her premature death in 1991. In 1985 Jean Forster was appointed to the staff of Northern College; subsequently several women have joined the teaching staff. Susan Durber was elected Mona Powell Research Fellow at Northern College in 1989, and wrote a doctoral thesis applying the literary theory of Derrida to parable criticism. Janet Tollington was appointed Director of Old Testament Studies at Westminster College in 1993. A further step was taken in 1998 when Catherine Middleton, who was already Associate Director, became Acting Director of Ordination Training and Chaplain at Mansfield College, Oxford, a post she held for a year before resigning because of ill-health, depriving the United Reformed Church of one its most able ministers. She died in May 2000 at the early age of 42.

Women are now fully accepted as staff and students in the United Reformed Church colleges, and feminist theology is taken seriously. But many issues relating to ministry and training remain to be faced in the new century. In her article published in 1990, based on questionnaires sent out in 1985, Helen Ashton reflected that the entry of women had so far had little impact on college courses.[24] This is probably less true in 2004 than it was in 1990, but there is still much to be done in building up the confidence of women as they seek to reach their full potential in church and society.

Chapter 5

On Not Keeping Silent in the Churches:
Women in the Pulpit

Preaching by women has long been seen as 'unfeminine.' When Betty Williams was ordained to Congregational ministry at Lytchett Minster in 1967 a friend wrote this oft-quoted remark of Dr Johnson's in a book given as an ordination gift: 'A woman's preaching is like a dog's walking on his hinder legs. It is not done well: but you are surprised to find it done at all'. Recounting that story Betty Williams remarked, 'Time will tell if my ministry has been well done but it has been good for me at least'.[1]

Throughout the centuries Paul's admonition in I Corinthians 14 that women should remain silent in church has often been quoted to justify opposition to women's preaching.[2] As the text is usually read now his stricture simply applies to not asking questions during a service but the advice has often been misused to attack women's ministry. The male minister of the City Temple Congregational Church in London, who welcomed the preaching of Anglican laywoman Maude Royden as his pulpit assistant during the First World War, received a regular stream of post cards referring him to this passage of Pauline teaching.[3]

Yet preaching has been such a major part of Free Church worship that to have barred women from it would have meant relegating them to the edge of what has been done Sunday by Sunday. To reflect on the Word of God through preaching has been seen as central to the work of ordained ministry in the Reformed tradition and most male ministers seem to have spent a lot of time preparing for it and doing it. Books of sermons by male ministers, well known, and not so well known, were common during the nineteenth century. As the Victorians began to build large new Dissenting chapels, capable of seating 2,000, so the appeal of massed congregations grew and preachers like R W Dale and Joseph Parker developed a style of preaching and a public profile to match the buildings.

Writing on English Dissenting history the Congregational historian Erik Routley complained about the way this had tended to lead to people treating the preacher 'much in the same fashion as the film-actor is now treated and to regard public worship as something like a respectable public entertainment'.[4] Adulation was further fuelled by the way the religious press published weekly sermons by the best-known preachers from the most important Free Church pulpits in London and elsewhere. At the time when women were first entering ordained ministry many male ministers clearly revelled in preaching. Sermons preached by women have rarely been published however.[5]

This is not to say that women did not preach until the twentieth century. As this study has shown, women have a long tradition in leading worship and preaching on the fringes of the Church. *The Christian Commonwealth* reported in March 1917 that 'women preachers are not so rare a phenomenon as reactionaries in the Churches would like as to suppose' and went on to give an account provided by Mrs Saul Solomon of her mother:

> She moved large audiences, especially great numbers of men of all classes, and won them for Christ. Her first splendid sermon on 'The woman of Samaria' was given in the Music Hall, Edinburgh, when I was a girl. Over 3,000 attended, and with wonderful results. My mother spoke in public in England and at the Cape till she was about 80 years old. She died in her 90th year, brilliantly happy, young and full of glory.[6]

Even so it was usual, where women did preach, that it would be to gatherings of women only and not normally in the church building but in the hall or Sunday School room. Times of revival allowed a certain relaxing of church structures, with an increase in women's activities, followed by periods of settlement and retrenchment when women once more took a lower profile and accommodated themselves to the dominant culture. One exception to this pattern was the growth of women's missionary auxiliaries which raised money for women missionaries, organised meetings that offered women missionaries a platform, and gave opportunities for women to speak in public in support of the cause. Susan Thorne's study of nineteenth century Congregational Missions has highlighted the importance of these outlets for women's activity at a time when evangelical churches typically kept them silent and excluded from positions of influence. She writes of the empowerment suggested by women's enthusiasm for hearing a speaker of their own sex addressing a female audience, and of the consequent regret which some women felt when women's and men's missionary bodies were amalgamated in the early twentieth century.[7]

It was in the context of a movement for revival in the Anglican Church during the First World War that the question of a woman being able to address mixed audiences became a matter of public debate. In 1916 the Church of England organised a National Mission of Repentance and Hope. Several Anglican laywomen, including Maude Royden, served on the Council responsible for organizing this venture. At first the Bishop of London, Winnington-Ingram, agreed that women might speak in church if no other building was available, on the condition that the audience was female and that the speaker stood in the aisle, not at the lectern or in the pulpit. This permission would apply for the duration of the Mission only. However, after protests from certain groups within the Church of England, Winnington-Ingram withdrew his permission.[8] This left many Anglican parishioners 'uncertain about the Church's official position towards women's speaking and teaching in church'.[9]

Mrs Lewis-Donaldson of Leicester, mentioned in *The Christian Commonwealth*, was one who 'preferred to speak from the lectern rather than from the pulpit'. She said that it was a terrible experience to preach in church as:

> There was a church atmosphere through which it was almost impossible to reach your audience. They seemed to have come to church believing that there was not anything for them to listen to.[10]

The suffrage movement had empowered and enabled women to take part in public debate, so that they were no longer generally expected to remain confined to the domestic sphere, as had been the case half a century before. The Suffragettes had also 'realised that preaching would allow them the opportunity not only to promote social and political reform but also to critique and combat the deeply rooted cultural sources of women's subordination'.[11] With the granting of partial women's suffrage in 1918 women entered a new phase as public speakers. For some people this meant that women, having achieved their aims, should be willing to return quietly to the domestic sphere. Others considered the doors were open at last and women were not ready to be silenced again.

Congregational Churches

When in 1917 the Congregational Union of England and Wales became the first Christian tradition in Britain to allow the ordination of women as ministers this gave a new validation to women's preaching ministry. However it is interesting to note the strong influence exercised on the first generation of Free Church woman ministers by the example of an Anglican preacher, Maude Royden, for whom ordination was not possible as she would not leave the Church of England. She had begun her preaching ministry in 1903, in the schoolroom of a parish church in Rutland, but by the time she met Constance Todd (later Coltman) in the Junior Common Room of Mansfield College in 1914 she was equally well known for her support of women's suffrage and her opposition to the First World War.

In March 1917, while ideas were forming for Claud Coltman and Constance Todd to minister in the East End of London as assistants of the Revd W E Orchard of the King's Weigh House Church, Maude Royden caused a national stir by preaching in another famous London Free Church, the City Temple. This church, which would later be described at its 1940 tercentenary as the 'Cathedral of Nonconformity'[12], had just been notified by the Revd Dr Joseph Fort Newton of Cedar Rapids, America, that he had accepted its invitation to become the minister. He did so on condition that he would only be expected to preach two sermons a week however, on Sunday morning and Thursday mid-day, hence the church's search for a regular pulpit assistant and its introduction of Maude Royden.

The *Christian World* reported that Maude Royden's first Sunday services in the City Temple pulpit had made a 'very pleasing impression'. The article detailed what she wore as well as the content, style and audibility of what she said, matters its readers presumably wanted to know about:

> Miss Royden was dressed in a dark costume, with a lace collar, and a hat the shape of which suggested a doctor's cap, as worn at one of the older universities. She entered sympathetically into the details of the service, which now includes a little more of the liturgical element than used to be the case; the General Confession, the Lord's Prayer and the General Thanksgiving were repeated on each occasion. Miss Royden's clear and musical voice could be heard distinctly throughout the building. Her moving sermon urged the importance of a spiritual view of life as distinct from the material view, though she put in a courageous defence of the scientific spirit.... Both in the morning and the evening there was an old-time crowd.[13]

That reference to larger than usual numbers at worship also figured in *The Christian Commonwealth* report of the same events. The journal reported that the number of men in the congregation was 'larger than had been anticipated' and remarked on the lack of any disturbances during the services despite agitation against Maude Royden from two daily newspapers.[14] It would seem that some people, perhaps sharing Dr Johnson's view of women preachers, wanted to hear one for the novelty value. Others presumably came because they supported the cause of women in ordained ministry. In April 1917 *The Christian Commonwealth* commented:

> Time alone will show whether or not the vast congregation that gathered at the City Temple on March 18 to hear a woman preach was composed of those who were merely desirous to hear and see a new thing. That this was the case has already been suggested in the Press, and no doubt will be insisted upon by those out of sympathy with the movement. The suggestion, however, will probably have little weight with the average man or woman who approaches the question with an open mind, for there is a growing conviction that women can no longer be excluded from the ministrations of the Church, and that they will contribute much that the Church greatly needs.[15]

In July 1917 the religious press reported on Maude Royden's preaching debut at the King's Weigh House Congregational Church, when Claud Coltman read the gospel and Constance Todd the epistle. Her appointment as pulpit assistant to Dr Fort Newton at the City Temple was confirmed that same month, with a ringing endorsement from the new minister himself. 'Many will profit by her insight and counsel, as well as by her vision and eloquence in the pulpit.' he said.[16] The appointment at the City Temple, which would last three years, began on the eve of ordination for Constance Todd and Claud Coltman, who were to maintain a lifelong friendship with Maude Royden.

When the City Temple's tercentenary history was written more than twenty years later the writer proclaimed that Maude Royden's time as pulpit assistant had banished from the mind of practically everyone any lingering doubt about the suitability of women for ministry. He noted the marked absence of an emotional atmosphere during her sermons. It is interesting to wonder whether this writer was keen to disassociate her preaching from any obvious feminine characteristics, lest these be seen to detract from the weight and significance of what she actually said:

> Her speech was incisive, lucid and, where easy assumptions were concerned, deadly. It was often the administration of cold logic upon wishful thinking. In another sphere she would have been an Asquith or a Simon elaborating arguments in a Court of Appeal, where any display of sentiment is an offence to determined dignity. The eloquence and persuasive force lay for the most part in the cumulative effect of evidence singularly lucid in its presentation.[17]

The impact of Maude Royden's preaching ministry on her friend Constance Coltman was in little doubt, as was shown by what the first Congregational woman minister wrote in her chapter on 'Women in the Free Churches' for Maude Royden's 1924 book *The Church and Woman*. Having surveyed the ministry of Post-Reformation women from Civil War Baptist circles onwards, through Quaker women preachers and women's ministry in the different branches of Methodism, Constance Coltman observed: 'The torch of women's ministry even among the Free Churches has often burned very low, but never without kindling another flame to take its place'.[18] She went on to describe the contemporary place of women in the different Free Church traditions:

> Reference here should be made to the very notable action of the City Temple in calling Miss A Maude Royden to be Assistant Preacher to Dr Fort Newton in 1917. Although an Anglican, Miss Royden accepted the invitation, and the fact that a woman of such outstanding genius was preaching regularly for three years from such a world-famous pulpit made a deep impression on the public mind and greatly forwarded the cause of the ministry of women among the denominations both in this country and abroad.[19]

The impact of this raised profile for women's preaching could also be linked to the call of the first Scottish woman to enter Congregational ministry. Between 1926 and 1928 Vera Findlay trained at the Scottish Congregational College in Edinburgh, the pioneer and at the time sole woman to do so. Her preaching skills resulted in her receiving a call to a church before her studies were finished.

> Her exceptional powers as a preacher won for her speedy recognition, and so impressed the Deacons at Partick Congregational Church, one of the largest Churches in the denomination in Glasgow, that she received a 'Call' from its members even before she had completed her University course.[20]

Another woman profiled in the 1929 pamphlet 'Women Free Church Ministers', the Revd Margaret Hardy, directly attributed her call to the power of Maude Royden's preaching. By then minister of Marshall Street Congregational Church, Leeds, Margaret Hardy had been the first woman student at Lancashire Independent College. Her biographer noted that her original career in journalism had taken her to Fleet Street in London:

> Whilst in London she came into contact with Miss Maude Royden, and often went to hear her preach in the City Temple. It was this experience which first led her to realise what a great vocation lay before women in the Ministry of Religion, and she soon came to the conclusion that Journalism was not her true vocation.[21]

In her autobiography *Don't Ask Me Why*, Kathleen Hendry described the context for her own entry to ministerial training at Lancashire Independent College in the 1920s. Her comment suggests the influence of Maude Royden had made a significant mark on the national consciousness, which had even reached young Kathleen as a schoolgirl in Manchester:

> The records suggest that the Congregationalists ordained at least one woman in 1917 and though Dr Maude Royden was not ordained she served as a minister and preacher when I was a schoolgirl.[22]

Despite the growing profile of women's preaching ministry, however, by the time the Congregational Union of England and Wales' Commission on the Ministry of Women reported in 1936 there were still only 45 women lay preachers in the Congregational churches. The commission recommended that this ministry be expanded saying, 'This is the kind of ministry to which a greater number of educated women should be encouraged to devote themselves'. It was the views which the ordained women (17 had been ordained since 1917) held about preaching which caused the report writers to profess greatest surprise. It would seem to have been the assumption of those on the commission that 'women are specially qualified for pastoral work'. The report went on to say, 'it deserves record that all the women, without denying that assumption, lay stress on their love of preaching and the necessary preparation for it, and one or two even express a preference'. Furthermore, adequate preparation time was recognized as being important and not something to neglect 'due to absorption in practical service'. Those on the commission concluded their consideration of the issues surrounding women's ordination by asserting:

> It is evident that these women at least would not be satisfied with any form of ministry which deprived them of the privilege of preaching to which they felt themselves called.[23]

Just as some men are remembered after their deaths as having been good preachers this has been the case for some women too. Edith Elizabeth Pyke Lees (who was also known as Mrs Pickles) was born Edith Kinnear in Ireland in 1874, marrying Congregational minister Albert Pickles in 1908. She was said to have been 'always interested in social and religious work and had done a considerable amount of public speaking before entering the ministry.'[24] Whilst her husband was serving as a chaplain in France during the 1914-18 war she had oversight of Stanley Congregational Church, Liverpool, where he was the minister. This included conducting the services as well as preaching occasionally in other churches in Liverpool. In 1924 her husband died suddenly and the congregation at Stanley invited Edith Pickles to succeed him. In her obituary it was noted that:

> She was a trained and practised speaker and had taken services at the church, especially during the 1914 war. She had also played an active part in Church affairs, both at Stanley and widely in south Lancashire.[25]

She was admitted to List A after submitting a thesis in 1927 and for seven years ministered at Stanley during which time 'church membership and attendances increased substantially and the church organisations were strengthened'.[26] The church was 'a busy organisation and carries on extensive work for men, women and young people'. This included a Sunday School, various men's meetings and women's meetings, guilds and societies. Her roles in the wider church included serving as President of the Christian Endeavour Union for Liverpool from 1922-24. She was also President of the Women's Guild of Christian Service for Lancashire. Her success was put down to 'a combination of two gifts – an ability to speak well on platform or in pulpit, and a marked aptitude for organisation, including a clear but sympathetic understanding of other people'. [27]

One of the first obituaries for a woman minister in the Congregational Year Book was that for the Revd Mabel Snowball, who died suddenly aged 62 in 1932. Her uncle, the Revd Arthur W Potts of Crewe, had founded the Christian Endeavour Movement in England and she had established it in Sunderland and then wherever she worked in the North East. Her obituary noted: 'She was a powerful preacher with an attractive style, and possessed a gift of human sympathy to a remarkable degree'. [28]

Dorothy Wilson (1893-1956), who had entered Mansfield College in 1924 and was the first woman to be awarded a distinction in the Oxford Diploma in Theology, was also remembered as a preacher. She was called to Carrs Lane Congregational Church, Birmingham in 1927 to become assistant minister to Revd Leyton Richards, one of the four ministers who had ordained Constance Coltman in 1917. Although recruited for her skills in religious education and work with young people, a profile printed at the time noted she was an 'impressive preacher' who had 'occupied the pulpit made famous by Dr Dale and Dr Jowett with a good deal of distinction'. One person had said of her preaching:

> Of all the women preachers I have heard she (Miss Wilson) seems to be at once the most feminine in tone and manner, and the least feminine in so far as that word implies a special mental attitude and atmosphere.[29]

This comment reveals something more of the attitudes and preconceptions encountered by women preachers in the 1920s and 30s, even from people who favoured their ministry. The extent to which such views still exist will be discussed later in this chapter.

It is interesting to note that a decade later, in 1938, Dorothy Wilson was again cast briefly in the role of assistant to a distinguished male preacher, this time the noted Methodist speaker and writer the Revd Leslie Weatherhead at the City Temple. Through her ministry, therefore, the congregations of two major churches in Congregationalism would have had an opportunity to make week-by-week comparisons between a woman and a man in the pulpit. Sadly ill health, in the form of spinal arthritis, cut short her public ministry; otherwise she could have played a far more significant role in the life of mid-twentieth century Congregationalism.

Eleanor Shakeshaft, whose minister husband died in 1941, was someone else whose preaching prowess lived on after her. She had been invited to carry on her husband's work by the congregation in Herne Bay, Kent, and in 1943 completed the ROM (Roll of Ministers) examinations. People remembered her as someone who had 'a great gift for preaching and who was tireless in her pastoral care both of her own congregation and of those in need in the community'. [30]

A little later, Edith Beatrice Boxall, a List B minister who qualified in 1949, shared joint pastorates with her husband, Kenneth Frank Boxall, at Petworth (1946-51) and Bursledon (1957-59). She was remembered for 'her undoubted gifts as a preacher'. Additionally she was an organist and musician and was involved in the Women's Guild Movement and the British and Foreign Bible Society.[31]

Women working overseas

Susannah Rankin (née Ellis), the first woman ordained by the Union of Welsh Independents in 1925, served all of her ministry with the LMS in Papua. She was described by her biographer, Laurel Gray, as 'a skilled linguist'. mastering Papuan languages, teaching reading and writing and preparing basic grammar books and storybooks during her long ministry. It seems that:

> her own experience of being taught in a language that was not her mother-tongue convinced Sue that if children became literate in their own language first they would find it much simpler to move to a second or third language.[32]

In her lifetime Welsh became the medium of instruction in many schools in Wales and during her ministry she preached in Welsh, English and several Papuan languages. At her first service on 11 May 1919 she recalled:

> Before the service the minister asked, 'Are you going to speak in Welsh or English?' I decided on Welsh because I knew if I started in English I would always preach in English.[33]

Later, it became her habit if preaching in English to write her notes in Welsh. Furthermore, the similarities between the vowels of Welsh and of Motu, one of the Papuan languages, helped her to become fluent in the latter. As to the content of her preaching, she wrote:

> I think in some ways we were wrong in stressing sin. Because Christ came to bring something more than freedom from sin. People who are not Christians don't have a sense of sin, so there's no real point of contact there. In Papua, it was no use talking about sin at first because people didn't know anything about sin. When they came into the church they started to grasp the ideas of justification and peace and grace. We missionaries talked to people most about fear, about bad spirits and the Good Spirit. Nowadays I think we should stress the kind of living that Christ brings. He came to give us Life, more abundant Life, Life in all its fullness.[34]

In 1972, which was also the centenary year of the arrival of the first LMS missionaries in Papua, Sue was awarded the MBE. She retired to live in Australia in 1976 and died in 1989.

Churches of Christ

There were women leaders in the Churches of Christ as early as 1912. Known as 'church sisters', their main tasks were usually with the women's meetings of the church in visiting, therefore they did not preach to mixed congregations. Some of the earliest were Miss E B Crawford (appointed 1912) and Miss Lydia Hunt (appointed 1913), however there were others before these. The development of more public ministry by Churches of Christ women, including leading worship and preaching, did not take place until the appointment of Etta Proctor (later Mrs Short) in 1939, who worked through the war. She was followed in 1948 by Jessie Baker, and then Beryl Langley and Mrs Gertie Gray, a widow. Mary Barr says of these women 'These three also did more work of a public nature but were still thought of by most as being available for women's work'.[35]

By the 1950s local churches began to hold 'women's services', usually in the evenings, although some churches had 'Women's Sundays'. On these occasions it was usually 'permitted' for a woman to be the preacher and for others to take part in the worship. Partnerships of married couples in local church leadership were also known. Mary Barr recalls, from her own family:

> My father-in-law was a Churches of Christ minister and my mother-in-law, who trained at Overdale, was always his 'partner' in the work he did. She was also prominent in the women's work of the Churches and did a lot of work preparing study notes, etc, as well as being women's treasurer. She must have been one of the first women to speak at an evening 'rally' of the Annual Conference before the 1939 war. When I was a child and a teenager in the church it certainly wasn't even thought of that a woman should do public work in the church apart from working in the Sunday School, but of course the 1939-45 war years changed a lot of attitudes and by the time I entered training in 1947 there was never any real opposition to women's work, though the full participation of women by presiding at the Lord's Table took a good few years to become a fact.[36]

Prejudices and Perceptions of Women as Preachers

The question of whether or not a woman preaches differently from a man has quite often been raised. Concerns about this may well underlie the comments quoted earlier about Maude Royden's cool logic or Dorothy Wilson's minimum of feminine 'mental attitude'. Perhaps some of those who reported on the first women preachers in the early twentieth century needed to reassure themselves and others that women's preaching could bear comparison with that of men in terms of thinking, learnedness and clear expression. To prefigure a concept from chapter 11 on 'Recurring Patterns in the Ministry of Women', some people may have needed to see women preachers as 'fictive men' in the pulpit, if not in other parts of their ministry.

The Free Church Chronicle, in 1997, reported the findings of a study carried out in the USA by Professor Lee McGee of Yale University, asking if congregations listen differently to a woman preacher. He concluded that they do but that this is often subconscious:

> In a word, many men do not like a woman telling them what to do, and so are at best ambivalent, and at worst hostile to a woman preacher and often without understanding why they are overtaken by such feelings.[37]

The research explored whether congregations listen differently to women preachers as compared with men and looked at three separate issues. One question was about sermon content, to see if this was different for women preachers as distinct from men. Another area of research considered whether women's preaching differs in style from that of men. Finally the study tried to identify any culturally-informed resistance to the voices of women as preachers amongst their hearers and congregations. The survey findings revealed that while women were seen as preaching personal, innovative sermons, men were regarded as being scholarly, informative and knowledgeable in their pulpit utterances. Women's delivery was regarded as being clear and sincere, whereas men were thought of as forceful, persuasive and loud. People perceived women's sermon style as highly personal and relational, evoking emotion in a congregation, whereas male preachers were looked on as distant and impersonal. The overall effect of a woman in the pulpit was of someone nurturing and compassionate, whereas a man in the same role gave an impression of being authoritative and formal. Finally, perceptions of the way women preachers delivered their message spoke of them being solicitous, hesitant and apologetic in appearance, whereas people thought a male preacher's delivery of his sermon related to his physical size.

McGee refers to what he terms 'cultural resistance' to women's voices: 'People cannot "hear" a woman preaching because it goes against their preconceptions about what is right behaviour in a church'. Or as the *Free Church Chronicle* put it: 'In other words, congregations are just not used to women preachers'.

Another insight into the different way people react to women who preach comes from the work of Rosemary Radford Ruether. She highlights the way the role of preacher has been seen in male rather than female terms:

> The preacher, as a speaker of the Word, is more abstract and cerebral. Traditionally, the symbol of Logos for Word of God has been male and hierarchical in Christian imagery. The Word descends from above the passive body of the people from the high (phallic) pulpit. One speaks of the 'seminal' Word, and the attitude of the laity in receiving it is to be one of passive receptivity. All this enforces a highly male symbolism of the preacher.[38]

Daughters of Dissent has confirmed there is still a lack of familiarity with women's preaching. More than 80 years may have passed since the first woman was ordained in Britain to a ministry that included preaching but male preachers are still seen as the norm. However evidence has also come to light suggesting that the novelty value of hearing a woman in the pulpit can draw people back to worship, or into a church for the first time, out of simple curiosity. The large numbers who flocked to the City Temple to hear Maude Royden's first sermons there have been replicated on a lesser scale in many churches up and down the country since 1917. As women have spread out into the highways and byways of church life, the arrival of the 'first' woman preacher in each area has often caused the local press to write an article, and a stir of interest to go around a community.

For instance, it merited a large picture and article in the *Aberdare Leader* when the Revd Jean Wilkinson was ordained and inducted to Providence Chapel, Mountain Ash in 1957, headlined as 'The first woman minister in Wales'. (Most people in Wales would have been unaware then, as now, of the existence of the Revd Sue Rankin as the true pioneer of women's ministry in Wales since her whole ministry had been exercised in the 'mission field'.) Jean Wilkinson's first service prompted another piece in the local press about the 'attractive 27-year-old' and it was noted that after the service she had the pleasure of welcoming several people back into church membership. Later that year *The Illustrated News* headed a photo feature about her with the words 'They flock to hear the petticoat preacher'. As well as a picture of her in the pulpit it also showed Jean Wilkinson on a Welsh mountainside, chatting with one of her scattered 'flock', farmer David Prosser whose home could be reached only by a trek along a muddy farm path. The clear message was that women preachers represented an attractive new image for the Church as a whole, bringing a more human face and a breath of fresh air.

With so little written about preaching by women it is difficult to assess whether or not the content of sermons preached by women differs from those of men, or whether women actually view preaching differently from men. Some women preachers see themselves as bringing a new wholeness to this part of ministry while others might claim that women have their own gender-based view of the Gospel and distinctive voice. An early Baptist woman minister, Violet Hedger, would seem to have been aware of this tension to judge by her comments on preaching quoted in 1929:

> 'All big truths,' she says, 'are many-sided, and women have their own contribution to make. I do not base the case for women preachers on the fact that in most Churches the women outnumber the men. That has really little to do with it. The important thing is that the woman's point of view should be expressed, and this can only be done by a woman.'[39]

Susan Durber and Heather Walton's book *Silence in Heaven: A Book of Women's Preaching* (1994) explored preaching by women at length, illustrated with sermons by 27 women, of whom six were ordained in the United Reformed Church. Explaining the need for the book the editors wrote:

> ...the fact that the 'word of God' has been heard for centuries from the mouths of men means that many women are especially conscious of both the difficulties and opportunities that fall to them as preachers and have begun to reflect upon them. This reflective activity is born of an awareness that to be a woman preacher is to be 'different'. The woman who preaches can assume much less about her own position and the tradition in which she stands than her male colleagues. As many of us have been made acutely aware, merely to speak from the body of a woman is to present a challenge to some congregations.

An entirely conventional sermon may take on new resonances if it is delivered by a person whose body presents an unconventional icon of authority.[40]

Walton and Durber stated that the book made opportunities for 'talk amongst women about their experiences of preaching... Most of us have never had the opportunity to speak with other women about this public but intimate concern.'[41] The authors had heard women preachers speak of the criticism they received on the pitch, volume and tone of their voices, as well as the way people expressed difficulties to them in following the content of their sermons. Walton and Durber concluded these reflected people's problems in hearing those who were usually silent and marginalised in church, or in re-ordering their convictions in the light of alternative perspectives.

Women Speak for Themselves

Sermons need to be prepared. In 1971 Dorothy Havergal Shaw gave a valuable description of the way in which she prepared for the weekly task of preaching. She read widely, to keep herself in touch with contemporary political and cultural events, as well as working on the theological texts:

> Taking the Sunday services is the most publicly noticed part of a minister's work. Preparation for this is time taking but there is nothing particularly masculine or feminine about it. I believe I used to take about thirty hours for two services. Now I timetable twelve and may take nearly twice that, and this does not include the Bible study in detail which I now timetable separately so that under pressure it can be omitted. In a faith which insists that a record whose age can be estimated in millennia not only has contemporary relevance but the basic information for satisfactory living, study of the text is inescapable. Is it really only female practicality which has made me protest when it was suggested that the modern theological student might by-pass one or both of the original languages to have more time for social studies? We need both, but of the two the social scene changes and to a great extent has to be learnt on the job in any case, while there is never time again for the learning of the basic linguistic tools. No natural linguist, I was feminine enough to shed tears over Hebrew at one stage, but the college syllabus which insisted that the grind continue has been justified by years of use. Other reading too, is necessary for a minister.[42]

We have very little information about women preaching in the Presbyterian Church of England. With less of a tradition of lay preaching than Methodists or Congregationalists, Presbyterian women do not appear to have had so many opportunities. Kate McIlhagga, who was Community Minister at St Ives Free Church and died in 2002, said:

I was the first woman to preach in that church and there were undoubtedly prejudices to overcome in the early days. Stress in the ministry is at last being acknowledged and dealt with.[43]

The link between facing prejudice in ministry and stress is something that needs to be explored further for women and men. Being the first to do something publicly as a woman, including preaching, is something people comment on. It can lead to some surprises for all concerned.

Elsie Chamberlain was the first Congregational woman minister to have a high public profile on the national scene, so much so that in many people's memory she is seen as the pioneer of women's ordained ministry. She became a well-known voice on the radio after she answered an advertisement and 'to her surprise was appointed to the BBC Religious Department' in 1950.[44] She worked there for sixteen years, broadcasting every week, including the Daily Service, prayers on Saturday night, and the daily radio programme 'Lift up your Hearts', as well as occasionally appearing on television. She said of the job:

> I have always regarded my job with the BBC as a missionary one, more so than any local church could offer. One of the problems the Free Church has to solve is how to avoid being involved with the faithful so much of the time that there is no time left to serve the people who don't go to church.[45]

She called sermons 'a tyranny'. In contrast to Dorothy Havergal Shaw's view that large amounts of time should be spent on sermon preparation she suggested several adventurous alternatives:

> Then there's the tyranny of the sermon. Don't mistake me, I like preaching them and I like listening to them (provided they say something). But how many of our ministers give hours to preparing two sermons, so that 90 per cent of the flock can choose which one they will have – the morning or the evening one? Again, don't mistake me! I do not think one hour a week is enough time for worship, if we are to keep our sense of values. But I don't think that even listening to *two* sermons a week equips us to meet the demands of life today.
>
> ...Would a question hour instead of that second sermon help prepare us? Would it give us opportunity to find out the things we ought to know but don't? Are the questions for women's groups to prepare, prior to a Rally, a step in the right direction? (I'm beginning to say 'no' to rallies – unless those participating will do some homework first!) Can we get several five-minute addresses from laymen on different angles of a subject as a matter for discussion? We might not 'like' it as much as a sermon, but is that the right standard of judgement? [46]

The extent to which it is still difficult for some congregations to be adventurous in worship, especially in respect of the sermon, is a measure of the tyranny she remarked on. In a 1965 context, Elsie Chamberlain's use of the term 'laymen' would have naturally been seen as including laywomen. This quotation raises, but does not answer, fascinating questions about how many women in a congregation would have considered themselves to have had something worthwhile to say in public worship, how much freedom the men in the congregation would have given them to do so, and what confidence might have been instilled by the sight of a woman leading worship.

Echoing Mrs Lewis-Donaldson earlier in the century, contemporary United Reformed Church minister Hazel Barkham wonders what people are expecting to hear in church:

> My preaching has been found to be too challenging. Congregations prefer simple emotive rhetoric with a warm flow of stereotypes to a genuine attempt to tackle some real aspects of Christian life and faith. I try to encourage them to think but they would rather be given a cosy feeling of being in a familiar warm cocoon of accepted beliefs. But I preach so as to encourage congregations to rediscover the Bible as the basis of a faith which demands social, personal and political action.[47]

Kirsty Thorpe likes the sermon to address a particular context:

> It's not easy to talk about [preaching] because it is so personal. When I was a single parent it struck me how much a liberation motif went through my preaching. Both Old Testament and New Testament were equally important, not just because the text is interesting in itself but to get people used to engaging with the text, and so they are expecting it to speak to them. I write sermons that come out of where I am now, so they can't be written long before they are preached because a lot can happen in a Friday or Saturday. It is very important to me not to say that there is only one interpretation. I want to make it clear that I have chosen one but that to have chosen another is not automatically wrong. I wonder if this is something women do more than men. Is it related to the bridging role that women often play in the family? As they bridge the different perceptions of people and events they learn to live with different truths which can never be totally reconciled.

Janet Webber began her ministry before the rise of modern feminism and she was initially 'very antagonistic' to it, saying she always saw herself as 'one of the boys'. She goes on to discuss the Bible, and the language of worship, demonstrating how her view of feminism changed:

More recently I think I can get inside what it feels like to be the kind of feminist who is haunted by God the Father, and who is anti-church because the Church is patriarchal. I can't entirely identify with this, but I accept it and understand it and sympathise with it. I would like us to be free in the churches to use him or her, Mother or Father, Sister or Brother or whatever about God, but I feel no compulsion to demand that it all be feminine. I find it amazing that the Bible is actually so positive about women, given its cultural background. It is quite remarkable that women even get a mention - and how much prominence they have for example in Luke's gospel! My attitude is to celebrate how good the Bible is in this field rather than be oppressed by how awful it is. So in leading worship, while I'm happy to pray to Mother God and use feminine images, I'm also aware that to say 'Our Mother who art in heaven' is offensive to some people, and that many women of my age and older are totally bewildered by this desire to call God 'Mother'. It doesn't enter their perception that there's anything wrong or deficient with calling God 'Father', and these people have to be considered as well. I'm perfectly happy to jolt people in worship, but I think I want to jolt them more in sermons than in prayers.[48]

Picking up the theme of the importance of the language of worship, Margaret Laurie also wrote:

Inclusive language? Yes, of course! But inclusivity is even more important for children, women and men (and for concessions like me!). Isn't language fun? In the 60s we campaigned hard to get rid of 'thee and thou'. At the time I was in N. Staffs where people used the singular pronoun in special friendship. To be asked 'What dust thee want for thee's tea?' was to be accepted almost as family. Genuine inclusivity is so important... for young, old and those with learning difficulties.[49]

On the same theme Doris Leyshon commented she found it difficult to find any description for God, male or female, but tried to use terms such as 'persons' and 'human beings' in referring to humanity, adding: 'Occasionally in a hymn where "he" predominates I change it to "she" in a following verse, endeavouring to keep the balance'.[50]

One way in which women's preaching has continued to grow powerfully during the first century of their ordained ministry has been through the influence of retired ministers like those just quoted. Retired women ministers in reasonable health have continued to exercise their preaching skills to some effect. Alice Duncan, who returned from missionary work in China to become a Congregational minister in 1952, served Congregational and Methodist churches in Wiltshire until a few weeks before her death in her early 80s.[51] It can even be an advantage to have more time to reflect on the topic of a sermon in a way that was not possible before retirement. Rachel Storr wrote:

> I still take services in the Tunbridge Wells Group of United Reformed Churches. I particularly appreciate having time to let sermon themes 'simmer' in the mind as I normally take one service a month instead of two each Sunday.[52]

Janet Lees describes her own approach to preaching in these terms:

> Like Elsie Chamberlain I love preaching, although my style has changed since I first began preaching in village chapels in Essex at the age of 18. Now in inner city Sheffield I have developed a particular way of approaching this weekly task. After my first visits to South Africa in the early 1980s, I adopted the discipline of using a lectionary, something I continue to do. Early in the week I look up the lectionary readings. As a former editor of the United Reformed Church prayer handbook I often already have some memory of a particular week's material. I let the lectionary readings lie about in my brain and return to them frequently in odd moments while driving my car, on the bus, or in any waiting time. This is my regular spiritual discipline, where I reflect and pray about scripture.

Conclusion

The narratives collected by Daughters of Dissent contain very few specific references to preaching. It is not clear whether this links with the view that preaching is a male activity. Does women's apparent silence about their preaching indicate that they undervalued its significance? Changing trends mean that there is now less emphasis on the sermon and more on the act of worship as a whole. There are many layers of silence still to uncover about the way women use their own voices in the church and this chapter is only a introduction to some of the issues which await further research. However, if pressed, very few of the women preachers mentioned here would probably have disagreed with Florence Frost-Mee's comment to a newspaper reporter in 1962: 'Yes, preaching is one heck of a job'.

Chapter 6

Peace and Justice

Peace

The twentieth century was a century of bitter conflicts, both global and domestic. Although many of these took place in other continents, Europe itself was the scene of two major wars and for a third of a century lay under the threat of nuclear destruction. In response to this, international co-operation in peacekeeping, and efforts to solve conflict by means other than violence, have gained strength. Women have been prominent supporters of both.

The relation between feminism and the peace movement has been the subject of much debate and discussion. On the one hand some have argued that women's intrinsic roles as nurturers and carers have made them concerned above all for the preservation of life, and therefore determined to find non-violent ways of resolving conflict. Their exclusion for so long from the centres of power has given them an instinctive sympathy with the victims of war. On the other hand, it has been pointed out that women's desire for equality with men has led them to seek to undertake roles hitherto confined to men, including military service. After the outbreak of the First World War many apparently peace-loving women activists became ardent supporters of the war. And if there has in the past been a gender difference in attitudes to violence, it has been argued that this was due to social conditioning rather than intrinsic nature.

This chapter will seek to show that the years when the feminist movement was strong have also been years which witnessed a strong peace movement, and that there has been an ideological connection between the two. The first third of the twentieth century was marked by the campaigns leading up to the granting of votes for women, and by the destruction brought by the First World War; parallel to this was a substantial international women's peace movement, with some links with international socialism. The last third witnessed a new and vigorous phase of the feminist movement which included several women's peace initiatives, the most public of which was the Greenham Women's Peace Camp. These feminist movements had an impact on the churches; the movement for the ordination of women had its greatest momentum in the first and last thirds of the century. During the middle of the century, years which were dominated by the Second World War and the ensuing cold war, the peace movement (including women's peace initiatives) did not die, but was pushed further to the margins in the face of the horrors of Nazism and the Holocaust. The chapter will also try to support the claim that women have a contribution to make to movements for peace and justice which can complement that of men (while recognising that both are needed). It may also become clear that women's efforts for peace have in the past been inadequately recorded.[1]

The peace movement in Britain began early in the nineteenth century, with the founding of the British Peace Society in 1820. Its most noteworthy general secretary in the nineteenth century was Henry Richard,[2] a Welsh Congregational minister who gave up pastoral ministry in order to concentrate on a public advocacy of arbitration as a means of resolving disputes. These ideas were being echoed elsewhere, and the number of international organisations devoted to improving relations between nation-states began to grow after 1870. One of these was the International Women's Suffrage Alliance (IWSA), founded in Washington in 1902.

It was not surprising that as women's suffrage movements gathered strength in different countries, international contacts developed. When war broke out in 1914 there was already an international group of women, growing in confidence, who realised that war threatened a collaboration they had already developed. From this there arose the idea of holding an international conference of women at the Hague early in 1915. In the autumn of 1914 a Hungarian member of IWSA, Rosika Schwimmer, and a British member, Emmeline Pethick-Lawrence, – technically they were enemies – had toured the USA together trying to promote support for an international women's peace movement. The result was the formation of the Women's Peace Party in America in January 1915. From this emerged the idea of an International Women's Peace Congress at the Hague in April.

The issue of whether or not to support this conference deeply divided the women's suffrage movement in Britain. The National Union of Women's Suffrage Societies, led by Millicent Fawcett, supported the war against Germany, thus prompting the more radical, pacifist members to leave. It was this radical group who supported the Hague initiative. The British government effectively stopped British delegates from attending the conference, except for the one or two who had already left England on an earlier date. Nevertheless it was a remarkable gathering of 1,336 women. Its immediate result was to commission a small group of women to visit the foreign ministries of countries at war with each other, a brave venture much criticised in the press. In the longer term, this conference proved to be the catalyst for the formation of the International Committee of Women for Permanent Peace, soon re-named the Women's International League for Peace and Freedom (WILPF – this name was adopted in 1919), which has consistently worked for peace since that time, more recently with the status of a Non-Governmental Organisation at the United Nations.

The outstanding figure at the Hague Conference was the American woman who was invited to preside: Jane Addams.[3] Jane Addams came from a Congregational/ Presbyterian background in Illinois; although she sat light to ecclesiastical authority, the inspiration of her work was Christian, and her ecclesiastical allegiance remained within the Reformed tradition. She did pioneering educational and social work in the first part of her adult life at Hull House, Chicago, a settlement which she founded, while the second half of her life was devoted chiefly to peacebuilding and humanitarian work. She was the first president of WILPF, and a supporter (though not an uncritical one) of the League of Nations. In 1931 she was awarded the Nobel Peace Prize jointly with Nicholas Murray Butler. Undoubtedly she was a great example and inspiration to all British women – and men – who shared her ideals of peace based on justice.

One of the first vice-presidents of WILPF was Maude Royden,[4] a life-long Anglican who had many links with Nonconformists. As a supporter of women's suffrage she was often a contributor to the *Free Church Suffrage Times* as well as to the journal of the Church League for Women's Suffrage; later, as a campaigner for women's ordination she was a colleague of many Nonconformists in the Society for the Ministry of Women. For three years, from 1917 until 1920, she was pulpit assistant at the Congregational City Temple where her gift for preaching matured. She was an ardent pacifist. In the early years of the war she and 988 other women signed an 'Open Christmas Letter' to the women of Germany and Austria. Her book, *The Great Adventure*, published in 1915, was a strong appeal for a positive view of peace: 'We peace people have made of peace a dull, drab, sordid, selfish thing. We have made it that ambiguous, dreary thing – "neutrality". But Peace is the great adventure, the glorious romance'.

During these years her pacifist activity was mainly channelled through an organisation whose membership was largely Nonconformist. The Fellowship of Reconciliation (FOR) arose out of a conference in Cambridge in December 1914.[5] Some leading Nonconformists, horrified at the way in which their denominations had abandoned any previous commitment to ideals of peace and had joined, often vociferously, in the general 'war fever', arranged to meet together in the fifth month of the war. They included a number of Quakers (from a tradition which had always opposed war), and two outstanding Presbyterian ministers who were both Vice-Presidents of the Free Church League for Women's Suffrage: Richard Roberts of Crouch Hill Presbyterian Church, and W E Orchard of the Congregational King's Weigh House. Richard Roberts resigned his pastorate because of difficulties with his congregation over his pacifist views, while Orchard, in contrast to most Congregational ministers, preached pacifist sermons in London throughout the war, and had an enormous influence on his own and a younger generation.

One of those whom he influenced was Constance Todd (later Coltman). It was as a student at Mansfield College, Oxford that she first attended the King's Weigh House and was drawn to Orchard's pacifist theology; and it was there that she was eventually ordained in 1917 with Orchard as the presiding minister. She was an early member of the FOR. In 1915 she responded to an appeal from Maude Royden to join a peace caravan through the Midlands counties sponsored by the FOR, an experience which eventually took an unexpected and unpleasant turn. At first the group met with curiosity and some support, but as they reached Leicestershire hostility grew, until at Hinckley they were surrounded by a jeering crowd who threatened violence, and so had to retreat to the nearest police station.[6] Constance Coltman was never an activist in the conventional sense, but she was a loyal member of the FOR throughout her life, offering a quiet but firm witness to non-violence as the authentic Christian way.

The connection between feminism and pacifism was already being highlighted before the end of the war. In 1915 Allen and Unwin published an anonymous work entitled *Miitarism Versus Feminism: An Enquiry and a Policy Demonstrating that Militarism Involves the Subjection of Women*, arguing that 'the subjection of women ... is essentially due to militarism'. Its authors were subsequently identified as Charles Kay Ogden, editor of the *Cambridge Magazine* 1912-21, and Mary Sargent Florence, a painter. One thousand copies were sold. Although it influenced only a small number of people at the time, the renewed interest in it which led to its being re-issued in 1987 suggests that the ideas presented were ahead of their time, and that they have something to offer at the beginning of the twenty-first century to the debate about peace and violence.

It cannot be claimed that Nonconformist women as a whole were sympathetic to the peace movement. The majority of Nonconformist ministers and church members, women and men, supported the 1914-18 war uncritically, and gave pacifist ministers a hard time; some of them were forced to resign. But the movements for women's suffrage, for the ordination of women, and for the peaceful resolution of conflict were all connected, and many women were involved in all three movements early in the twentieth century.

Maude Royden resigned from the FOR in 1919 because she felt its emphasis was too negative. But she remained a pacifist until 1940, and was active in many peace efforts in the 1930s, including the Peace Pledge Union. Although Hitler's activities persuaded her that the evils of Nazism were worse than the evils of violence, she remained committed to the ideals of international mediation and arbitration.

As Europe recovered from the traumatic experiences of the First World War, hopes for peace were pinned on the League of Nations and other international organisations. This interest was shared by a much wider group than those who belonged to pacifist organisations. In the 1920s many Congregational Women's Guilds affiliated with the World Alliance for Promoting International Friendship through the Churches. In the following decade they helped to promote the Women's International Disarmament Appeal. When Lady Spicer died in 1934, her family endowed a Jessie Stewart Spicer Memorial Fellowship, to enable individual women Congregationalists to travel in the furtherance of international peace and understanding.

The threat of Nazism overshadowed attempts at peacemaking after 1938. There was a core of people, amongst whom the Quakers were prominent, who remained faithful to pacifism. Allowance was made for conscientious objectors, who were treated with more sympathy than in the previous war. The FOR maintained its witness in a low key, and with a smaller membership, giving much attention to planning for reconciliation and reconstruction when the war was over.

The renewed peace movement after recovery from the war was focused on opposition to nuclear weapons. The Campaign for Nuclear Disarmament (CND) was launched in January 1958. At Easter the first Aldermaston march took place, and was then followed by marches each year until 1965. Among the marchers were Claud and Constance Coltman, then in their later 60s, together with a distinct Quaker group. There was a short-lived women's group within CND, and also a more permanent Christian CND. But there was no strong link at this point between feminism and peace activism.

The revival of a strong feminist peace movement took place in the 1980s (though in the 1970s the formation of the Peace People in Northern Ireland was a women's initiative). It can be dated to the late summer of 1981, when a march from Cardiff to Greenham (the proposed base for Cruise Missiles) under the banner, 'Women for Life on Earth', took place. Meeting both opposition and indifference from official authorities, a few women almost immediately set up camp on the perimeter of the base. Although many men were present at first, and their support was welcomed, within six months it had become a camp for women only; it was felt that this was the best way to sharpen the witness. There followed several years of non-violent protest and many confrontations with the police. The camp dominated the media headlines in the early 1980s, and networks of support grew up all round the country.

One of those who took part in the protests both at Greenham and at Alconbury was Hazel Barkham, who was ordained as a non-stipendiary minister in 1983. She experienced some violence from the police personally at Greenham. She continues to share in non-violent protests against nuclear weapons, and in 1999 attended the Hague Appeal for Peace conference. In her ministry she preaches 'so as to encourage congregations to rediscover the Bible as the basis of a faith which demands social, personal, and political action'. She is now the secretary of the United Reformed Church Peace Fellowship.

Greenham (and other peace camps) evoked strong reactions from both women and men. The churches were divided on the issue. When Hazel Barkham was arrested at Alconbury, some of the elders at her church in Derbyshire were shocked and quoted passages from Paul's writings about obeying civil authorities. Early in 1983 Kate Compston, a United Reformed Church minister, wrote an article for *Reform* (published in the February edition) entitled, 'A quiet rage against dying,' an account of her visit to the rally at Greenham on 12 December 1982. The occasion impressed her deeply, especially 'the power, the impact, of "weak" non-violent action'. The letters which followed from this article, especially in the April issue of *Reform*, expressed strongly-felt opposing opinions.

In 1975 the Helsinki Agreement between Eastern European states and the West had included cultural and educational contacts among its objectives. This had encouraged members of the government-sponsored Women's National Commission to consider exchanges between East and West European women. It was Elizabeth Charles,[7] a United Reformed Church representative on the Women's Council of the Free Church Federal Council, as well as a representative on the Women's National Commission, who took the initiative. After extensive consultation and endless visits to East European embassies in London, she managed to organise and lead a delegation of eight Christian women, representing the National Free Church Women's Council, the Women's Guild of the Church of Scotland, the Mothers' Union and the National Board of Catholic Women, to Poland and Hungary, in September 1980. They were entertained by both church and secular women's organisations. This was followed by reciprocal visits by Polish and Hungarian women. In 1984 another British delegation visited East Germany. These visits did much, not only to promote individual friendships, but to build up mutual understanding, and prepare the way for co-operation at the end of the cold war. All these exchanges were led by Elizabeth Charles, who exercised great perseverance in overcoming obstacles, and enormous energy in organising and conducting the visits.

Apart from the fact that the Cruise missiles eventually left Greenham – and what part the women's camp played in this will be much debated in the future – Greenham illustrated in a very public way the connection between feminism and anti-militarism. In 1988 (September) a letter appeared in *Reform* signed by four men and one woman thanking the women of Greenham for 'representing our collective conscience'. It is significant that amongst Virago's re-isssues in the mid-1980s were Virginia Woolf's feminist-pacifist tract, *Three Guineas* and the originally anonymous *Militarism versus Feminism*.

Two of the most able and effective members of the Fellowship of Reconciliation in the second half of the twentieth century have been John and Elnora Ferguson, Congregationalists who became members of the United Reformed Church, and in later years members also (jointly) of the Society of Friends. Both were active members of the United Nations Association and of the FOR from the time of their student days in Cambridge; Elnora was also a member of WILPF. When they returned from some years abroad in 1969, they became for 20 years joint editors of the FOR's *Reconciliation Quarterly*. Elnora Ferguson was elected chair of the National Peace Council in 1987 and served for five years. Since her husband's death in 1989 she has continued to be an active member of the peace movement as well as of the local ecumenical scene in Birmingham. Most recently she has been one of the chief promoters of the Bradford Peace Museum, and chair of its board of trustees since 1998.

As has been pointed out in chapter three the United Reformed Church has adopted an equal opportunities policy which discourages organisations of women alone. However this has not prevented inter-denominational groups of women meeting together to discuss matters of particular concern. As a new century dawns, the issue of violence against women, on a national and an international scale, is high on their agenda. It is a subject which has long been ignored or even condoned in many churches, and it does seem that it will be women who will have to persevere in keeping this issue on the agenda until churches are really prepared to make a stand. Peacemaking at all levels, domestic, national and international, must be high on the agenda for humanity in the twenty-first century.

Justice

Women have always been active in philanthropic work, and in alleviating the suffering caused by injustice. It has required both education and access to power to bring into focus their more positive commitment to justice and challenge to existing structures. One can point to some outstanding women, such as Octavia Hill, Josephine Butler and Elizabeth Fry, who worked successfully and against great odds for a more just treatment of humanity in the years before women were given the vote. They were exceptional people. In the twentieth century a much wider group of women began to campaign for all kinds of reform. Here we will highlight the contribution of four women, two of them lay and two ordained, whose Christian commitment within the United Reformed Church traditions led them to work for social justice in different contexts.

Margaret Bondfield (1873-1953),[8] for many years a member of the Congregational King's Weigh House Church in London, was an immensely energetic woman who became the first woman Cabinet minister. She was the tenth of the eleven children of William and Anne Bondfield of Chard, Somerset. Her father, a lace designer and foreman worker, could remember the unrest and controversy (in which he had taken part) surrounding the Reform Bill of 1832, and had been greatly influenced by the local Congregational minister, John Gunn. Her mother was the granddaughter of a Wesleyan Methodist minister. Both her parents were devout Nonconformists with Radical political interests. After a limited education in a Board school and a spell as a pupil teacher, she moved to Brighton when she was 15 as an apprentice in a draper's shop. Here she experienced the 'living-in' system – accommodation in dormitories providing no privacy, and with no provision for recreation. She joined Clifton Road Congregational Church, where she met and was greatly supported and encouraged by Louisa Martindale. When she moved to London 1894 she was appalled at the living and working conditions of shop assistants; she herself was working 76 hours a week for an annual salary of between £15 and £25. At the first opportunity she joined the National Union of Shop Assistants, and contributed a regular article to its magazine under the name 'Grace Dare'. She discovered skills in public speaking at Union meetings, and her vitality and obvious integrity helped to break down prejudice against women activists.

She was introduced to the King's Weigh House, which had recently moved from the City to a new building in Mayfair on the Grosvenor Estate. On the surface this appeared to be an exclusively prosperous area, but almost out of sight in the side streets were flats and other buildings inhabited by poor families and young shop assistants.

When one of the church deacons told Margaret Bondfield that membership of a trade union was incompatible with church membership (a remark she never forgot), she had no hesitation in choosing union activity. However, the minister at the time (Alexander Sandison) and his wife were more sympathetic to her attempts to improve conditions for other shop assistants.

In 1897 she was commissioned to write a report on the conditions of work in London shops by the Women's Industrial Council. This led to her being appointed assistant secretary of the Union of Shop Assistants in the following year. In 1899 she was the sole woman delegate to the Trades Union Congress Congress in Plymouth, where her speech on behalf of women shop assistants made a great impression. She joined the Independent Labour Party and shared platforms with leaders such as Keir Hardie and Ramsay MacDonald. In 1906 she helped Mary Macarthur to found the National Federation of Women Workers. When she visited the United States for five months four years later, she formed a lasting friendship with Jane Addams. In 1914 W E Orchard became minister of the King's Weigh House. He was a great supporter of her trade union and political activities; he also encouraged and inspired her to think and read more widely. He described her as 'one of the great women of the century'. Like him she opposed the war and associated herself with the women's peace movement; she was elected a member of the executive of the Women's International League in 1915 and in 1917 was a leader of the Women's Peace Crusade.

In her autobiography, written towards the end of her life, she reflected:

> Dr W E Orchard, at the King's Weigh House Church, was the influence that induced me to think and explore. Up to this point I had suffered the impact of experience almost passively. But in his sermons and lectures Dr Orchard opened up a new world of adventure – a spiritual world – an introduction to the mystery and dynamic force of prayer. ...

> ... I began a course of reading, and this brought to me a sense of the quality of the service given to the world by people like the Lady Julian of Norwich, Catherine of Siena, the Quaker saints, Josephine Butler, Evelyn Underhill and that great host of dedicated lives. My everyday Trade Union work took on a deeper meaning.[9]

When the franchise was extended to women and women became eligible for election as Members of Parliament, she was encouraged to seek election, though this did not mean the abandonment of her trade union activities, which were always the focus of her professional life. In 1920 she was Labour candidate for Northampton, and was finally elected in 1923, the year in which she was also elected chairman of the Trades Union Congress. A year later she was Parliamentary Secretary to the Ministry of Labour in the short-lived first Labour government. When Labour returned to power in 1929 she became the first woman Cabinet minister as Minister of Labour, steering an unemployment insurance bill to the statute book with skill. She lost her seat in parliament in 1931 but continued trade union work until 1938, when her activities were concentrated on research and social work. In 1948 her achievements were recognised in her appointment as a Companion of Honour.

At the end of her life she was able to reflect on the ideals which had always inspired her work. After pointing out that nineteenth century Christian churches had concentrated on personal salvation, she went on:

> Christians are waking up now to the consciousness that they have not placed sufficient stress on that other aspect, which is equally definite in the Gospels – the social side – the belief that our Christianity is not merely a spiritual and mystical and personal religion, but is quite definitely a social scheme – and what is more, a scheme for the proper and just management of the whole world. It is only to the degree in which we love our neighbour that we can know anything of the love of God. The personal life of the Christian has to be a social life.[10]

That reflection is equally relevant half a century later.

A fellow-member of the Labour cabinet of 1929 with Margaret Bondfield was William Wedgwood Benn (1877-1960), Secretary of State for India. His background was Congregational – his grandfather, Julius Benn, was a Congregational minister. His wife, Margaret, then an Anglican, was to exercise a considerable influence on public affairs, nationally and internationally. Margaret Benn (later Lady Stansgate) came from a very different background from Margaret Bondfield. She was born in Scotland of agnostic parents who had a deep interest in politics. From the time her father became a Liberal MP in 1912 and the family moved to London she was near the centre of British political life. After her marriage in 1920 to another MP, William Wedgwood Benn (he was created Viscount Stansgate in 1941), she and her husband shared a commitment to justice and international understanding.[11] For Margaret especially, this had a profound biblical basis. When she was asked near the end of her life to choose a book which had had a profound influence on her for a TV programme, she selected George Adam Smith's *The Book of the Twelve Prophets*.[12]

> I explained that what comes burning through the words of the prophet Amos is his great passion for righteousness and justice. From him I learnt that there can never be social and political harmony in a country unless there is social and political justice. Society will not endure if it is founded on wrong thinking and wrong doing, and religion is of no value if it is indifferent to these things. The Old Testament is full of the idea of the necessity of a just society and it is not sufficiently remembered that this idea comes originally from the prophets of Israel.[13]

This interest had been deepened by study (which included learning both Greek and Hebrew) at King's College, London soon after her marriage. Her son, Tony Benn MP, testified to the influence this interest and conviction had on the upbringing of her family: 'For my mother, spiritual teachings naturally went hand in hand with social justice'.

During the 40 years of her marriage she travelled all over the world with her husband and shared all his political life, while at the same time maintaining her interest in theology and strengthening her support for the ordination of women. She was a founder member of the Society for the Ministry of Women in the Church, of which she became a Vice-President, and regularly attended Maude Royden's Guild House. In 1945 she chaired a Church of England committee on the training of women for service in the church. Three years later she was invited to be a consultant on the status of women at the first assembly of the World Council of Churches in Amsterdam in 1948. The experience of learning that her views were regarded as suspect by some of the Anglican hierarchy led to her becoming a convinced Congregationalist.

After the death of her husband in 1960 she continued the friendships the two of them had made with liberal Israeli scholars and politicians, in particular with members of the Hebrew University in Jerusalem, and in her eighties was made a Fellow of the University. In Britain she was an active supporter of the Council of Christians and Jews, of which she became a vice-president.

She chose not to follow the majority of her fellow-Congregationalists into the United Reformed Church, but became the first President of the Congregational Federation. Throughout her life she held a deep conviction of the biblical basis of social justice which had a lasting influence on her family and a wide circle of friends all over the world.[14]

Mary Webster (1923-69)[15] was born into an Anglican family in south east London, but became a Congregationalist when she felt a call to ordained ministry. She was an early student at St Paul's House, and followed this by reading philosophy at King's College, London and theology at St Hugh's College, Oxford. After passing the Congregational Union examination, she was ordained at Twyford Congregational Church, Berkshire, in 1950. As a minister in pastoral charge, and through her own experience both of a slight disability and of looking after ailing parents, she became conscious of the difficulties and hardships facing many single women who had to combine earning their own living with looking after elderly dependants. She herself had had to give up pastoral charge after only four years in order to look after her parents, combining this with teaching Religious Knowledge in a girls' grammar school and preaching nearly every Sunday. Before her mother died she had to revert to part-time work. In 1962 this experience inspired her to propose the formation of a National Council for the Single Woman and her Dependants. She lobbied MPs, women's groups, churches and prominent individuals, seeking their support. The response was mixed, but from women in her own situation it was overwhelmingly favourable. She gained enough support to enable the new organisation to be launched in November 1965, just before she herself underwent treatment for cancer. In the three and a half years that were left to her she saw the organisation able to appoint a full-time director, and the opening of several branches. Holidays for the elderly to enable carers to enjoy a break, conferences to promote bereavement counselling, and support groups were organised. Many of her ideas, such as attendance allowances and protection of pension rights for carers have subsequently been accepted and enacted in statute. What has now become the National Carers' Association is a tribute to her work.

Yvonne Workman (1943-91) was a person of whom her former tutor, Richard Harries,[16] wrote that she 'managed to hold together in herself the personal, mystic quest, with a deep concern for the environment and issues of peace and justice'. She had a long and sometimes difficult personal journey towards ordination in the United Reformed Church. Her early years were spent in Northern Ireland; she attended Larne Grammar School before studying Home Economics in Belfast. After marrying Wesley Workman, a United Reformed Church minister from Northern Ireland, she worked and travelled with him in Europe and the United States. In 1978 they moved to England, where she worked for a time for Christian Aid. Gradually she was drawn to the study of theology and enrolled for a degree course at King's College London. Despite ill health she gained a first. Now convinced of a call to ordained ministry, she spent a final year of training at Mansfield College Oxford. In 1988 she was ordained to a part-time ministry at Wheatley United Reformed Church, and was appointed part-time tutor in Ethics at Mansfield. Just before her ordination service, she was diagnosed as suffering from cancer.

During the last three years of her life, her pilgrimage as a person and as a theologian underwent an intense flowering, alongside continuing medical treatment. In 1989 she attended, as a United Reformed Church delegate, the meeting of the World Council of Churches in Basel with the theme, 'Justice, peace and the integrity of creation'. This experience made a deep impression on her, not least the fact that she with other delegates was housed in a Swiss underground nuclear shelter. She returned with a deeper vision of the inter-relation between a theology of God the Creator and a commitment to social justice, peace and care for the natural environment. Here the academic study of theology which she had found so fulfilling, and which had evoked such a creative response from her, was combined with a spirituality which owed much to her own Celtic roots. During her short period of teaching she had a deep influence on both staff and students at Mansfield. It was largely due to her inspiration that when Mansfield College established an inter-disciplinary centre for the study of environmental issues in 1992, a distinctive feature was a focus on ethics and values as a foundation for the study of the social dimensions of environmental issues.

After Yvonne Workman died early in 1991 a fund was set up in her memory at Mansfield, to promote the study of issues important to her. Although she had written so little, and the doctoral research which she began had made very little progress because of her illness, her influence and inspiration live on in the lives of her students and those to whom she ministered.

When she was President of the National Free Church Women's Council in the 1990s Janet Wootton, minister of the Congregational Union Chapel, Islington, chose as the cause to be supported during her term of office a day centre for homeless women. As a preacher and hymn writer she has, like many others, drawn inspiration from the Magnificat as a proclamation of God's justice in the coming Kingdom. She used it as the starting point for a hymn written for Christian Aid in 1995:

Moratorium on Magnificat

When Mary heard her cousin say
God's promises would be fulfilled
She looked towards the coming day
And sang a song to change the world.
This is the way the world will be
When God takes on humanity.

But while the poor support the proud
And tyrants thrive in lands and homes
And while the hungry people crowd
Around the mighty on their thrones:
While greed and need go on and on
How dare we think of Mary's song?

And when it comes to you and me
To show the world a God who cares,
We duck responsibility
And hide ourselves behind our prayers.
Till we have faced our common wrong
How dare we think of Mary's song?

Now face to face with Mary's Son,
Who healed the sick and took the blame,
We'll let God's promise call us on –
And then we'll never be the same,
Then we can sing with heart and voice,
In God my spirit does rejoice.

Chapter 7

Ecumenism

The word 'ecumenical' is derived from a Greek word meaning 'the whole inhabited world', not only all humanity but the whole of creation. Thus the international ecumenical movement of the twentieth century grew from a shared concern for overseas mission in the early years of the century into a more encompassing programme for 'justice, peace and the integrity of creation' at its end. Although there were ecumenical conferences in the late nineteenth century, it was the Edinburgh Missionary Conference of 1910 which was the first to bring together formal delegates (as distinct from a gathering of interested persons) from the major non-Catholic churches of the West. What had made this gathering possible was the work of the Student Christian Movement (SCM) in fostering confidence between denominations over the previous generation. Since the societies represented included zenana missions and women's missionary associations, a number of women delegates were present, and a few women were also included among the delegates of the main denominational missionary societies.

The First World War interrupted the momentum of ecumenical co-operation which resulted from the Edinburgh Conference, but once the war was over, new conferences and organisations were planned. The International Missionary Council was founded in 1921,[1] a World Conference on Faith and Order followed in Lausanne in 1927, and another on Life and Work in Oxford in 1937. Two years later a world war interrupted but could not stop the movement which led to the formation of the World Council of Churches at Amsterdam in 1948.

World Council of Churches

One of the features of the World Council was its inclusion of lay participants, and therefore of women, though they were few in number at first. The growing recognition of the place of the laity in the Church has usually helped women to take a more active role. One of the most outstanding women among those who gained ecumenical experience in the SCM in the earlier years of the century was Kathleen Bliss (née Moore)[2], who came from a Congregational background. After studying history and theology at Girton College, Cambridge and playing a leading role in Cambridge SCM, she married Rupert Bliss, then an Anglican; they worked in India for the London Missionary Society before the Second World War, primarily in the educational sphere.[3] In middle life she became an Anglican but her ecumenical commitment was undiminished. During the war she assisted J H Oldham (who had been responsible for the actual organisation of the Edinburgh

Missionary Conference) in editing the *Christian Newsletter,* an important forum for those concerned about the reconstruction of society after the war; she became editor herself in 1945. Oldham was her mentor and one of the greatest influences on her life. She was a person of immense energy and ability, and went on to become one of the small number of women who played an outstanding part in the development of the World Council of Churches (WCC). Another was Ruth Rouse (1872-1966), a Girtonian like Kathleen Bliss, who also came from a Nonconformist background; she had been a delegate at Edinburgh in 1910. For 20 years she was a travelling secretary for the World Student Christian Federation. She was a special visitor at Amsterdam, and was joint editor of the first comprehensive history of the ecumenical movement.[4]

Since the foundation of the World Council of Churches in 1948, society and the role of women within it, has changed dramatically. Yet the Christian churches, whatever their professed intentions and ideals, have been slow to include women on anything like an equal basis in their councils, and reluctant to give real attention to the unjust structures which oppress women. Half a century later, the debate still continues. The issue of the ordination of women has been a divisive one throughout the history of the Council. While the planning for the inaugural meeting at Amsterdam was under way, the organising committee realised that the status and contribution of women was one of the important issues facing the churches, and 'The Life and Work of Women in the Church' was listed as one of the four main 'concerns'.[5] In preparation for the debate, an enquiry was sent to all the participating churches, asking them to record something of the life and work of women within their membership. The report of this enquiry revealed while there was a deep division on the issue of ordination, there was agreement on the need to integrate women's organisations into the main structures of the churches, on the need for an improvement in the availability of training for women church workers, and on the desirability of including more women in the councils of the Church. The importance of the last was revealed within the membership of the Council itself, for women formed only a very small minority. The English Baptists, Congregationalists, Churches of Christ and the Presbyterian Church of England had no women at all among their delegates, although the Congregationalist Elsie Chamberlain attended as an accredited visitor. The Methodists did rather better with women forming 25% of their delegation, and the Church of England achieved 20% (though most of these were alternates). Only 19 women had voting rights at Amsterdam.[6] It took a further half century before anything like equal representation was achieved.[7]

The committee on 'The Life and Work of Women in the Churches' at Amsterdam was chaired by a remarkable woman from the Indian Syrian Orthodox Church, Sarah Chakko (1905-54), who as a student and later had gained experience of ecumenical life in the SCM and the World Student Christian Federation.[8] In 1948 she was principal of Isabella Thorburn College, an American Methodist College in Lucknow. The consultants to this committee were (Lady) Margaret Stansgate (an Anglican who was soon to become a Congregationalist) and Olive Wyon[9] of the Presbyterian Church of England.

The 'alternate' committee on the same theme was chaired by Lady Stansgate and the secretary was Kathleen Bliss (who also chaired the alternate committee on the laity). These committees recognised that the issues raised were important for the whole church and not just for women. Kathleen Bliss was asked to prepare a fuller report based on the material submitted to the conference. The result was *The Service and Status of Women in the Churches* (London: SCM, 1952) – a wise and challenging work which still has relevance – to which she added an analysis of the interaction between Church and society in the twentieth century. The changing role of women in society required new thinking from the Church. 'When the churches are in a desperate position for lack of man-power, all sorts of service is gladly accepted from women; when the situation is eased, theological reasons against women doing this kind of work are at once raised'.[10] The Church, she argued, having helped to promote the education of women, should not now be surprised if this led them to question the way the Church treated them: '...this is the process by which the Church's life is renewed: out of its good endeavours arise those who can urge the Church on to other and better endeavours'.[11] Having noted that few theologians had reflected seriously on the significance of women's contribution to a doctrine of the Church, what was now urgently needed, she claimed, was to give women greater access to theological study in order to enable them to 'think theologically'. Both men and women had been created to become 'persons in the true sense of the word', and it was on the relations *between* men and women that the position of women in the Church depended. 'The question for the future is how the immense achievement of the work of women for women and with women can be made fruitful in the life of the whole Church,' adding, 'This is not a women's question, it is a Church question'.[12]

The consultation and the report that followed stimulated a process which is continuing into the twenty-first century. The WCC now established a Department on the Co-operation of Men and Women in the Church, whose first director was Madeleine Barot of France.[13] When the second meeting of the World Council of Churches took place at Evanston in 1954, the Congregational Union included the Revd Elsie Chamberlain among its delegates and Dorothy Biggs among the accredited visitors; the Baptists included the Revd Gwenyth Hubble[14] among their delegates and the historian Dr Marjorie Reeves among the accredited visitors. This time 38 of the voting delegates were women. Kathleen Bliss again played a leading role; she was one of the four women elected to the central committee of 100 members, she chaired the section on the laity, and she helped to draft the final message. The department on the life and work of women in the church was now renamed 'the Department on the Co-operation of Men and Women in Church and Society'.

In 1955 the Central Committee of the WCC reported: 'If the implications of the co-operation of men and women in all doctrinal and practical issues of the Church were generally recognised by the member churches and the departments of the World Council of Churches, there would be no further need for this Department.' However, the need for it was demonstrated by the fact that although the overall proportion of women members of the Assembly was increasing, there were no British Congregational or Presbyterian women among the delegates to New Delhi in 1961 or Uppsala in 1968, despite official pleas for more women on WCC councils and committees. Time and again reference was made to the slow progress of women's representation in the committees of the WCC.

Attitudes finally began to change in the 1970s, as it was realised that little had actually been altered in practice between 1948 and 1970, and that many new issues had arisen through the influence of the feminist movement. The number of women delegates now began to increase: 22% of the delegates overall at the fifth Assembly in Nairobi in 1975 were women, and of the four delegates from the United Reformed Church, two – Sheila Rudofsky and Eileen Steel – were women. In addition, the emphasis now shifted to include issues of social and economic justice for women. The title of the Assembly's report was *Breaking Barriers*.[15] The feminist movement was gathering strength and could not be ignored (though it could be resisted). As women were beginning to study theology in greater numbers, feminist theology was developing rapidly, especially in the United States. There was also growing awareness of the inferior position, in regard to wealth, education and employment, of women on a global scale, as well as of the degree of violence which women experienced. This was being highlighted through the United Nations Commission on the Status of Women. Here was a huge challenge to the churches. At Nairobi a debate on the treatment of women in the context of justice – 'Women in a Changing World' – led to the sponsoring of a major programme on 'The Community of Women and Men in the Church'.

Regional meetings around the world were held in preparation for a WCC conference in Sheffield under this title in 1981. Although the United Reformed Church delegate was male (the Revd Martin Cressey, principal of Westminster College, Cambridge), the fact that he was Moderator of the General Assembly of the United Reformed Church for the year 1981-2 indicated that the denomination regarded the issue as important. The report of the conference, edited by Constance F Parvey, was published by the WCC in Geneva under the conference title in 1983.

In the light of the Sheffield conference, the Executive of the British Council of Churches established a working party of ten women and five men on 'The Community of Women and Men in the Church' in May 1982. Amongst the working party were Stephen Orchard, a United Reformed Church minister then employed by the British Council of Churches, and Norah Morgans, an elder of the United Reformed Church in Wales. The United Reformed Church can take some credit for the fact that it was the only denomination to make a financial contribution to the group's work. The group's remit was to follow up the concerns raised by the Sheffield conference and to engage in dialogue with feminists. From the beginning the group discovered, had they not known already, that this was a highly emotive issue; some dismissed it as trivial with a strength of feeling that belied the claim, while others expressed their pain in a tone which their opponents characterised as 'strident'. They found that in all churches, women were on the margins as far as power structures were concerned (most especially in churches which did not ordain women). They also identified the use of language as a crucial factor in alienating women from the Church. 'It is virtually impossible to find the experience or identity of women explicitly celebrated or affirmed in traditional church language'. They called on all the churches to review their ethos in order to discover what message they were conveying to the world about community. They also unanimously recommended that the British Council of Churches should create a post, at least half-time, to monitor progress within its member churches.[16]

In the same year as the Nairobi conference, the United Nations began its Decade for Women, in which the churches played little part, though Elizabeth Charles, a United Reformed Church laywoman, attended the mid-Decade United Nations World Conference at Copenhagen in 1980 as a representative of the Free Church Federal Council and the British Council of Churches. However, at Vancouver in 1983, where over 30% of the delegates overall were women, 300 participants took part in a four-day pre-assembly women's meeting, and it was within the context of debates on peace and justice that there was a renewed call for women's participation in church structures. At the end of the United Nations Decade the central committee of the WCC, late in the day, decided to promote an Ecumenical Decade of Churches in Solidarity with Women 1988-98. In Britain this Decade was launched at a service in Liverpool in which Ruth Clarke, a United Reformed Church laywoman, and Kate Compston, a United Reformed Church minister, took a significant role.

At the next meeting of the WCC, in Canberra in 1991, when the countries of the West and the Middle East were embroiled in the Gulf War, greater efforts were made to include women in the leadership of the Council. Of the 826 delegates, 46% were lay, 35% were women. Every committee and grouping had two moderators, one woman and one man. The English Methodist Pauline Webb took a leading role. Elizabeth Welch, a United Reformed Church minister, was appointed to the Central Committee for the next seven years. It was a black American woman, the Revd Jacqueline Grant, who delivered the sharpest challenge to the war then being fought. And it was a Korean woman theologian, Professor Chung Hyun Kyung, whose address was the most challenging and the most controversial. At the same time many women delegates expressed disappointment with the churches' response to the Decade of Churches in Solidarity with Women.

The World Alliance of Reformed Churches[17] had been slow to follow these initiatives. Not until 1983 did reference to 'The Community of Women and Men in the Church' feature in any of its reports; one and a half pages were devoted to the subject in a report produced in 1983, *Called to Witness to the Gospel Today*. However, this was followed in 1992 by a more determined effort to take the issue seriously with the launch of its 'Programme to Affirm, Challenge and Transform Women and Men in Partnership in Church and Society' (PACT).

In 1993 a group of women prompted the WCC to sponsor a visit by two men and two women to each member church to report on the effects of the decade. The general conclusion of their report was not optimistic: 'With the rare exception, it would be fair to say that the Decade has not been one of churches in solidarity with women ... Rather it proved to be a Decade of women in solidarity with women.'[18] They called for the churches to be more direct in renouncing violence against women, and to take more positive steps to include women's participation in decision-making.

Before the eighth assembly at Harare in 1998 more than 1,000 women and about 30 men met for four days to mark the end of the Decade of Churches in Solidarity with Women, and to discuss what still remained to be challenged. They recognised that while there had been much progress, many churches had resisted change. Again they drew attention to the violence, and the economic and sexual exploitation that women still suffered in many parts of the world, and called on the churches in the form of a letter ('From Solidarity to Accountability') to make explicit their condemnation of such injustice, which was still to be confronted. When the letter was presented formally to a plenary meeting of the Assembly, nine recommendations for implementing the elimination of discrimination against women were accepted. However, the adoption of inclusive language and the ordination of women continued to be contentious issues.[19]

Ecumenical Ministry

Within the UK, Congregational, Presbyterian and Churches of Christ women have shared in solidarity with women of other denominations who found a calling to ordained ministry frustrated by church authorities which refused to test it in the same way as for men. The Women's World Day of Prayer, initiated by an American Presbyterian woman, Mary Ellen Darwin James, in 1887, had brought women of different denominations together since the end of the nineteenth century, and gave women the opportunities to lead worship which they might otherwise not have had. At the same time, it made little impact on the Church as a whole. A more recent movement is the Fellowship of the Least Coin, founded in Asia in 1956, through which women in more than 50 countries collect the least coins of their currency to support projects all over the world.

The Society for the Ministry of Women (for a time it used the name the Society for the Equal Ministry of Men and Women in the Church) was founded in 1929 by a group of Anglicans who had been involved in the League of the Church Militant (whose original object was equal suffrage for men and women, now achieved) and a number of Free Church members. Its constitution was approved at a meeting of over 100 people in Central Hall, Westminster, presided over by Maude Royden, in May 1929. Later that day a public meeting including both men and women, chaired by Irene Parker Crane[20] of the London Missionary Society, launched the new society. 'The Society has come into being because of the conviction which is growing in the minds of men and women that the present position in the Church is contrary to the mind of Christ;' so stated the original notice. The Anglican Maude Royden, now a well-known public figure, was the first president; Constance Coltman was the sole woman minister among the vice-presidents. From the beginning it was ecumenical and Congregational women played a leading role, giving encouragement to fellow members who could not yet seek ordination because of church policy. Within a year there were members not only from all over the United Kingdom, but from China as well. The Society has continued to offer support throughout the church debates of the twentieth century on the ordination of women.

Later in the century, when the issue came to the forefront of church politics, some Congregationalists and some members of the United Reformed Church joined with their Anglican colleagues in the Movement for the Ordination of Women, whose immediate main object was eventually achieved with the acceptance by the General Synod of the Church of England of women to the priesthood in 1991. However, the fact that there is a significant group within the Church of England which is unable to accept the validity of women's priesthood means that fellowship and solidarity are still needed.

There has also been a particular fellowship among ordained women of different countries, particularly through the International Association of Women Ministers, which meets annually, usually in the United States, though in 1987, the year in which a United Reformed Church minister, the Revd Patrice Sessions, became the first European president, it met in Bristol. In 1991 it met in Edinburgh. The Association was founded in 1919 in Missouri in order to provide 'an enabling fellowship' among women ministers, and to encourage women to take up the work of ministry. Its quarterly journal, *The Woman's Pulpit*, has been published continuously since 1921. Florence Frost-Mee has played a particularly important role in this Association, attending its conferences and serving on the executive board. As the churches of other countries have debated the issue of women's ordination, so Congregational and United Reformed Church women, among others, have given their support. Late in life, Constance Coltman learned Swedish so that she could correspond with Swedish women hoping for ordination. When the first three women were ordained in the Swedish church in 1960 she visited and formed friendships with each one.

Women with a strong sense of call to ordained ministry have sometimes been willing to change their denominational allegiance in adult life in order to use their gifts appropriately. Both Constance Coltman and Dorothy Wilson had their enquiries about ordination rebuffed by the Presbyterian Church of England in the early decades of the twentieth, but found acceptance at Mansfield College, Oxford for education and training for Congregational ministry. Irene Shewell Cooper (1902-70) was an Anglican whose call to ministry led her to become a Congregationalist. She never had a pastorate of her own, but preached regularly and collaborated with the Revd Romilly Micklem in producing a book of prayers and responsals – *Responsals* (1947).[21] Clementina Gordon was a colourful character who moved from Anglicanism to Congregationalism for a similar reason, and held pastorates in Wivenhoe and Witney. She was also well known as a very capable sailor. Rachel Storr, who was ordained in 1949, followed a similar path and continued to preach well into retirement. 'I became a Congregationalist because the call to the ministry became stronger than allegiance to any one denomination. (How glad I am that I did not wait for the C of E to ordain women priests!),' she wrote in her eighties.[22] Ivy Jeffers (1900-95) was an Anglican who worked with her husband in show business (he was a comedian, she played the cinema organ). After her husband's death she became a lay preacher and was eventually ordained a minister of the Congregational Church at the age of 68, on 17 July 1968.[23] She continued her ministry in the East End of London for many years.

Lay Women

Many lay as well as ordained women have been involved in ecumenical organisations. Rosalind Goodfellow was a vice-chairman of the British Council of Churches from 1985 until 1990, and later chaired the Commission on Inter-Faith Relations of the successor to the British Council of Churches, the Council of Churches in Britain and Ireland (later Churches Together in Britain and Ireland). She was chairman of the Free Church Federal Council (during her tenure of office the name was changed to the Free Churches Council) from 1993 until 1997. Ruth Clarke was one of the two United Reformed Church representatives on the Church Representatives Meeting of Churches Together in Britain and Ireland, and has served on its steering committee. She is also president of the National Free Church Women's Council, and is an active member of the Ecumenical Forum of European Christian Women, which brings together representatives of women's organisations (in the case of the United Reformed Church, representatives from the network of women and men) from all parts of Europe to discuss issues of common concern.

The ordination of women and the use of inclusive language are issues which still deeply divide the churches, and are a challenge to the new century. To those who suggest that the question of the ordination of women should not be pursued until the Church is reunited, some words of Constance Coltman written in 1920 may still be relevant:

> Only as each Church, according to its own light, draws nearer to Him who is the one Truth, will the Churches find themselves side by side. Those who shrink from acting on the truth they themselves have glimpsed because others have not yet seen it, are committing the real sin of schism by separating themselves from the Truth, who is the Head of the Church. They are denying the operations of the Holy Ghost.[24]

Chapter 8

'Shout Sister, Shout'[1]:
The Voices of Black Women

Io Smith, a black woman pastor in the Pentecostal tradition in the UK has said: 'It is very difficult being a woman and black within a white system'.[2] So where are black women in the white system of the United Reformed Church? For, as Haideh Moghissi has pointed out, 'In any setting where uniformity, vanity and conformity are celebrated to intimidate and silence dissenting voices, to speak out loudly is a victory in itself'.[3] Whilst the denomination may be proud of its part in the Dissenting tradition, it has not always managed to give voice to dissenting voices from within that tradition, as the church became an increasingly safe and non-radical institution. A white middle class denomination now struggles to listen to other voices, including those of black women. From such a wide field this chapter concentrates on the relationship between Britain and the former Caribbean colonies and the voices of descendants of the latter.

Statistics do not advance us very far if we want to understand the struggle and place of black women in the United Reformed Church and its predecessors. Marjorie Lewis-Cooper[4] has pointed out that black people may not even be listed on the official membership rolls of local churches and some church officials are very threatened by the idea of monitoring for racial equality (see page 123 for her response). At the United Reformed Church General Assembly in Southport in 1999, monitoring of the gender, race and disability of representatives attending was made for the first time. In an Assembly of several hundred people only four representatives were black.

So we have to turn from statistics to narrative if we are to hear the story of the struggle of black women for full participation in the Church. We have to hear it in the context of the story for black people's struggle for full participation in British society and in the knowledge that black women world-wide do engage in fruitful theological discourse. Called 'womanist theology', this stream of theological work is related to feminist theology, in that they both have the experience of women as their starting point. However, womanist theologians' main critique of feminist theology would be the way in which white feminist theologians have all too often ignored the struggle, experiences and work of black women. The relationship between history understood by and written about by black women, as distinct from that of white women writers, has been discussed by Catherine Hall:

> Black women presented a challenge to white women as well as developing
> their own historical project. White women must find out for themselves how
> different racisms, each with their contingent historical conditions, arising

from the colonial and imperial ventures of the last five centuries, have been and continue to be central to British history and an understanding of British society. It was not the task of black women to teach white women this, any more than it was the task of women to teach men: oppressors should learn about their own forms of oppression. The understanding of difference is a task for us all.[5]

She goes on to assert that racism, imperialism and colonialism are the issues that white women in Britain have to explore because they have formed our identities too. To hear the voices of black women within the United Reformed Church and its traditions is therefore something we all need to do. It is not a project to benefit black women or even women as a whole but something with which the whole church needs to engage: 'The "Empire" is not just out there, it is inside us too'.[6]

Marjorie Lewis-Cooper has referred to this challenge using imagery from the Hebrew Scriptures, as the need to 'rewrite the script of Sarah and Hagar'.[7] These two mothers of the Genesis narrative:[8] Sarah, the wife, and Hagar, the black concubine, of Abraham are depicted as rivals. It is Sarah who insists that Hagar is sent out of the camp with her son Ishmael to wander in the desert. Lewis-Cooper illustrates this age-old struggle with examples of black and white women failing to work together for racial justice and 'sisterhood' in the present. She wonders how this conflict can be negotiated and reconciled when black women are still 'caught in the middle' particularly in socio-economic terms.[9]

To hear the story of the ministry and contribution of black women to the United Reformed Church we need to go back beyond the Britain of the 1950s, when the period of most recent migration to the UK from the Caribbean was beginning, to explore the experience of the African diaspora under European colonialism several centuries earlier. We need to acknowledge that black people have lived in Britain for centuries such that by the mid-twentieth century 'there were already black communities [in Britain] that could trace their ancestry back a couple of centuries'.[10] Britain was involved in the Slave Trade from the 1500s and as black people settled in Britain so racism[11] grew. As early as 1596, concern was being voiced about the growing numbers of black people in the country. On 1 July 1596, Queen Elizabeth 1 published an open letter to town officials about the repatriation of black people. This letter gave them authority to deport black people and was given further weight in 1601 by a second proclamation. Black people were said to be 'a drain on the public purse'.[12]

Although Elizabeth I's attempt to deport all 'blackamoors' from England did not succeed, the black population in England in the seventeenth century was small. By the eighteenth century their number, out of a total population of about nine million, has been estimated at about 15,000, most of whom were household servants. Though racist remarks were often made verbally, and racial prejudice was common, racism as an ideology did not appear until the middle of the eighteenth century.

In 1750 the *London Magazine* published an anonymous article which described 'the people called Negroes' as 'the most remarkably distinct from the rest of the human species', and in an essay on 'national characters', published in 1753, the philosopher David Hume wrote, 'I am apt to suspect the negroes... to be naturally inferior to the whites.'[13] This contributed to a prevailing view that Europeans were the superior race.

The Slave Trade had begun in the sixteenth century and was finally abolished in 1807. However, slavery itself remained legal in the British Empire and, in 1823, people began to campaign for its abolition in both local and national organisations.[14] The first three women's anti-slavery societies were formed in Birmingham, Sheffield and Calne (Wiltshire)[15] in 1825.[16] Taking the example of Birmingham, the prosperity of which owed much to the Slave Trade but which was proud of its anti-slavery movement, Hall describes how the women's and men's groups[17] worked differently on the same agenda. She concludes that whilst the work of the female society was more radical than that of its male equivalent, with immediate abolition as its main aim, the way in which the men's society worked was more typical of other middle-class voluntary movements of the time which were part of the whole struggle for power and recognition by white middle-class men in the first half of the nineteenth century. The work of the women's group displayed some similarities with the public arguments against third world debt and in favour of fair trade deployed at the turn of the twenty-first century.

> The women used informal networks to inform their particular public on the distinctive horrors of female slavery; they organized meetings in their own homes (the homes always recorded in the minutes in their husband's names), produced albums and workbags, sold anti-slavery pamphlets and books, risked derision by visiting house to house in Birmingham in an effort to dissuade women from buying slave-grown sugar, raised money to free particular victims whose stories had become known through anti-slavery channels, organized what in effect became a national women's anti-slavery network.[18]

Corfield points out that anti-slavery work was 'one of the few avenues open to women of conscience in early nineteenth-century society'.[19] He reported the work of a Leicestershire Quaker, Elizabeth Heyrick, whose 1824 pamphlet, *Immediate not Gradual Abolition of Slavery*, was critical of more cautious aims and policies. This work received wide circulation, comment and criticism over the next ten years.[20] She saw the link between the local poverty of British farm workers and the slavery in the West Indies, condemning the government for laws and a justice system that oppressed the poor. Her arguments were not dissimilar to those advanced today about the links between unjust trade arrangements and poverty, both local and global. Unfortunately she died in 1831 before seeing slavery abolished.

Tracts and pamphlets were a well-used strategy of the anti-slavery campaigners.[21] Women's anti-slavery groups often heard speakers on the particular situations of black women, but few of these women found their way into print in their own name. One exception was Mary Prince[22] who was the first recorded black British woman to escape from slavery.[23] When slavery was abolished in the British Empire on 1 August 1834 the struggle for the full human rights of black people in Africa and the African diaspora had only just begun.

Most of the black people living in Britain in the nineteenth century were very poor. The majority were seamen, attracted to British ports by the prospect of casual work and thus mostly remain anonymous. The city of Cardiff with its large port and dock area, has a long history of multi-racialism. The membership of the Hannah Street Congregational Church was affected by expanding migration from the docks district at the end of the nineteenth and in the early years of the twentieth century. A local history recorded that 'people of foreign extraction' were 'taking the place' of white residents in the Hannah Street area even before the church there was formed. Clarice Smith[24] ministered there from 1909 to 1912, after which the preaching services were discontinued, but the Sunday School remained open. The comment that 'the church and congregation inevitably dwindled, but a nucleus of friends remained faithful to the cause and maintained a brave fight for years to carry on the work'[25] suggests that the local church felt embattled by the racial mix around it. The premises were sold in 1917.

By the end of the nineteenth century black people were beginning to come to Britain to study for professions. Sylvester Williams (1869-1911), for example, was a Trinidadian who came to London to study law in 1896. A year later he founded the Africa Association and was instrumental in calling the first Pan-African Conference in London in 1900.

Another, who came to London in 1904, was Harold Arundel Moody (1882-1947).[26] A Jamaican, he was a member of North Street Congregational Church in the capital Kingston, a church supported by the largely Congregational Colonial Missionary Society.[27] He enrolled as a medical student at King's College, London, where he distinguished himself as a brilliant student. But he soon found obstacles to his profession because of his colour. Eventually he set up a flourishing medical practice in Peckham, married a white English nurse, and joined a Congregational church in south London. Often consulted by younger immigrants who encountered racial prejudice, he finally resolved to take more formal action on their behalf.

The League of Coloured Peoples was founded in 1931 at a meeting in the YMCA headquarters in London, with the aim of achieving equality of opportunity for all. Moody was elected president, and from its inception the League had close links with Congregational churches and with the Congregational Union, whose premises housed its first office. 'We believe that all races, creeds and colours have their part to play in evolving a new social order and system', declared the editorial of the first issue of the League's magazine, *The Keys*,[28] in July 1933. Members of the League came primarily but not exclusively from the countries of what was then the British Empire.

From the beginning women were prominent in the League's organisation. There were two in particular: Una Marson,[29] and their librarian, Stella Thomas, who was the first West African woman to be called to the Bar. Whereas Stella Thomas returned to West Africa, Una Marson spent some of her life in Britain and some in Jamaica. Una Marson, like Harold Moody, was a Jamaican, born in 1905, the youngest of nine children of the Revd Solomon Marson, a Baptist Minister, and Ada Marson. She came to England, originally for a long holiday in 1932, and for the first time in her life experienced both 'street racism' and discrimination in her attempt to gain employment. She found lodgings in Peckham, London with the Moody family, and was soon acting as unpaid secretary to the League of Coloured Peoples and attending a local Congregational church. She organised social events and meetings, and by 1934 was editor of, *The Keys*, building up its circulation to 2,000. She became well known as a speaker at numerous women's organisations, and by 1935 her reputation was such that she was invited to represent the Women's Social Service Club in Jamaica at the twelfth Annual Congress of the International Alliance of Women for Suffrage and Equal Citizenship in Istanbul. Her speech on the second day of the Conference was reported in the *Manchester Guardian*, whose correspondent wrote that a 'woman of African origin from the former slave world of Jamaica brought a new note to the assembly and astonished them by the vigour of her intellect and by her feminist optimism'.[30] She had literary and journalistic skills that she used to further the cause of black people, both in Britain and in Jamaica, and during the Second World War she worked for the BBC's Empire Service. After the war she went back to Jamaica where she was active as a publisher, journalist and social worker until her death.

The League of Coloured Peoples continued in existence until about 1950 and did much to improve the lot of black students and others in Britain, through lobbying MPs, writing to the press and organising public meetings. Moody travelled all over the country speaking and preaching. Inevitably some of the younger members felt that The League was not radical enough, and there was a good deal of conflict. Nevertheless, The League has an honourable, if under-reported, place in the history of campaigns to combat racism in Britain in the first half of the twentieth century.

A better-known event in that history occurred on the 22 June 1948 when the *Empire Windrush* docked at Tilbury, and 492 women and men arrived from the Caribbean to begin to make Britain their home. Men made up most of the first wave with women and children coming later.[31] The initial experiences of those women and men are now being documented and amongst these there was the common experience that the newcomers rarely found a welcome in the British churches. Phillips and Phillips comment: 'In Britain the official denominations were cold and unwelcoming, especially the Church of England, to which many of the immigrants, ironically, already belonged.'[32] Many people remember being asked not to return to the church of their choice:

> After the service I was greeted by the vicar, who politely and nicely told me: 'Thank you for coming, but I would be delighted if you didn't come back'. And I said, 'Why?' He said, 'My congregation is uncomfortable in the company of black people.'[33]

Other mainstream churches were equally unwelcoming on the whole. Yet the urge to worship God, to offer personal and social support to each other, to meet the community's needs for marriages, funerals and the like meant that 'Pentecostal churches, created and run by immigrant groups and individuals in their own houses, sprang up to fill the gap.'[34]

Even then the response of the mainstream churches hardly altered in the 50 years to the end of the twentieth century. For example, after the Deptford Fire, in which 13 young black people died in a house in New Cross, South London in January 1981, Ros Howells[35] said, 'The churches were silent'. She goes on: 'It took the energy of the black people to begin to put the pressure on them, to say something, to do something'. It is this silence in the churches to which we must now turn our attention.

Io Smith came to Britain from Jamaica in 1957, aged 19 years. She says:

> The call was 'Come to Britain. The buses need you. The hospitals need you'. There were many, many areas of work that were advertised. The invitation extended to whoever would come. There were no immigration rules. There was no visa control. The invitation was wide that there were prospects in Britain.[36]

It was also in 1957 that Clifford Hill came to be minister at High Cross Congregational Church, Tottenham. This church was situated across the road from the Tottenham bus garage and next door to the Prince of Wales Hospital where some of the new arrivals would in time find low paid work. Like some churches in similar locations, the racial composition of the congregation gradually changed. Clifford Hill produced several publications on racial issues. In an article in *The Congregational Monthly* in 1965 he noted:

> The young men who formed the bulk of the immigrants in the early 1950s have been joined by wives and sweethearts. They have married and produced children in this country, and can no longer be regarded as migrant workers.[37]

In these few words the presence of black women in their own right was recognised for the first time, by a white male writer from within the church.

There were those in the British churches who were only too conscious of the inadequate response to the immigrants. At the Assembly of the Congregational Union of England and Wales, in May 1965, the Life and Work Committee introduced a resolution on behalf of the Christian Citizenship Group. The resolution was approved after 'prolonged discussion'.[38] The wording of the resolution declared that 'all men are equal in the sight of God,' where 'men' was considered to embrace both genders. It included a call to 'our ministers and congregations to take positive steps to ensure greater understanding of the needs and problems of coloured immigrants, and to foster deeper bonds of friendship between them and the churches' and declared furthermore that the CUEW welcomed the 'proposed legislation making discriminatory practices on the grounds of race or colour an offence punishable by law'.

This support was reiterated in the reports of the 1968 Assembly in which the CUEW welcomed 'measures by H M Government designed to ensure that the immigrant and his children receive the same treatment as the native-born citizen and his children'.[39] The gender exclusive language of the day made women, both black and white, invisible in church and society. Once again churches were encouraged to do all they could to welcome and support 'local organisations which engage in the work of reconciliation between different races'.

Yet how this was to be done was clearly more difficult for some churches to grasp than others. Eventually, at the 1972 Assembly, it was noted that 'a study folder of material prepared in co-operation with the Training and Mission Department' would be available by that summer for use locally during the autumn and winter of that year. Material from the British Council of Churches Community and Race Relations Unit was also commended.[40]

However, there were those who had realised earlier that material of that kind would not be enough. In 1963 Thomas Camsey, minister at Trinity Congregational Church, Brixton since 1956, wrote in *The Congregational Monthly* about ministry and mission at what he called 'Wit's End Corner' in Brixton, South London describing it as 'Brixton, where, said Gomez the former West Indian test batsman in an interview with Peter West at the Oval, "there are more West Indians than anywhere else in the world" (the West Indies excluded, I presume)'.[41] Camsey wrote about a ministry to black people in Brixton at that time issuing what he described as 'a cry from heartbreak corner' as he sought to marry, baptise and minister there, concluding: 'In my youth I dreamed of the mission field. Now, the mission field half fills my parish'. This view was the common currency of the time. Mission was not the everyday task of each church member in their own context as the church now understands it, even if it does not practise it. Rather it was done overseas or as 'home missions' with very poor people in other parts of Britain. He went on to conclude his piece with a call to service in this 'mission field' of black Britain:

This is a challenge to the whole Church of Jesus Christ. I move that we search Jamaica for a man of God; for one born and bred, where these were born and bred, a man trained to be a minister of God to serve his own folk. Let us bring him to work with the man at Wit's End Corner, let us bridge this gulf with a dual ministry, black and white in harmony, a visible demonstration that the Church is a family, a practical means of showing that we all care for the brother in Brixton, SW2, as we have cared for the brother in Brixton BWI.[42]

It was the beginning of the idea of partnership in mission world-wide that would in future be translated into the policy of the Council for World Mission.[43] But that was to come later. For now the only question was 'Who would hear the call?'

Marjorie Prentice Saunders

In the language and attitude of his time, Camsey had called for a man. The one who came was a woman; Marjorie Prentice Saunders, known as Madge. Born in Galina, a small district on the north coast of St Mary, about three miles from the capital Port Maria, her father was 'the manager of the Carron company', in charge of the wharf to which the ships came. She was a member of the Presbyterian Church in Jamaica from birth and might have been born during the first Synod meeting in the Kirk at Port Maria. The Revd T V Prentice, from Scotland, was the moderator of the Synod and she was born about an hour after her parents left the Synod meeting, as her mother felt the baby coming. Madge Saunders said of her mother at her birth:

> She thought I was a boy and offered me to the Lord while I was in her womb. In those days women were not in the forefront of church work. The following day when the Moderator heard that a baby was born he said it should be named after him, so I was named Marjorie Prentice after the moderator.[44]

Madge Saunders grew up in a family who were involved in the Presbyterian Church:

> I have always felt attached to the church. I went to Sunday School as a little girl. I was always playing at church and doing things connected with church. At the age of twelve there was a United Evangelistic meeting at the Port Maria Baptist Church and I answered the altar call and gave myself fully to the Lord. I became a full member of the Presbyterian Church at the age of twelve. From then on I devoted my whole life to serving in the church in whatever way I could.[45]

She was trained for ministry at the Bethlehem Training College, concentrating on work with children and young people and with developing basic education in Jamaica.

According to Saunders, it was the Revd John Wint who brought the request for someone from Jamaica to serve with West Indians in Britain, after a visit to St James', Sheffield, in 1954:

> A request was made for a man from Jamaica to work with the immigrants [in Britain]. Revd Wint said the one person he would recommend was Madge Saunders, a deaconess in Jamaica. Revd Gillespie, in Sheffield, wrote to the church in Jamaica requesting me to come to England to work with immigrants. However, I heard about the letter several weeks after it came to Jamaica and I was annoyed that I was not informed about it sooner. I said that I would go. On the first of December 1965 I was dedicated and commissioned at the Union of the Congregational Church and the Presbyterian Church [in Jamaica]. I left my well furnished home and went to England to work in Sheffield with the West Indian immigrants.[46]

Thus one of the first acts of the newly formed United Church of Jamaica and Grand Cayman was to commission Saunders as a missionary to England. She had already served the Presbyterian Church of Jamaica as a full time women's worker for 17 years at the time.[48] She had a lot of experience in the Caribbean Girl's Guildry[47] both in Jamaica and at camps in Cayman and Haiti, as well as in Sunday School work.

Of her early days in England she wrote:

> I arrived in England on December 31 in the middle of winter in this foreign land to find no home prepared for me in Sheffield. After three months of inadequate accommodation I found a 'flat'! As I had come to serve my people I felt this new experience of 'settling in' had prepared me to understand one of the difficult plights of my country-folk.[49]

Indeed this situation was not unexpected as 'she already knew about racialism in Britain: proposals to restrict further immigrants into England; banning of unskilled workers; "sorry no coloureds" notices accompanying accommodation advertisements'. [50]

Marjorie Prentice Saunders was ordained as a deaconess in the Presbyterian Church of England on 26 January 1966, and served at St James Presbyterian Church, Scott Road, Sheffield, for about ten years. Of this period she said:

> I enjoyed the team-ministry and the sharing and fellowship with other members of the team. As part of this ministry, I was asked to concentrate on community work. This made me more available to work in race relations and go to schools and colleges, and be on the boards of governors and managers. I was constantly being called upon to give talks and to interpret certain cultural behaviour patterns.[51]

Of the work in Sheffield, both the particular difficulties she encountered and the successes she said:

> One [of the tasks] was to give the immigrants the confidence to be themselves. Another was to help them respect themselves and others and understand the new society in which they had gone to live. So I wrote the little booklet called 'Living in Britain' in which I told immigrants how to become adjusted to the British way of life.[52]

The booklet, published by the British Council of Churches and The Society of Friends, was later translated into Urdu and Bengali and gave basic advice about immigration law, work, housing and education.[53] She found that 'the British ministers of the churches who had migrants in their areas were not at first sure how to approach the West Indians' and through talks, study groups, conferences, working on committees with the Social Services, Police and Education Departments, radio and television work, she 'tried to bring about understanding and respect for the immigrants as people, who need no special treatment, only wanting to be treated as human beings'. [54]

Madge Saunders was active in work with children and young people, both in Sheffield and on her return to Jamaica. Of her work in the UK she said:

> To further help the process I had conferences with school teachers to help to break down discrimination in schools, and classes for West Indian children at my flat on Saturdays. I helped to break down the barriers in the school system'.[55]

Madge Saunders returned to Jamaica after ten years in England. Selem Fagan, one of the Elders of St James', Sheffield, remembers her ministry:[56]

> She came to Sheffield in 1966 as a Deaconess, and she was later ordained to the ministry. She was very instrumental in the church and as leader of the Sunday School. She promoted the Girl Guides' group that was very active. Her involvement also included a women's group in and around the church for many years. She was an asset to the Revd Robert Gillespie who sponsored her into the country to help with the growing number of Afro-Caribbean people who were coming into Sheffield.

> She was also the president of the West Indian Community Association that plays a very important part in the life of Afro-Caribbean people in the city. She also took part in the Sheffield Committee for Community Relations, which also served the ethnic minorities in the city. Her service as a whole spanned over nine years in this city, for which we are very thankful.

Madge Saunders was ordained to the ministry of Word and Sacrament on her return to Jamaica, at the Salem United Church in Islington St Mary, on 18 January 1976. More recently the Madge Saunders Conference Centre in Ocho Rios was named after her, of which she said:

> When this centre was to be built we were at the Synod in the Cayman Islands but there was no money for the building. But after praying over the matter, God told me at the Synod that we should not borrow the money from the bank because we have the money. The money came forth from the Synod. People just gave, gave, gave! And I gave all I had and we were able to build that centre.[57]

Although retired she remains committed to an active life in the church, living out her earlier declaration that:

> The church must go into top gear in its training programme for leadership, visitation, group study and social outreach. She must be the window looking into the needs of the Community, giving support and co-operation wherever possible and never failing to give the Christian Witness.[58]

Black women in Britain

As regards black women in the public eye, many of the pioneers or first generation are still living and active. These include: Lydia Simmons, in 1984 the first black woman mayor in Britain; Tessa Sanderson, Olympic gold medallist, who was made an MBE in 1985; Janet Adegoke, in 1987 the first black woman to be mayor of a London Borough (Hammersmith and Fulham); Patricia Scotland, the first black woman Queen's Counsel in 1991.

In 1987, amongst the one Asian and three black MPs elected to Westminster was Diane Abbott,[59] who said: 'It's a bit like starting a new school'. By 1995, when the Asylum Bill came onto the statute books, Diane Abbott said, 'Immigration and asylum has become a bogus way of talking about race'. The bill and its forerunners have had a profound effect on the lives of black women coming to Britain as these following two examples from the lives of ordinary black women, known to the author, illustrate:

> Mary came from Tanzania as a student and I met her in Oxford, where she was attending the Church of the Holy Family, Blackbird Leys.[60] I do not know the whole of Mary's story but she did have family in Tanzania and had been in the UK several years when detained, for overstaying a visa. During that time she had worked at several jobs and had been a regular member of the Holy Family Church. She and Stephen, a local white person, announced they would get married and I lent Mary my wedding dress for the occasion. A few

weeks later she was detained by immigration officials at her place of work: the local social security office. By this time I had moved to Twickenham, which is reasonably near Heathrow airport. Mary was held at the Harmondsworth detention centre awaiting removal to Tanzania, and Stephen used to come to stay with us at weekends so that he could visit her. Harmondsworth was bleak. We tried to offer what support we could: postage stamps and telephone cards, paperback novels and sanitary towels. Eventually, after several months and all avenues exhausted, Mary was given a date on which she would be taken back to Tanzania. We sat together in the visiting room and cried. She was 'returned' to Tanzania in 1993.

Jane came from Uganda where she and her daughters had witnessed the violent deaths of her husband and sons at their home in the early 1990s. For a time she attended Twickenham United Reformed Church and her daughters went to local schools. For several years she struggled to obtain the right to remain in Britain for her and the children (her youngest daughter had no memory of Uganda, having left before she was three years old) given her justifiable fear that their lives would be a risk if they were returned. The local churches were amongst those who supported her campaign. Several times she was given dates on which she should expect to be removed to Uganda. At one point, knowing we had been involved with other asylum seekers, she asked us what she could expect if the immigration officials arrived at her home. Given the number of occasions on which black women had been injured or killed when officials had entered their homes,[661] and her own family's experience in Uganda, her fear was understandable. Her older daughter was having nightmares about the death of her father and brothers in Uganda, and Jane considered moving to a different address so that, if officials did come to detain her, the girls would not have to witness this too. Thankfully she was not detained and eventually she was granted 'exceptional indefinite leave to remain' just before the 1996 General Election.[62]

The experiences of black women like Mary and Jane continue to be repeated throughout 'Fortress Britain' from the closing years of the twentieth century into the beginning of the twenty-first, but the women themselves rarely have a voice.

Black women at work

'Black women are one of the most invisible groups in our society' wrote Elizabeth Nash, about black women employed in the NHS in the 1980s and 90s.[63] Tizeta Powell came to Britain from Jamaica in 1962 and settled in Sheffield.[64] She says:

> When I came in 1962 I couldn't get a job and me and my friend, we went to see Mr Gillespie.[65] He gave me a reference and I got a job at the [Northern

General] hospital where I work now, because people used to put up notices saying 'No Blacks', you see.[66]

Black woman have made up a significant part of the work force of the National Health Service for the 50 years of its existence: 'without those who came to Britain between 1948 and 1971, our hospitals would not have coped with the demands made on them.'[67] The NHS is easily the largest employer of black people in the UK, and most have unskilled or semi-skilled jobs, while those who nurse are concentrated in the lower grades. The link between these low paid jobs and the lives of black colonial women has not gone unremarked. Enoch Powell, when Tory Minister for Health, welcomed West Indian nurses to Britain. But, as one commentator has observed:

> The jobs these black migrants came to fill, jobs in which they still predominate – driving tube trains, collecting bus fares, emptying hospital bed-pans were [and remain] invariably the unglamorous ones at the lower end of the labour force.[68]

Whilst nursing training and the organisation of the National Health Service has undergone, and is still undergoing, major changes, the fact that most black women already occupy the lower paid jobs means that their prospects are very unlikely to improve. Their skills and abilities continue to be overlooked, they are still to be found servicing the carers in this and other types of service, which means that according to Nash, 'black women's skills and expertise are systematically undervalued and all their work is counted as "service" and given less worth, however, well they exercise care'.[69]

In spite of the fact that 'Black women through the centuries have been formidable leaders'[70] the double oppression of race and class that black women in Britain face has still to be addressed, not least by the churches to which so many still belong. One step that needs to be taken, according to Marjorie Lewis-Cooper, is what she calls 'Recapturing Memory':

> In order to take a step across the threshold of racism to the reign of God, we need to recover the unedited memory – to rewrite history and include some important bits that have been left out of text books and information that is inaccessible to many.[71]

In respect of the history of nursing she says:

> The story of Florence Nightingale's work in the Crimea is well known. Less well known is the story of Mary Seacole, a Jamaican nurse born of a Scottish father and a Jamaican mother. Mary Seacole financed her own way to Britain, but her offer to nurse British soldiers was rejected by the British army. She financed her own way to the war front and distinguished herself for her professional and compassionate nursing of soldiers.[72]

Part of the University of the West Indies in Kingston, Jamaica, is named after Mary Seacole.

A case study: St James' Presbyterian Church, Sheffield.

In 1998 St James', the smaller of two Presbyterian Church of England churches in Sheffield, celebrated its hundredth anniversary.[73] The church is small, having 20 full members and about a dozen other regular attenders. The congregation ranges in age from two to 94 years with about half the members being black and half being white. Black members of St James' have described it as a welcoming church:

> St James' opened its door, and has kept them open for the downtrodden, the depressed and the lonely. When no one else wanted us St James' let us in. We could join in whatever was doing and we could also have time for ourselves. I am still part of the fellowship that is St James'. The house of the Lord should be there for all to share and that's what I found in that church. That's what I still find, nearly forty years later. No matter who you are or where you come from you'll find a welcome.[74]

Indeed, Madge Saunders described it similarly: 'The St James' Church to which I was attached came to be regarded as the mother Church, for she had from the first critical days welcomed and served the immigrants'.[75]

It was during the 1950s and 1960s that West Indians began to move to Sheffield, invited by the British Government to work in Britain and to rebuild the economy after the war. As the West Indies is made up of many islands the various groups of West Indians should not be considered uniform. In Sheffield the majority of West Indians were originally from Jamaica, and the next largest groups are from Grenada, Dominica and Trinidad. At first most moved into Pitsmoor (the current electoral ward name is Burngreave) but have gradually spread out to other parts of the city.[76]

One source of information on the period is the Minutes book of the Diaconate[77] that records the visit in 1954 of the Revd Wint, who acted as the intermediary to Madge Saunders' introduction to St James'. The 'services for coloured people' had already started and a leaflet had been printed to advertise them.[78] These services continued for several years and in 1961 the local Free Church Council began to explore the possibility of appointing a chaplain to immigrants.[79] By 1962 Stewart Brown the first black deacon had been appointed[80] and a large number of weddings for West Indian couples had been celebrated. In 1964 Stewart Brown went on to become the first West Indian to be appointed to the eldership in a Session of the Presbyterian Church of England.[81] It was also in 1964 that the first mention of a deaconess from Jamaica appeared in the Deacons' Minutes book. Finance was obviously a consideration for what was then one of the few genuinely working-class churches in the Presbyterian Church of England.[82] A deaconess committee was set up to oversee the financial management and the youth fellowship contributed £2 to this fund.[83] It was further recorded that the deaconess's expenses were to be given priority over fundraising for the East London scheme, which the church had a long history of supporting.[84]

When Madge Saunders came as a deaconess to Sheffield in 1966, she recalled it was a large 'highly industrialised city with factories of iron, steel and metal goods, a city world famous for its cutlery' and 'The West Indians were not afraid and still are not afraid of hard work as they took their places in hospitals, steel works, and in transport, as bus drivers and at railway stations.'[85] It was soon after her induction that Madge Saunders was noted as having taken the chair of the deacons' meeting for the first time, on 23 February 1966.[86] At the time of her appointment there were about 100 members on the church roll of St James', although it is not certain what proportion of those members were black. The financing of the ministry of the deaconess continued to surface from time to time. It was agreed that retiring collections from West Indian weddings should be used 'specifically for the work amongst West Indians by our own deaconess', although the amount given to date was recorded as negligible.[87]

The Christian Education Committee began in 1966, and was chaired by Madge Saunders, to introduce new initiatives like family worship.[88] At the annual general meeting of the congregation in 1967 she organised a programme and discussion around the questions 'Where are we going?' and 'What is the future of St James?' This was a far-sighted move.[89]

By the Christmas of 1968 Madge Saunders had returned to Jamaica for home leave. The deacons agreed to send her Christmas greetings at a cost of 30 shillings.[90] In the following year the advice and friendship centre that had been part of the chaplaincy to coloured people was moved to St James. The staff were available on Monday evenings, Wednesday mornings and Friday evenings and included both Christian ministers and a medical doctor. The deacons agreed to 'standing the expense so far, so long as it is a service for the community and not just for immigrants', which suggests, at the very least, ongoing tensions between the black and white members at this stage. This was increased when the Sheffield *Morning Telegraph* report suggested that the service was 'for immigrants only'. Mr Gillespie was charged to clarify with the newspaper that it was 'part of a scheme for the general community'.[91]

As the 'Mother Church' of the West Indian community, many baptisms, weddings and funerals took place at St James', and preparation of families for baptism was one of the duties of the deaconess. Madge Saunders described a typical ceremony thus:

> A typical Christening took place on a bright Sunday morning at St James' Presbyterian Church, Scott Road, Sheffield. There was a large turn-out of relatives and friends, occupying the front seats of our small but friendly church. The service begins at 10.30 but mothers and babies generally arrive half an hour later and assemble in a small back hall to await the Session Clerk who at the appointed time reverently leads them up the aisle to the Baptismal Font prepared with warm water, as is necessary in this climate. There are

usually three or four babies to be christened... This is not the end of the Christening celebration as in the afternoon the Minister, Deaconess, relatives and friends are generally invited to a Christening party at the parents' home when a beautifully decorated cake is cut and refreshments served'.[92]

But the work of St James' did not end with the baptismal service. Madge Saunders also described one of the many community 'outreach' activities of the church:

A Playgroup 'for all nationalities', is held each Thursday morning in the Church and Hall from 9.30-12 noon. Youngsters from 3 years old learn and play together and prepare themselves for their entry into Infants School. [93]

The playgroup began in 1967, with the approval in principle of the deacons' meeting.[94] It would aim to take 20 local children for 39 or 40 weeks a year and would pay £10 towards running expenses to the church, but the deacons warned that 'they must make it pay its way'. The treasurer had to be a church member and the books to be properly audited. However the opening was delayed until new heating had been installed.[95] The playgroup struggled in 1969 when it was reported that it was 'said to be losing money' and 'past irregularities in the playgroup accounts' were discussed at the deacon's meetings. Madge Saunders considered taking on the running of the group, but this proved not to be necessary when a Mrs Eastwood took on this task.[96]

Today, the Burngreave ward in which St James' is situated, is home to the highest number of black residents of Caribbean origin in the city, and is probably the most ethnically diverse part of Sheffield.[97] It is also one of the poorest electoral wards in the UK, and a programme, called Sure Start, to enhance the development of pre-school children funded by central government began there in January 2001. The successor to the playgroup that has already been described, the St James' Carers and Toddlers group, continues to meet the needs of local families on Tuesday and Thursday mornings. St James' was one of the Sure Start neighbourhood centres, from 2000-2003. It is the base of a project to promote early speech and language development, called Let's Talk.[98]

Madge Saunders worked in partnership with the then minister of St James', the Revd R C Gillespie. In 1968 St James' faced the prospect that Mr Gillespie might be called to a church in Liverpool. She chaired the meetings at which the congregation discussed this. It was noted that Dr Moll said he was 'irreplaceable, particularly with the people from overseas'.[99] The move did not proceed and Mr Gillespie stayed at St James' until his retirement. He died in the early 1970s whilst Madge Saunders was still working at St James', and she assumed leadership of the congregation at that stage. Before she returned to Jamaica at the end of 1975 she was presented with a silver plaque by the West Indian Community Association in recognition of her work in the community.

In the Millennium New Year Honours List for 1999/2000, the name of Mr Stewart Llewellyn Brown, an Elder of St James, was announced as having been awarded the MBE for services promoting race relations in Sheffield. This was only half of the story, as those who remember his late wife, Icilda, affirm. They were partners in this work for many years, and a room in the Day Centre at the West Indian Social Club, SADAACA, was renamed in their honour in December 1999.[100]

Conclusions

In a visit to the Yorkshire Synod of the United Reformed Church in 1998 Marjorie Lewis-Cooper noted that of the 83 churches (out of 127) providing statistics about membership in regard to race there were recorded a total of 43 black members and 4,979 white members. Of those members 758 were white Elders and just eight were black. The figures were not broken down in respect of gender.[101] She went on to note that:

> In general there was good participation of black people at congregational level in some churches, notably Trinity, Leeds; St James', Sheffield; and Headingley St Colomba's, Leeds. Black people in these churches have served as secretary, treasurer, pastoral visitors, Sunday School teachers and members of the [church] council.[102]

Further she urged that, as part of the recapturing memory strategy mentioned earlier, 'The province should properly document and celebrate the work of Revd Madge Saunders and Revd Gillespie in Sheffield'.[103] This was just one of the aims of a visit by a group of people from St James' to the United Church of Jamaica and the Cayman Islands, at Easter 2002, when they stayed at the Madge Saunders Centre. At a reception, hosted by the United Church of Jamaica and the Cayman Islands, to celebrate Madge Saunders' long ministry, she fondly remembered Sheffield and 'her Sheffield people'. She recalled racist graffiti being painted on her flat door and an interview with the local newspaper about the remarks Enoch Powell had made about immigrants. It had been a struggle, although there was clearly much to celebrate: she still had the scissors, made of Sheffield steel, which the Mayor had presented to her before her return to Jamaica.

However, there is still much more of the story to recapture than this part of the Daughters of Dissent project: there are other voices to be heard. The United Reformed Church has benefited from the leadership and skills of other black women, both through the Council for World Mission and within the denomination, yet their number is small. At Westminster College, in June 1999, in a session on 'Women's theological contribution from an African perspective', Janet Llewellyn, a black British woman said:

What I look for in a church is, clarity [of expression]: I need things to be concrete. I also look for passion, for enthusiasm, for people who are like me, which is more about culture than colour; rather that we speak the same language. And I also look for evidence that my colour and gender won't be held against me.[104]

So far the United Reformed Church has made little effort to provide such evidence. We all need to participate in 'establishing the visibility of black people in all the structures of the church and ensuring that black people's perspective is given an equal footing to that of white people' by making 'their stories heard, their experiences visible': what is required is 'an honesty and openness that can foster depth in relationships and true community'.[105]

There is a rich history of the contribution and role of black women in our churches if we look for it. In some parts of Britain this history may go back further than in others. Those congregations that can look back to the time of the slave trade, perhaps in larger British seaports, may find their history differs from churches in places where black people are as yet small in number. Even an 'all-white church' has something to learn from the history and contribution of black women to the United Reformed Church. Often black people are present in the local community but not in the local church. It is not enough for those who consider themselves a part of the liberal white majority to say, 'I don't see you as black', thinking that is a compliment and sufficient action to take against racial discrimination. In 1987 the denomination issued a Declaration on Racism in which it was stated that 'The United Reformed Church pledges itself, as it shares in action against racism, to monitor and review at regular intervals what progress is being made in church and society'.[106]   To fulfil this pledge the church must 'listen to the voices of black people'. It is clear that much more listening has still to be done if we are to completely 'rewrite the script of Sarah and Hagar' in relations between black and white women.

A Response

This paper was given by Marjorie Lewis-Cooper (now Marjorie Lewis) to the Daughters of Dissent Conference, Mansfield College, Oxford, 19 September 1998. [107]

The fact that I am a black Jamaican woman working in racial justice in the UK will inevitably colour the comments that I have to make. The first major issue I want to look at is that of women in leadership. It has already been pointed out that in the early years of movements of dissent and/or pentecostal fervour in the church there was an acceptance of women in leadership but that this acceptance was challenged or changed once the movements became institutionalized or were engaged in wider ecumenical discussions. I have been reading recently some reflections on the work of Marcus Garvey. Marcus Garvey worked in the early twentieth century primarily with a project that you could generally call 'racial uplift' looking at Africans; he was a Jamaican but his work was international. There is a particularly interesting article entitled 'Women and the Garvey movement in Jamaica' by a feminist Jamaican writer called Honor Ford-Smith.[108]

She pointed out that in Jamaica in the 1930s and 1940s the feminist movement was in fact nurtured within this Garvey movement that was focussing on racial uplift for black people. From the beginning, the movement itself had provisions for women in leadership in the context of this wider objective of racial uplift for people in Africa and the diaspora. But one of the interesting things is that the women in the Garvey movement were influential not only in the movement itself but went on subsequently to assume leadership in other organisations – in feminist organisations, in the trade unions and in political parties. Now, I ask, to what extent did the female leadership of the churches influence wider social and political institutions? Did women in fact find space in those institutions to exercise the gifts of leadership that the church withdrew? Is it possible that the church in providing some theological and practical formation for women remains an old wineskin, making it necessary for women, empowered by the Holy Spirit, to find their actualisation in new wineskins? And I really want to take up that question because it has a lot of implications about how we see God working and how we think the Holy Spirit is active through our denominational structures.

In both the Garvey movement and the experience of white British women in history there was some evidence of asymmetry between the stated philosophy or theology of a kind of restricted women's role and the praxis. In the case of the Garvey movement there were women's organisations. They had, constitutionally, a woman vice-president from the very beginning, but women could and did hold any office. However, when you read Honor Ford-Smith's paper as to how they identified the women's role it still had to do with the domestic sphere and with philanthropy. But, and I quote her work on 'Women and the Garvey movement in Jamaica', 'political practice sometimes outstrips the theoretical limits of a stated philosophy and a study of that practice ultimately leads to a wider analysis of the problem under study'. So I think there is a deeper question. Once these women were restricted in terms of the public exercise of the ministry or a retraction of the progressive theological position, what happened? How did they cope? What was really happening in practice? These questions have not received satisfactory answers.

The issues of silence and invisibility have been raised in other chapters. Certainly one major problem for black women in the United Reformed Church and other mainline churches in Britain is the reluctance of the Church and the wider society to name racism. As people from the Judaeo-Christian tradition we know that every demon must be named before it can be forced to surrender its power and then exorcised. This we have to face. It can be argued that the church absorbed the dominant sexist view of the wider society and I want to suggest that there is a parallel process. The church in its process of institutionalisation in Britain has absorbed the prevailing value of racism as well as sexism. Black women today are still being rendered invisible. This invisibility takes many forms. Some of them I have identified in my rapid tour of the Synods of the United Reformed Church, though the analysis is not complete. Some examples of this invisibility are the existence of many black women and men who have been attending our churches for many years but have not been received into membership, and therefore they are not on the official members roll. So some years hence, if somebody tries to find out about black people in the church and takes up the list of the members, their names are not even recorded.

There has also been a refusal by some congregations and leaders to co-operate with the Equal Opportunities committee and with the Multi-Racial, Multi-Cultural programme to provide statistics and other information on minority ethnic persons in the United Reformed Church. I remember a lovely district secretary who said to me, placing her hands on both my cheeks: 'My dear, you are so beautiful. I love you. I have nothing against you. But I don't see colour. I am sorry. I will not respond to the list of questions that you have asked'. So even though statistics are of limited use, the reality is that we do not even have a complete set of statistics for the United Reformed Church. If you look back to the Assembly Report for 1997 you will see a note on the Equal Opportunities committee that indicates that the percentages and the figures relate only to those churches who responded: there is some silence.

There is also, it seems to me, unease about special interest groups for minority ethnic persons and of course for women. I have raised it with the moderators and had some fierce arguments with the Multi-Racial, Multi-Cultural Management Committee on this issue. I was amazed that there was no official women's organisation in the United Reformed Church. I realized that people were worried about where I was taking the 'black thing' – getting black people together. 'We don't really want a grouping of black clergy do we?' they said. I said: 'What?' then discovered that there was no women's organisation and my voice went up a couple of octaves. But I think that this issue may be deeper than it appears at first and may extend to issues outside the United Reformed Church. It may have to do with the way in which British society exercises control by sometimes giving the form but not the substance. The reason I am suggesting this is that in looking at the *Windrush* documentaries there was a very interesting section on the Labour Party; my voice went up further decibels again when I discovered that the Labour Party had voted against black sections. What is it in this society that sees a threat in interest groups when some of us from where we are coming would see that as essential?

I think also in trying to grapple with issues of silence the dynamics of things like culture, ethnicity, social class and people's practical experience have to be brought into this equation because they can also further entrench the silence and invisibility of black women. Again I will just give a few cases from some other areas. As far as discourse anaylsis is concerned, one of the most significant things is that oral tradition is very important for black people. That is not heard and is often not recorded or validated by the predominant way in which white society accepts knowledge. Black women's spirituality is also seen as invalid and therefore not brought into the arena of discussion. There is also a tendency of many black people to edit information when it is shared in groups that include white people. So if in a discussion you have a mixed group to discuss racism you may not discover what is really happening. We also found, particularly within work done on my women's group in Jamaica, that there was an advantage that educated middle class women had over working class women in terms of the way in which they communicated, whereby the middle class women were better at facing passionate arguments rationally. The working class women were not happy with what was happening but couldn't find the words to say it. There is also, I think, a lack of faith that the white church is genuinely committed to the racial justice agenda. One of the areas I definitely want to do some more work in is the question of post-traumatic stress. In some cases people who have been victims of traumatic experiences including racial abuse deal with it by shutting down, blanking out that experience. I am wondering to what extent that is part of what is happening. There is also the knotty question of the feminist/womanist debate and how open white feminists are to hear what black women have to say.

The physical aspect of black women in leadership also needs some analysis. What are the mechanisms for nurturing the faith and call of black women within the United Reformed Church? There was a case that came to my attention of one woman candidate who had been actively discouraged by a male minister when she indicated she wanted to candidate for ministry. Information was withheld from her about the process and the long and short of all of the manoeuvrings was that it took her ten years between the time she felt a call to ministry and the time she actually entered the formal process of candidating. It is also a matter of concern that most of the black clergy, both women and men, have had their basic spiritual nurture overseas. Even Marlene Brown,[109] who you could say is acculturated, spent the first nine years of her life in Jamaica. If you ask her, as I did, about her spirituality, she still has memories of what happened with her grandmother in Jamaica before she came to this country aged nine. The scattered distribution of black female clergy within the mainline churches is in part being addressed by the Association of Black Clergy, but this female network is in its very early stages. One of the interesting things that happened was that I felt frustrated with *Reform* when I tried very hard but unsuccessfully to get an article on Madge Saunders published there. I thought it would have been important in the context of *Windrush* to talk about the one United Reformed Church that I have been able to find that was proactive in having ministry to the black community.

Finally, I want to leave two challenges with the Daughters of Dissent. The first is to do with young women. We are ageing feminists and womanists and there has got to be space made for younger women in order to hear their stories and to share their experiences. The second is the question: What is the nature of the commitment of Daughters of Dissent to the full participation of black women in this project and what are the mechanisms that are put in place to ensure that participation?

Chapter 9

Life Lines

Introduction

Many of the women who recorded their memories as part of this project began with their earliest recollections and gradually brought their stories up to date, while a few of them offered instead a collection of scenes or vignettes. Whatever the pattern by which they have emerged all of these stories have shown a great ability to bring the women's experiences vividly to life. In many cases the storytellers were near or over retirement age when they wrote or were interviewed and their contact with Daughters of Dissent came close to the end of their lives. This gives their stories a particular power, as well as raising questions as to whether what they shared would have been lost if they had not been invited to record it.

What follows has been drawn from the original material gathered by this project, supplemented by other accounts drawn from books, magazines and journals. In piecing the stories together to make a continuous narrative it has been possible to reflect on the way some familiar patterns have emerged from several stories while other experiences have been unique to each individual woman. When various women can be seen to have responded differently to apparently similar situations this causes one to ask whether women in ministry can be said to have a common story at all.

American minister and theologian, Nancy J Ramsay writes from her observations of contemporary ordained women in the United States: 'Whenever clergywomen gather, our stories disclose the challenging ways truth, power and love emerge in the daily practice of ministry'.[1] She outlines the various skills a woman in ministry must use in the different situations she encounters, concluding:

> Often we must summon the courage to speak truth to power and wonder how to do so in our own voice. Daily we discern how to exercise power authentically, discriminate between behaviours that offer care and those that encourage dependency, and negotiate the call to love self and neighbours.[2]

Some of the women whose stories follow would probably never have dreamt of being able to share their faith journeys with an all-female group, but despite that they still had to negotiate living out a call to love self and neighbours. Their accounts are grouped to follow a pattern from childhood to adulthood and later years.

Growing up to ministry

Many of the women whose stories of leadership have been gathered by Daughters of Dissent received strong encouragement during childhood to think about a possible role in the Church and encountered significant experiences that started them moving in this direction. For some women, members of their own family were the powerful catalyst or subtle influence that caused them to explore a call to service. In certain instances close relatives did their best to dispel a vocation, or tried to re-focus it in a direction they considered more suitable, with varying degrees of success.

In the case of Helen Rose (Nella) the mantle of the mother was handed on to her daughter. At 88 years of age she described herself as one of the oldest survivors of Presbyterian women's work, having been London North Presbyterial Secretary of the Women's Missionary Association (WMA) and the Women's Home Church Association (WHCA), and later chair of the Settlement Committee:

> My mother, who died in 1938, was in her day a member of the Settlement Committee and a keen supporter of the WMA, so I was brought up under the shadow, as it were, of women's work.[3]

Many other women ascribed family influence to their decision to be involved in the work of the church. Mary Osborn (née Darlaston), who entered Mansfield College for ministerial training in 1934, found protection and warmth in her home and church life. She had a role model in the shape of her father, George Ernest Darlaston, one of the four ministers who ordained Constance Coltman. He ministered at Park Chapel, Crouch End in London from 1912. For young Mary the experience of growing up in that congregation was like being part of a large extended family with many friends among the girls and boys as well as plenty of adopted 'aunts' and 'uncles':

> For me, church and home were always very closely bound together. It was at a very early age that I began to see the significance of this friendship between Church families. …. Later, when, at Mansfield, I was thinking and talking of the Church, the memories of these occasions were very dear to me as a vivid treasury of what a church should be. I was deeply thankful for the fellowship of Park Chapel, and I longed to have an opportunity to help to lead people to realise such fellowship in other churches.[4]

The closeness of the church family had been borne in upon Mary Osborn during the First World War as the pews on Sundays were emptied of 'big boys' who later visited the house in their khaki uniforms to say goodbye. Only a few months or weeks later they would be followed by grieving relatives who came to speak to her father behind the closed doors of the drawing room. Mary Osborn could not single out one moment when she had decided she wanted to become a church member but aged 14 she had asked her father if she could join his communicants' class. The church meeting in 1924, when she joined Park Chapel, was a 'wonderful experience' for her and she found deep meaning in the simple ceremony of receiving the right hand of fellowship:

> I remember my gladness when he [her father] came to me, took my hand in his firm grasp, and looking at me with a twinkle in his eye, spoke my name, 'Mary'. [5]

Looking back on the transition from childhood faith to adult service in the Church, Mary Osborn considered her early role as a Sunday School teacher had been a critical influence on her deepening commitment. She had begun work in Sunday School when she was 14 and the leader of the Primary department had asked if Mary could help the Beginners' leader:

> I loved little children, and I found their response to her stories of Jesus very moving. Soon I was given a little class of my own, and I attended a weekly training class. Our leader, a professional teacher, made it very clear that regular attendance on Sundays and at the training class were both expected of us. I was fascinated by child psychology, by the biblical background, and by the art of story-telling. My own home preparation for my class each Sunday quickened my love for Jesus, awakening my response to his call to his disciples to 'Follow me'. Working on how to tell the stories as vividly as possible, so that my pupils would see everything as clearly as possible made those stories all the more real to me, and contributed to my desire for Church Membership.[6]

Mary Osborn represents an early example of a woman who followed her father into ordained ministry, a pattern to be expanded more recently as daughters have also begun to enter ministry in succession to their mothers. Dynasties of male ministers, where several brothers or male cousins and male members of the next generation have all become ordained ministers, have often had quite a high profile in church affairs. This makes it all the more strange that the fact of three daughters following their father into ministry should hardly have registered in the life of the Congregational Church.

When Joyce Painter died in December 1998 aged 82, it was noted: 'Joyce was the daughter of a Congregational minister, the eldest of three sisters who were all ordained'.[7] She had trained as a teacher, and developed worship skills within a group of young people in Carrs Lane, Birmingham, before studying at Western College, Bristol. During her ministry in Chalfont St Giles she married the widowed organist and gave up pastoral charge a year later in 1965. One of her younger sisters, Margaret Knee, had died aged 78 in September 1998. She, too, had switched from teaching to ministry, working first as the

CUEW secretary for children's work before several pastorates. No mention was made in her obituary of having two ordained sisters. Their father Edwin Knee's obituary simply stated: 'He is survived by his wife and three daughters'.[8] The third sister, Dorothy Knee, was ordained to non-stipendiary ministry in 1990. These silences suggest an undervaluing of the handed-on tradition of women's ministry.

Ideas of becoming a minister can surface at a surprisingly early age and find their expression in play. Like Mary Osborn and the Knee sisters, Kathleen Hendry (née Hall) grew up in a manse, so she took for granted the routines and activities of that sort of home. She was the daughter of a Wesleyan Methodist minister and had a pre-First World War childhood memory of playing at ministry, aged four or five:

> On Sunday evenings my brother, who would then be three or four, and I played Church. He was the congregation and sang the hymns and I the preacher until I fell off the pulpit stool and sprained my ankle.[9]

Sue Rankin (née Ellis)[10] remembered how she had developed story telling skills during childhood when, as the family sat around the fire in the evening, her father would sometimes ask her to tell the rest of the family what she been reading. She, too, played at preaching. In adult life she would discover how the voice she had found in play and within the family could be used in worship and teaching:

> I often played at preaching. Staggering up the stairs with the big family Bible in my arms I would rest it on the curved rail of the first floor landing and preach to my imaginary congregation below. Many times the Bible fell over the rail while I was holding forth.

> When did I get the idea of becoming a missionary? I can't recall a time which I did not dream of becoming a missionary. My friends took it for granted. Missionaries often told us their stories at chapel. Mrs Bowen's brother worked in India with the London Missionary Society. Each time he came home on furlough he visited us. We children were fascinated by his tales and the little carved monkey on a stick that he gave us. I decided that God had called me to India.[11]

Doris Leyshon traced the roots of her vocation back to her childhood reading of the First World War magazines that were stored in her bedroom at home, which aroused a lifelong concern for pacifism:

> I used to take these out and look at the pictures when I was four, five and six and was profoundly moved. I thought how dreadful it was and the roots of pacifism were planted then. Later I became a member of the Fellowship of Reconciliation. [12]

Margaret Gibson

Agnes Lewis

Constance Coltman

Mary Collins

Edith Pickles

Muriel Paulden

Margaret Fullerton

Middlewich Ladies Bible class 1920s

Elsie Chamberlain

Margaret Stansgate

Alice Platts

Mary Evans

Mary Webster

Dorothy Spence

Kathleen Hendry

Janet Webber

Jean Wilkinson

Elsie Jones

Eleanor Shakeshaft

Joan Duncan

Mary Segain

Mary Barr

Madge Saunders

Ruth Clarke

Catherine Middleton

Yvonne Workman

Rosalind Goodfellow

Janet Wootton

Sheila Maxey

Marjorie Lewis

Wilma Frew

Elizabeth Welch

In the 1940s she would be what she later called with hindsight a 'reluctant missionary' to India with the LMS, thus fulfilling her grandfather's expectations and those of others in the family. She returned to train for ministry at Brecon College in the 1950s.

The impossibility of seeking ordination in one's own church tradition does not stop a young girl from experiencing a call to ministry as Hilda Pettman's story showed. Brought up in an Anglican family she announced in 1905, at the age of six, that she had been called 'to be a clergyman'. Her mother persuaded her that this was impossible so she compromised by going to Ceylon as a missionary. On her return in 1929 she joined a Congregational Church and in 1930 applied to become a minister, at which point her previously generous Anglican godmother stopped paying her an allowance.[13]

Cold water was also poured on the vocation of Florence Frost-Mee when, aged 17, she voiced her sense of having received a call to ministry at a service in Romford Congregational Church. After everyone had tried to put her off, and finding her way blocked in the 1930s, she settled initially for teaching but later came back to explore ministry in 1945 as a young widow.[14]

For contemporary Congregational minister Janet Wootton the call to ministry came at the age of 13, while listening to her lay preacher father. He was preaching on the parable of the talents and spoke powerfully of the call to develop and use the gifts which God gives:

> I pondered my own awakening abilities. I knew I had a loud voice! I also enjoyed reading the Bible. At that point, two things happened: a quiet, matter of fact voice said very simply, 'You are going to be a minister', and my heart was filled with a tremendous love for the people who would be my congregation. Both experiences were overwhelming and have remained with me. I came out of the service saying that I was going to be a minister. Everyone said that I would soon grow out of it. People soon started saying that it was an inappropriate ambition for a girl.[15]

Joan Duncan came to ordained ministry after retirement age and reflected back on the significant influence her parents had exercised on her life choices. Both were Anglicans and Sunday School teachers, who had been introduced to the Quaker tradition while employees of the Cadbury family business in Bournville. They worked alongside Quakers in social and educational fields while continuing to value the Church of England and its sacraments. Joan Duncan had a wide range of early experiences including Sunday School at the Friends Meeting House and later the Congregational Church. Music was important:

> From the age of five I had piano lessons from Mr Joseph Engelmann, a fatherly Jewish gentleman who used to bring the Passover bread to share and left me with a life-long appreciation of Jewish rites and ceremonies.[16]

Her education included St Joseph's Roman Catholic School, where she attended Mass, the effects of which obviously caused some parental concern:

> It was when I made myself a little altar on the mantelpiece of the bedroom I shared with my sister that my parents decided to seek a second medical opinion and Dr Marguerite Sheldon came into my life. It was she who introduced me to Guiding with its allegiance to God.[17]

The influence of family can, of course, draw people away from church involvement. Janet Webber's family were acutely uncomfortable when forced into church attendance:

> I was brought up more or less as an agnostic and surrounded by a family sense of embarrassment if we ever found ourselves in a religious situation. Yet, as a small child when on rare occasions I went to a service without my family, with someone who wanted to worship, I enjoyed it. However, I remember that I proclaimed myself firmly as an atheist when I was about ten. Looking back, my faith started as a working hypothesis, although I wouldn't have put it in those words at the time. My sister was a research scientist, six years older than me, so I knew all about working hypotheses and experiments and testing things. I decided that the hypothesis 'God' was more likely than the hypothesis 'not God', and if that was so and if God by definition is the most important thing, person, whatever, that could ever be, then what one had better do is pursue this hypothesis 'God'. So at the age of 14 and a half this is what I did. I pursued the hypothesis with great devotion. I went to church three times on Sundays, I read my Bible every day, I joined the Bible Reading Fellowship, I attempted to pray.[18]

Her exploration of faith continued in a similar style:

> I started going to a Congregational church because it was the least off-putting of the churches which I'd been to for Guide Parade services. I became a church member when I was 15 and a half, but I knew I wasn't a proper Christian. I raised this with my minister. I told him that I believed in God, but that I had only got as far as revering Jesus as a man - and had read enough by then to know that that wasn't what being a Christian was. Being a Christian was being in the presence of the risen Christ who died for me, and none of that had happened for me. So I told him where I was and he said, 'That's all right, you're committed, you want to journey on this way, that's a good enough basis.' So now I went to Church Meetings. The youngest person apart from me was 45 and there were some very cantankerous 70 year olds. Discussions were often very acrimonious and very confused, with people not seeing the wood for the trees. My very first sense of the aweful responsibility that God

lays upon you was having to stand up in Church Meeting, because I could perceive the issues more clearly than anybody else, and had to say so, at 16 or so. It was terrifying.[19]

Thus Janet Webber claimed her own voice and used it in church for the first time.

Into adulthood

The accounts this project has gathered about the stories of churchwomen in early adulthood reflect a vast range of experiences. Some women found their ministerial vocation young, had it recognised relatively quickly, and had begun work within the Church well before their late 20s. Some women spent the early decades of their adult lives in other ways for a variety of reasons. For a number of women this was quite simply because they had not yet experienced a call. In certain cases women spoke of having met with insuperable obstacles when they expressed a sense of calling in their youth and of taking time to explore other avenues before returning later in life to try again. Another group of women found events like marriage and motherhood changed their sense (or the Church's sense) of their ability to fulfil their vocation in early adulthood, and so their ministry had to wait until their circumstances and the social outlook were more favourable.

In view of the difficulties faced by any young woman trying to enter ordained ministry at the start of the twentieth century it is all the more remarkable that so many of them managed to achieve this quite quickly. The story of Sue Rankin's journey from the chapel life of the Welsh countryside in the early 1900s to a powerful teaching and pastoral ministry in Papua shows how determined she was to develop and use her own voice. During her first teaching job at the Anglican school in Llanfyllin the Rector dubbed her 'Little Miss Independent', a sign of the strong difference between church and chapel in Wales at the time: she loved Bible stories, the Rector preferred catechism and the headmistress emphasised 'the syllabus'.[20] The young would-be missionary had firmly decided not to train as a teacher, preferring to wait for the response of the LMS to her letter offering herself for service. Eventually Mr Griffiths, LMS secretary for Wales, gave her the news the LMS board were considering her offer. When Sue Rankin doubted if she could afford the university fees for the training he told her: 'If God wants you as a missionary, the door will open. Just be ready.'[21]

When it came to it, her fees at Bala-Bangor College of the University of Wales were paid for her by the Church but to pay for her own board she preached every Sunday. She recalled later:

> Some very generous churches in the slate quarrying area of Carnarvonshire [sic] paid three guineas for three services. That meant I had enough for my

needs for the week and to buy a book as well. When once I preached at a place, I was always asked to come again. I guess it was the novelty of having a missionary girl to preach. The hostesses enjoyed over-feeding me. 'To keep me strong enough to go to the mission field', they said.[22]

She graduated in History and Philosophy and went on to theological training, emerging as the first woman to be awarded a Bachelor of Divinity degree from the University of Wales. Despite six years of study, however, she decided against being ordained in 1925 before leaving for her first LMS appointment:

> Finally the day came when I was to be dedicated to the work. I felt that I should not be ordained before I went to Papua because the Papuan church might not be willing to accept a woman minister. The posters went out reading: 'Dedication Service'. I told the college staff and my minister that it was to be a dedication service, not an ordination. I thought I had convinced everyone....
>
> My minister conducted the service and the charge was preached by my college principal. I was asked to tell how the Lord had prepared me and led me to offer for missionary service. The Revd Ifor Huws brought greetings from my fellow students. I knelt and the ministers present prayed, dedicating me to the preaching of 'the glorious Gospel of the blessed God'. Mr Richards asked me to bring my ordination certificate to be signed. 'But I was not ordained', I replied. 'Too late, it's done, my dear, we had all decided on it', he smiled. He produced a piece of paper which all the ministers signed, and later attached it to my ordination certificate.[23]

This story raises a lot of interesting questions. On one level it could be seen as illustrating the Church's failure to listen to talented women and respect their views. Some might object to the rather patronising way the male clergy apparently decided between them what was best for their first female student, even omitting to tell her what they were doing until after it was too late. One might ask why 'Miss Independent' failed so lamentably to get her own wishes respected in the matter of her ordination even though she had stated her case very clearly. It should be said however that Sue Rankin's biography does not suggest she met with resistance as a woman minister or ever regretted having had her wishes overruled. The Papuan people later gave her a title of their own choosing, 'Sinabada' (big mother), in recognition of her work raising the status of women in society, and in linguistics, teaching, preaching and healing.

For Janet Webber the initial call to ministry that she had felt aged 16 faded and on leaving school she refused to go to university, choosing to work on a farm instead:

But by April of that year, 1952, I began to have the feeling that I was not being fully used, that there were whole areas of me that were stagnant. It was quite vague, but it wasn't just that my brain wasn't being used, it was wider than that. So I got in touch with Westhill College in the Selly Oak group of Christian colleges in Birmingham. I was interviewed in June and accepted as a kind of open student, exploring possibilities – and my father agreed to pay for me, without knowing what might be the outcome.[24]

At Westhill, Janet Webber came to personal faith and was encouraged to develop her devotional life by the principal, H A Hamilton. When she announced she had decided to train for social work he suddenly asked her 'What do you want to do?' and before she knew what she was saying she replied 'I want to read theology and be a minister'. The first test of her call followed:

I was duly summoned for interview – Solihull Congregational Church, a large room with 17 men in black suits and dog collars lining the room, and me. I was just 21. They turned me down. They said I was inarticulate, which I was. They were not convinced this was a call. To his credit, the District Secretary contacted me and said, 'We don't want you to think this is turning you down for ever. You need more experience; why don't you go and work in a church for a year, and we'll see how you get on.' As far as I recollect, I thought I was turned down because I was too young and inexperienced. I don't remember any feeling that it was because I was a woman.[25]

In 1954 she reapplied for ministry and was accepted but fell foul of the rule imposed by many colleges that women ministerial students must have a professional qualification already in case they could not find a church to call them. Janet Webber refused advice to begin by going to teacher training college for two years and of the 11 colleges she wrote to only Cheshunt College, Cambridge would accept her without a degree already. She later reflected on the reason why women were expected to have another career to fall back on:

Of course in the Congregational, and now United Reformed Church, system nobody is guaranteed a job which means no one is guaranteed ordination, but in those days most churches had never considered having a woman, even though there had already been women in our ministry for over 40 years. Moderators were tentative about it, too. For years I argued with Moderators that they shouldn't ask churches whether they would consider a woman. As a denomination, we accepted women, and so they should not apologise for us, but simply offer a name, Janet Webber, as matter of factly as they would Tom Jones. But Moderators went on asking that question for many years – perhaps some still do![26]

The call to ordained ministry may come early on in a woman's life but without a sense of immediate urgency. It was a big disappointment to Mary Evans' family, especially her grandmothers, when she decided to stay and help on the family farm in the Vale of Glamorgan near Cardiff, rather than go to college on leaving school. That was not the end of the story however:

> Although I was glad to leave school, and to help at home, in so many ways the autumn months of that year [1937] gave me space to think. This thinking made me conscious of something within me that was not quite right. There was an unspoken, almost unthought of current pulling me again and again towards the idea of full time commitment within the Church of Jesus Christ. Should I offer myself to the London Missionary Society? Because of my background I thought this was the only opening in full time service for women. I had never been very brave, and remembering the Missionary books with pictures of savages, jungles and flies I knew I would not have that kind of courage!
>
> I was in a secret turmoil. The crisis came, one Sunday during evening worship. There was a preacher, but out of a sudden quietness that evening in the atmosphere I became aware of a presence surrounding me and a calm that gave me, through my mind a definitive directive. 'Christ was 30 before he began his full time ministry. Stay where you are.' This was the kind of assurance I had been searching for and I believed God had spoken to me as clearly as he had to Moses at the burning bush. You may think I only heard what I wanted to hear! I was 34 years old before I was able to offer myself for training for full time ministry.[27]

For contemporary women who receive an urgent call to ministry, the obstacles in terms of recognition, funding and training are considerably less than those which confronted their pioneering sisters at the start of the last century. In the 1980s Mia Hilborn (née Kyte) received her call to ministry in her early twenties and was able to put it to the test in the most direct way, receiving an enthusiastic response:

> As a new Christian, I was sitting on a bus in Nottingham, and passed a United Reformed Church. I felt God telling me I was to go in there and tell them that God was calling me to be a minister. So I went in, and said to someone, 'Excuse me, I hate to bother you, but God has told me to be a minister here.'

She was taken seriously. After three years at theological college she was ordained and ministered in the church for five years as her first pastorate.[28]

Despite having felt an early call to ministry, aged 13, Janet Wootton still experienced a 'devastating theological onslaught on several fronts' in the years that followed. In the evangelical Christian groups she joined at university she wrestled with Paul's teaching on women. When she worshipped in an Anglican church after her marriage the priest told her a woman could not represent Christ, and suggested she join the Church Army where she could do a lot of good. She has written:

> All the time, the power of that experience of calling would not go away. If it had not been so definite and dramatic, I think I would have given in to the siren voices of dependency. As it was, the force of vocation met the theological hostility head on, and I battled and battled to understand. It was never in doubt that I would be a minister, but was I damned?

> That was the point at which, in desperation, I told God I needed an answer. I gave him (he was definitely a 'him' in those days) a deadline – the end of that year – the year 1976. I prayed and prayed. 'You *have* to give me an answer'. Eventually, that quiet, matter of fact voice spoke again. Isaiah 40: 13, it said. Aha – my answer! Trembling, I opened my Bible. My whole future depended on this. Isaiah 40: 13 reads, 'Can anyone tell the Lord what to do?'

> That was my answer. It was not what I was expecting, but I relaxed. I don't have to answer all the questions. Simply, I have to follow my calling. As I have done so, I have learnt to read the Bible in new ways, which rediscover female imagery of God, and show how distorted the churches' teaching has been down the ages.[29]

Sometimes it takes a while for a sense of call to be put into words but those around the young woman concerned are not surprised at all when she makes her announcement. Liz Byrne, who would go on to become second director of the United Reformed Church's National Youth Resource Centre at Yardley Hastings, felt she was being addressed directly when in her late teens she heard the North Western Provincial Moderator preach at a service to inaugurate a new group of churches. Tony Burnham asked when was the last time any of the churches gathered there had sent anyone to train for ministry. At the time Liz Byrne was planning a career as a music teacher and £1500 of her parents' hard-earned savings were due to be spent on a euphonium to take with her to college. When she tried to explain that her future might not be in music teaching her parents waited on events. That Christmas, when she came home having set her heart on ministry, they simply said 'Yes, we know'.[30]

Early entry into ordained ministry does not automatically bring with it the ability to identify and use one's own voice but it does allow a young woman the chance to grow into her role as she learns to deal with those in the congregation and the wider world who are two or three generations older. Commenting on a portrait of a 28-year-old woman minister, American pastoral theologian Nancy J Ramsay asks how this woman can: 'hold onto her rightful authority when she thinks it is questioned, and at the same time acknowledge the inevitable limitations of her brief life experience?'[31] Of course young male ministers must also find their own voice but since we live in a societal and church setting where men have traditionally been given far more unquestioning respect than women this is a wholly different challenge for them.

Commitments: juggling church and family

For the first generations of women ministers the clear expectation was that marriage would mark the end of any paid and publicly recognised vocation. There were notable exceptions to this rule, most significantly Constance Coltman the first Congregational woman minister herself, though her continuing in ministry alongside her husband after motherhood was probably on the basis of sharing one stipend. At her funeral Lady Stansgate affirmed Constance Coltman's ability to combine her various roles: 'The ministry reinforced the marriage, as the marriage did the ministry, and motherhood as well as all that it meant in itself was found to be yet another qualification for ministry'.[32]

The fact that this example of ministry, marriage and motherhood did not conclusively change expectations for other women in the church is evident from their stories. Eva Gibbons, who trained at Lancashire Independent College and was ordained in 1931, married fellow Congregational minister Walter Lazenby the following year. Her pastorate ended when he moved churches in 1935, after which she 'continued her ministry in less official ways', partly through encouraging the women's organisations in Northamptonshire, Cheshire and Lancashire where her husband served.[33]

As a young minister in Shaw during the 1930s, Kathleen Hall was painfully aware of the different responses to her decision to marry Dr Jim Hendry, the handsome young Scot at the local surgery:

> For several months we met secretly. I knew that if I married I would have to leave the ministry – even my teacher friends had to resign when they married. Consequently, when we announced our engagement on New Year's Day 1937 we faced questions and criticism. Hadn't I taken vows on my ordination that I was now breaking? Even my good friend Mr Platt said he always sacked his secretaries if they got engaged, as their minds were no longer on their work. Some church leaders accused me of letting the side down; hadn't the critics always said women in the ministry would pack up and get married? It might have been different if I were to marry another minister. But our love for each other was irresistible and we agreed together that if God still needed me as a minister in his Church the way would eventually open.[34]

When Kathleen Hall went to see the Moderator to announce her engagement and consequent resignation from pastoral charge he insisted she must drop use of her maiden name in the *Congregational Year Book*. The way back into ministry opened up nine years later, when the minister who had succeeded her moved pastorate, leaving Shaw Congregational Church in vacancy:

> The deacons invited the Moderator to discuss with them the church's future and made the suggestion that perhaps for an interim period I might act as caretaker-minister. He replied that was a bad idea – if they wanted me back, why didn't they ask me to return as fulltime minister? The deacons felt I wouldn't be willing as I most certainly didn't 'need to work'. [35]

The deacons were wrong, however, for when the Moderator visited them both Jim and Kathleen Hendry thoroughly supported the idea of a return to ministry. This was agreed on the basis of a reduced stipend of £300 per year because of Kathleen Hendry's unique circumstances as a woman minister married to a doctor. Jim Hendry bought his wife a car, paid for extra domestic help and laughingly said it was costing him money for his wife to work, but he did not mind that. Sadly, only three years later in 1951 he died leaving his wife with two daughters, one of them adopted. Their handsome income stopped overnight and the deacons, to their credit, immediately raised Kathleen Hendry's stipend to £400 per year. She continued in ministry, despite comments like that from one man who said, 'I should think you'll give up preaching now'.[36]

Marriage to a Free Church layman was one thing, but marriage to a clergyman of another denomination was quite another, as the experience of Elsie Chamberlain shows.[37] In 1939 she had been due to marry Anglican curate John Garrington, whom she had met while both were studying theology at King's College, London, but then he fell ill. The engagement was broken in 1941 under pressure from Mrs Chamberlain and the need for him to become a priest. After the Second World War, as John Garrington hunted unsuccessfully for a move into priesthood, Elsie Chamberlain intervened with the Bishop of London. She even offered at one point to resign her pastorate on marriage and seek confirmation in the Church of England, presumably to counter suspicions in some Anglican quarters that she was seeking entry to the priesthood by marriage to a curate. They eventually married in 1947, thanks to the intervention of Lord Stansgate, Secretary of State for Air, whose wife Margaret had become a friend of Elsie Chamberlain's while both were studying at King's College. Lord Stansgate spoke to the Lord Chancellor, who had certain livings in his gift, and within days John Garrington had been offered one. Their daughter writes in her biography of Elsie Chamberlain:

> Throughout his subsequent priesthood John never had much preferment and it seems probable that he was never forgiven for marrying a Non-conformist minister. It was felt that Elsie, being an ordained Free Church minister,

could not devote one hundred per cent to the duties required of a vicar's wife. She would be ministering to her own church members and thereby serving two masters.[38]

For Daisy Beryl Russell, marriage to fellow Congregational ordinand Harold Bennett in 1948 while he was still at Yorkshire United Independent College meant that despite already being ordained herself she experienced being relegated to the role of minister's wife before he had even finished training. Although she was ordained and inducted to a church in September 1948, it was unfortunately to the one where her husband had been student pastor the previous summer, and the congregation were inclined to continue treating him as their minister. Once he was ordained she was the 'minister's wife' and ministers' wives were not paid. It was exactly 30 years before she was inducted to another charge.

During his second, more northerly, pastorate a village church invited her to take their Harvest services. She pointed out that, although she had not been given a fee for taking their earlier Anniversary service, on this occasion, being a professional, she would like one. She added that she did not mind if they got someone else who would not expect a fee and they took her at her word. Poor public transport gave her very little chance of taking supply services and continuing her preaching ministry. Things got worse:

> When my husband was wanting a move, the Moderator came to visit us. He did not know I was an ordained minister! He came back a year later, and still did not realise I was a minister. One of the churches my husband was offered was Newark. There was no other Congregational church within 15 miles. He was even discussing curtains with the church secretary on the phone, when I told him that if he went to Newark he would go on his own! Whether I was right I don't know. A few years later the church closed.[39]

In the 1950s Janet Webber was asked at an interview exploring her call whether, as a young single woman, she intended to get married in the future. She replied by questioning the assumption that marriage need prevent a woman from continuing in ministry, once a youngest child was of school age. A few years later Betty Williams discovered how difficult it could be for a wife and mother to answer a call to ministry:

> Having completed the Certificate course in Lay Preaching in 1959 I felt called to full time ministry and approached my Moderator. His reaction was, 'A woman with a husband and three school-age children aspiring to the ministry – impossible! Go away and study for the Lay Preachers' Diploma and see me again if and when you complete it.' Two years later I approached him once more to be told, 'I never expected to see you again!' At interview with Province Committee (all male) I was asked, 'What will your husband do for clean shirts if you become a minister?'

Over the years I have found both pastoral work and preaching immensely satisfying and rewarding, although the tensions and stresses between family and church commitments were at times severe. It was particularly difficult for our youngest child who sometimes complained, 'I hate the Church. It takes my mummy away just when I want her'.[40]

Jacky Smith, who trained at Western College, Bristol, in the early 1960s, married a fellow student. Throughout their ministry they adapted to particular church circumstances and the needs of the family so that she could continue to fulfil her call, even if she did not always receive the pay and recognition that would probably be expected today.

I married Paul Robert Smith at the end of my second year. Paul had left Western and taken a church and I continued my course and eventually we went to Nottingham as joint ministers for one stipend. It worked very well. I also taught RE at a local technical college for seven hours a week. Paul mainly wrote the sermons for us whilst I did any schemes. After two years we had our daughter Helen and moved to Sleaford and I went as Paul's assistant. Although I still did lots of church work I also began building a family. We adopted a mixed race baby boy, followed by two more later. Later Paul went into teacher training college at Lincoln for four years. He taught at Brigg and we looked after the tiny United Reformed Church which was about to close. Later we moved to Yorkshire into three churches and I remained a wife and mother, although I did loads of church work and again at another church.[41]

As the twentieth century drew to a close the power of marriage and motherhood to stall or permanently obstruct a woman's publicly recognised and financially rewarded ministerial career had largely diminished. Even now any group of women ministers can tell stories about introductions to prospective pastorates where Elders asked them inappropriate questions about how they could properly care for their husbands and children as well as minister effectively to the congregation. On the surface, however, the Church has accepted that ministry, marriage and motherhood can be fruitfully sustained alongside each other and are not mutually exclusive. Maternity leave legislation has made it possible for women to combine motherhood with work, though questions remain as to whether there is too much pressure on women to return to work quickly, and what the effect is on small children of being cared for by someone other than the mother. It is not unknown now for the husband of a woman minister to stay at home full time and care for their pre-school children, thus challenging those people whose main expectation of a woman minister's husband is that he should be in paid employment.

The traditional pressure to give up paid ministry on marriage or motherhood may no longer be there but today's women ministers meet different challenges from the ones faced by many of the early woman ministers. Now there are widespread expectations in the Church and in society at large that professional women should be able to sustain a balance between commitments with conflicting demands. Kate McIlhagga summed this up well as 'women's ability to juggle: work and worship, nappies and agendas, meetings and mothering, marriage and ministry'.[42] Her own journey into ministry began with youth work in the Church of Scotland in the early 1960s, when ordination was not open to women in that denomination and the chance of joining the Iona Community had been ruled out 'because George MacLeod said the loos weren't convenient!'[43] She married and had children but continued to grow through her involvement with the Student Christian Movement:

> As I reflect on that period in the early 60s, on ground broken, on preparation made for so many things, I realise how much I owe the SCM in enabling me as a woman to take my place in meetings and conferences; to have a say, when so many women's voices went unheard and women themselves were invisible. It was only later that I learned the value of listening as well as having the courage to speak. It was also a period of pressure: the pressure felt by being the first woman to preach in a particular church or to chair a conference. Like most women I had to learn to resist the temptation of trying to be better than my male colleagues in order to prove my worth.[44]

It took 21 years for her call to ordained ministry to reach fruition and for 13 of those years she combined marriage and motherhood with part-time youth and community work. Having married a minister she followed him to different places. When he served a new church on a housing estate in Sheffield there were no expectations of her as minister's wife, so she could develop her own ministry based on her gifts and training. As she did so she found motherhood had eroded her confidence and swamped her selfhood. When ordination approached she learned she was suffering from cancer:

> 'But I'm being ordained,' I said feebly to the group of serious men. 'I can't have cancer. I haven't got time for operations.' 'The lump is malignant,' was the reply. I went white, the student red, my husband green and the surgeon's black face remained sympathetic but firm. They were very good at reassuring me about the wonders of breast prosthesis, but not too hot on talking about what I wanted to talk about – the dreaded C word. How often those in the caring professions answer the unasked questions while ignoring the deeper pleas for help.[45]

Kate McIlhagga was in her early 40s when she was ordained although she had known for many years that she had a call to ministry. It has always been true that some women have come to ministry as a second or third career, either because they may not have experienced a call earlier in life or because the opportunity to train and change direction did not present itself earlier on. Joan Peters, the third woman to be ordained by the Presbyterian Church of England, spent ten years as a hospital almoner and ten years teaching divinity before she began training for ministry in 1968. She explained the reasons for leaving behind her previous careers:

I couldn't speak in the name of Christ. In the hospital, a woman came to me heartbroken at the loss of her husband and I couldn't comfort her as a Christian outright. I couldn't speak of Christian duty to those who consigned their old people to geriatric wards without question. When you are teaching religion, you are showing your wares, telling children on their immature basis, to 'take their pick'.[46]

For Jessie Clare (née Halfpenny) ordination training followed directly on two years of working as a Mission Sister (deaconess) at Salford Central Mission, between 1956 and 1958. The Manchester Congregational Board supported three such ministries in Manchester and Salford with funding from its Women's Auxiliary. She was paid £150 per year and allowed to do other part-time work to supplement her income. Referring to her entry in the *United Reformed Church Year Book* she remarked that her role as a Mission Sister was 'the one ministry I exercised which is never mentioned'.[47]

Ella Gordon sensed a call to ministry early in life but was turned down by the Church of Scotland when she offered for ministry as a double graduate in her mid 20s because they were not yet ordaining women. Instead she served as a missionary in Manchuria and Nagpur between 1936 and 1949, during which time she also took theological training containing all the elements needed for entry to the ministry. She, too, found that diaconal work could provide a step on the way to ordination, but the waiting must have taken its unseen toll:

> Back home, deeply frustrated but neither rebellious nor with any weakening of her sense of call, she taught science in Glasgow in Woodside Secondary School. In Cambridge she had been in touch with leaders of the Women's Home Church Committee of the Presbyterian Church of England, and with the significant work of the Church Sisters who had been a part of the Church's life for many years. She was recruited in 1952 and appointed in North Shields where the newly united congregation of St. Columba's was trying to establish work in a large new estate on the west of the town.[48]

Although she entered ministry later in life, Ella Gordon was over qualified, with her three degrees. Other women, with different family circumstances, have found it hard to get the training they want and need. Frances Chambers came to Christian faith in her 40s from what she terms atheistic humanism, initially through existentialism and then from a spiritual experience. She took the ROM (Roll of Ministers) course and was ordained in the Congregational Church in 1971 just before the United Reformed Church came into being.

> Because at that time, although I was accepted as being suitable for training in New College, I could not get a grant – even more essential for a mature student who was a widow with a child at school – my training had to be with tutors,

with one term of my last year at Westminster College. However, I had really good co-operation and help from New College, and my tutor was excellent, and I realised at Westminster that my training was well up to standard.

Have I experienced discrimination? Yes, from one or two of my United Reformed Church colleagues, including from one because of my ROM training, that I must have been too dumb to go through college. Yes, from a Moderator who played the record of it being difficult to place a woman, although I was aware that the church my name had gone to had specifically asked for a woman – my tutor had done some researching and discovered that. None at all from any of my Anglican colleagues with whom I had excellent relationships, and always a good welcome at Deanery and Diocesan Synod.[49]

Joan Duncan grew up in an Anglican family and she learned from her father's support of the Liberal Party the importance of not transferring her allegiance if she believed the way she had chosen was right. As an adult, however, she did change one important allegiance. Having been confirmed in the Church of England in 1940 she transferred to the Presbyterian Church in Australia 15 years later when she and her husband Neil went to work for the Flying Doctor Service. This change caused problems in the 1950s as Brother Les Whereat, an Anglican priest in Australia, explained to her:

He told me that because I had transferred to membership of the Presbyterian Church I could no longer take Communion in the Anglican Church! He had been told by his churchwardens to inform me of this. He could not convince me that I had made a mistake in deciding to worship with my husband in his church. When I mentioned that I turned regularly to my Bible for guidance he asked me how I knew that the devil was not guiding me? My only answer was that I .....had faith that God was in fact guiding me just as much as a Presbyterian as when I was an Anglican..... When Neil heard what had happened I think he expected me to be totally shattered – but such was my 'blessed assurance' of God's promises that I had spent much of the day in Bible study and could find nothing to suggest that my baptism and confirmation were not all that was required for me to present myself for Holy Communion wherever and whenever two or three of us were joined together in prayers and remembering particularly the sacrifice which our Lord had made on our behalf.[50]

The move to discovering and using her own voice was a key moment in her journey towards ministry. Joan Duncan was finally ordained to non-stipendiary ministry in September 1984 aged 66, to serve as associate minister at Crowborough United (Methodist and United Reformed) Church. Amongst others the Anglican Suffragan Bishop of Lewes, Peter Ball, gave the right hand of fellowship. When all the Crowborough churches held a day of celebration of their unity Cormac Murphy O'Connor, then Roman Catholic Bishop of Arundel, was chairman of a lunchtime meeting of ministers. Joan Duncan asked him 'How long do we have to wait before we can "break bread together"?' His reply, with a smile, was 'Some of us are getting a little impatient'.[51]

The minister wants a wife

It is clear from these stories that women ministers have often experienced marriage and family life as at best complicating factors in their fulfilment of a call and at worst downright obstacles. This leads on to considering how and where single women (including spinsters, widows and divorcees) find support for the pressures of ministry they experience. Some women in earlier generations of ordained ministry chose to put their calling first and remain single at a time when paid work and marriage were regarded as mutually exclusive for women. The personal cost they paid for fulfilling their vocation, in terms of limited income, poor accommodation, stressful work and resulting ill health is hinted at by an appeal which appeared in a column Constance Coltman wrote for *The Sunday at Home* journal in 1931:

> A letter has reached me from a Congregational woman minister, who has been working single-handed in the East End of London for the past seven years. She feels that owing to the growth of the work the time has now come when she urgently needs the assistance of a part-time deaconess or other trained worker. She could offer a bed-sitting room and other amenities of her own little home and a sum of 10s. weekly in addition.[52]

This minister was probably Mary Collins, who had been called to North Bow Congregational Church in 1923, and would retire in poor health two years after this appeal, aged only 59.

Another single woman minister who worked in an area affected by economic deprivation was Muriel Paulden. She spent much of her ministry in community-building, firstly through the training and Young People's centre at Berkley Street, in Liverpool 8, and the work of the re-planted congregation there with its uniformed organisations, Sunday School, Nursery School, prayer group and women's guild. Her next venture, St Paul's House, of which she was Warden from 1946 to 1957, was a community of Home Missionaries. One great strength that St Paul's House offered its women students was the prayer support and practical help that continued throughout their ministry, coupled with annual return visits of two separate weeks to the community house in Liverpool to share experiences and reflect on the future. Every summer, students would visit the different County Unions on mission tours that often proved to be recruiting grounds for the community. Mary Evans was introduced to the possibility of becoming a Home Missionary by this means:

In 1954 the Secretary of the East Glamorgan Congregational Council invited me to plan a programme for a St Paul's House Liverpool student, who was coming to South Wales on an advocacy tour. She was a woman! I had never heard of St Paul's House or Revd Muriel Paulden. I was now 34 years old! Life was fairly easy. There were plenty of friendly men about, but having secretly vowed I would never marry a farmer there was no real romance in the air! For ten days I toured around the District with June Davis, and could hardly believe the story I was hearing. A college to train women for ministry! Why had I not heard something of this work before? After the first evening I felt I wanted to immediately go to Liverpool and offer myself![53]

It is impossible to say how many of the women who studied at St Paul's House would have thought of entering any form of ministry without the presence of an all-female, supportive community to train in and return to as a home base. They all entered as single women and the community tended to frown on marriage as a potential waste of their training. Once in ministry the challenges faced by St Paul's House women were not just spiritual and emotional. To live alone in a manse could be hard work physically too. Mary Evans experienced the bitter winter of 1963 while in her first ministry, at Wotton under Edge, and had to dig herself out of the manse eight times. Living in poorly heated accommodation, driving long distances to meetings and services, can take their toll on all ministers but at least a member of St Paul's House knew herself to be upheld by the prayers of others as she struggled. In the 1972 Congregational Year Book, just before the advent of the United Reformed Church, there were six names listed as members of St Paul's House. Two of them were unmarried and in ministry, one married and in ministry, and the other three 'N, now married, are not at present seeking further Pastoral Charge'.[54]

When St Paul's House closed in 1965 the then Warden, Alice Platts, wrote of this 'Experiment in fellowship' for *The Congregational Monthly*:

> Of all the churches served, not one could be said to be easy. All the Home Missionaries could have suffered badly from loneliness, but it is interesting and significant that not one has been ill, not one failed, not one dropped out – except to be married or to resign for quite specific reasons. This experiment in fellowship has been the strength and stay of us all.

> To be able to slip away from one's church for a few hours or longer, to be able to talk things over with someone, to be able to get things in their right perspective again, to talk, and in the talking, to see new possibilities, to be able to laugh at something which seemed so forbidding, to know that there were people who were praying for you – this is what fellowship has meant and means, and this is what has made it possible for so many of us to go on.[55]

Support to continue in ministry is not only to do with being able to get away and see things differently but also the quality of friendship offered by those in the local church. Margaret (Winifred) Taylor, wrote of her experience that single women ministers receive less help on a personal and practical level than their single male colleagues:

> I am sure if I was an un-married male minister I would be invited out much more often, but because I am a woman no one thinks that I would enjoy company and a meal cooked for me occasionally.[56]

Issues of loneliness in the manse and a need for personal support for women ministers emerged when the Congregational Union of England and Wales gave its response to a World Council of Churches study 'The Co-operation of Men and Women in the Church' in the early 1960s (see chapter 10 'How this story has been told'). There was a well-meaning recommendation in the final CUEW report about the need for domestic help, so that women ministers could do the job they had been called to, but no suggestions about how they might afford this on a stipend. Florence Frost-Mee, who had been recruited to join the group that wrote the report, told an interviewer in 1975 that she got up early to get her domestic chores out of the way by 9 o'clock, which implied that she for one had no paid help.[57] Another idea in the report to the WCC was that some women ministers might find companionship and help by sharing their home with a family member or friend. This more practical proposal has been the way some women ministers have countered the loneliness of ministry though figures show that in contemporary British society more and more people are living alone.

Mary Wyatt was a single woman aged 49 when she was ordained in 1960, becoming in effect a non-stipendiary minister before the category even existed. She lived with her elderly mother:

> I had a full-time job with J Lyons & Co Ltd, as a librarian in their laboratories and a frail old mother at home, so was glad to be in the SW Middlesex Group of Churches with John Taylor as Group Minister (full time), David Skidmore (local pastor, later ordained), Arthur Burgess (lay preacher). Churches: Gunnersbury, Brentford, Isleworth. It was a blessed time. In June 1962 my mother died and a year later I offered for the full-time ministry, saying I should prefer to leave London where I had lived all my life.
>
> For some months no one seemed very interested in me, until I was introduced to North Avenue, Chelmsford. They had happy memories of the ministry of women (Eleanor Shakeshaft and Reita Searle). I was a part time (hon) industrial Chaplain with Marconi's, which I found very rewarding. I was welcomed particularly as a woman. I also formed a very close relationship with the Cathedral clergy.[58]

This study has already referred several times to questions of poor health among women in ministry. Current levels of clergy stress and ministerial burnout in all denominations are worryingly high among both men and women. It is not known whether ordained women are reported as suffering more from health problems than men, nor is there anything known about the effect of marriage or staying single, motherhood, divorce or single parenting on stress levels among them. However it is hard to escape the impression that some single women ministers suffer ill health partly because they work under extra pressures which a man would not encounter. For instance, Ella Gordon's outward lack of rebelliousness about the Presbyterian Church of England's long-delayed recognition of her call to ordained ministry could explain why she worked so hard in her first pastoral charge. It may also have caused the ill health which made her leave pastoral charge to teach at Selly Oak Colleges in 1966, and to retire two years later, just short of 60. A former colleague has written:

> A bald record does not do justice to the ability and dedication of this gracious woman. As a pioneer of women's ministry she knew that she was watched and that makes for loneliness. As she in turn watched the slow acceptance of women's ministry in other Churches there was no sense of triumphalism in her mood, just humble costly faithfulness to her sense of call and a quiet acceptance of the difficult pastorates which fell to her care.[59]

It can be tough for a minister to live alone, whether a man or a woman, but one added burden single women may carry is the veiled expectation that they should fulfil two roles, that of the minister and the minister's wife. The traditional model of the minister's wife as a quiet, dutiful helpmeet who runs the home, presides at the women's meeting and makes sure her husband is equipped in every practical and emotional way for serving his flock, is fast disappearing. However, it is not unknown for women ministers to be asked to take on the role of the minister's wife as well as the visible leadership parts of ministry. Sheila Thorpe, who went into ministry in her 50s as a widow, relates a story from the 1980s:

> Before my first Christmas in ministry the wife of the Anglican curate I was working with in an LEP [Local Ecumenical Project] came up to me with a list and asked how many mince pies I was able to make – apparently they always had home made mince pies with the refreshments after service at Christmas. I asked her what she wanted me to do – prepare for leading worship or make mince pies? She was a bit taken aback. I don't think for a minute she asked the Vicar if he was going to make mince pies! The following autumn she presented me with a large plastic bag of potatoes to peel for the Harvest supper – I just handed them back, saying something like 'What do you want me to do with these?' She didn't ask me that sort of thing again and in the end the cracks about not having home made soup for the ministers' fraternal when it met at my manse stopped too.[60]

During the twentieth century British society underwent enormous changes in terms of attitudes towards women's paid employment and marital status, many of which confounded and confused the prevailing expectations of women's role in the church. Even a comparatively recent article, 'What do we owe to spinsters?', which appeared in *The Congregational* Monthly during 1966, seems to have come from a different world. The writer quoted Government predictions that by the close of the century the predominance of women in the population would have ended. He assumed this would mean the virtual disappearance of spinsters since every woman who wanted to would be able to marry, and he feared this would mean they stopped attending church:

> And how will it be for the church when spinsters are no more? Unencumbered with families, an army of spinsters has undertaken for years our missionary work, the teaching of our children in Sunday Schools, the leadership of our uniformed organisations and the maintenance of good standards in choirs.[61]

As the new millennium dawned, women outnumbered men more than ever within congregations, many of them married but attending church without their husbands. Though married women now probably make up the largest group among ordained women, there are still single women in leadership roles, some of them spinsters or widows and others divorcees or women whose marriages have come to an end since entering ministry.

Another style of ministerial household, which would have been quite unforeseeable in 1966, is that of an ordained minister with a same sex partner. Janet Webber, who retired in 1997, 'came out' as a lesbian when she was 60 and spoke out for gay and lesbian ministers within the United Reformed Church during the inconclusive discussions on the issue in the late 1990s. Her last five years before retirement were spent in two District appointments as her high profile at this time as a lesbian meant that calls to pastorates were no longer forthcoming. The parallel between the reluctance of pastorates to call women in the 1950s with their reluctance to call gays in the 1990s is very strong. As a young minister, at the time thinking herself heterosexual, she had found the loneliness of single ministry very stressful. She lived alone until 1973, after which the support of a partner helped her through some very difficult situations in an inner London pastorate:

> There are certainly advantages for ministry in living on one's own – cries for help can be answered, day or night, without anyone worrying as to where one is – pastoral calls can stretch out into a mealtime for instance, and lead to a greater sense of togetherness. But to return to an empty house after some really good, and therefore exhausting, Sunday services has often overwhelmed me with a tension which it is difficult to release on one's own, and it is even worse to be alone after a turbulent Church Meeting, and try to make a rational assessment of what has been happening![62]

A recent development, which symbolises a new attitude towards the work stress experienced by male and female clergy of all denominations, is the way some ordained people now join trade unions. This is a clear departure from previous practice whereby clergy were expected to accept unquestioningly the pay and conditions decreed for them by their denomination. Hazel Barkham comments:

> I was pleased that MSF[63] set up a clergy section because I'm certain that there is a role for a union in the Church. It's a social justice issue: just as the Church is promoting social justice we should be securing just conditions of service for people in the Church. Women especially have been unfairly treated on a number of issues, such as bullying, stress and isolation. So I'm pleased to chair the MSF executive meetings.[64]

Power, relationships and finding one's own voice

In the early 1950s, when Ella Gordon formally sought acceptance for ordination from the Presbyterian Church of England, she wrote on her application form: 'I feel unworthy of that high calling, but frankly it is not on the grounds that I happen to be a woman'.[65] This quotation vividly suggests the problems, both for candidates and the Church, of singling out gender as a factor when a person is led to ministry. Things get even more complicated when one tries to untangle the influence of gender on the manner in which ministers fulfil their call, both in terms of their self-identity and the way they relate to women or men. Because women's domestic role has always revolved around nurturing, supporting and developing the skills of others, there has often been an expectation in the Church that women ministers would concentrate on the pastoral care aspects of their role more than the prophetic, preaching and teaching sides.

A number of women have clearly focused on the social work side of ministry, though whether this was through choice or because of the expectations of ministerial colleagues, their congregations and society at large is impossible to say. When Daphne Jones first came to Cardiff in 1978 as a minister's wife she was employed initially as a social worker at the teaching hospital before being ordained in 1981.[66] Madge Saunders, answering the call to work with West Indian immigrants in Sheffield during the 1960s, brought to the job her wide experience as a travelling organiser for the Church in Jamaica. The community soon called on her for wisdom, support and advice:

> The greatest problem I had to tackle was the Church. When more than ten immigrants went into a church, the host people in the community left the church. This caused a financial crisis in the church and so whenever this happened they sent for me. This took me all over Sheffield and Yorkshire. Thank God that the immigrants listened to the advice I gave them and

while I was there we had no racial problems. The churches began to take responsibility for the West Indians and the immigrants began to find their niche in the churches to which they were attached.[67]

Much of her work was aimed at giving the immigrants confidence to be themselves, and at breaking down barriers between racial groups and within the school system. Her booklet, *Living in Britain,* helped new residents adjust to the British way of doing things and her influence was felt through the Race Relations Committee, links with other denominations and broadcasts on the local radio station.

Mary Webster, whose pioneering work in championing the needs and rights of single women carers with dependants gave birth to the National Carers' Association, was another woman minister who took the social and pastoral care side of ministry very seriously (see chapter 6 on Peace and Justice). She had gifts in leading worship, preaching and Christian Education too, but the experience of having to give up pastoral charge to care for her parents may well have influenced the emphasis she placed on pastoral ministry. Her early death, at the age of 45, followed a long illness.[68]

Kate McIlhagga was described in a book on women's ministry, three years before her death, as having 'lived and worked on the exposed borderlands between happiness and sorrow, hope and despair'.[69] She wrote of the way response to one particular pastoral concern, that of bereavement, featured in her ministry:

> I learned how important it is to grieve, to ask for and accept help, to allow the tapestry of bereavement to be woven: sadness and fear, anger and pain, numbness and searching form its pattern in each individual life until the tasks of mourning are complete. I learned how men, in trying to protect women from pain and unpleasantness, will often deprive them of important grieving tools, like viewing a body where it is appropriate. I learned to be silent in the face of appalling grief and rage, but to be there, to hold and to stay. So many bereaved parents experience the rejection of those who 'don't know what to say' or the insensitivity of those who say, 'I know how you feel.' You don't need words and you can never know how another person feels. Do women have a special ministry in bereavement? Some do. Some men who are prepared to wait and listen and weep do as well.[70]

There are other areas where women's ministerial gifts seem to be especially valued at times. Hazel Barkham considers the presence of a woman minister is particularly appreciated where situations of abuse and domestic violence exist. Women whose husbands have abused their children were more ready to talk their feelings through with her than with a male member of the clergy. She also likes children:

I enjoy being a school governor with responsibility for children with special needs. Coming back on a coach from swimming and talking to a six year old girl about the first children in the world makes me hope I am talking to a future theologian.[71]

Mary Evans' many ministerial gifts centred on building up individuals and communities. She was a popular speaker, reckoned to have covered every Young Farmers club and Women's Institute in South Wales and many far beyond. She was highly active in the youth work of Congregationalism in Cardiff and its surrounding rural areas, organising social functions and sports, 'networking' between people in different places long before the word became popular. In 1966 she came to Grand Avenue Congregational Church in Ely, Cardiff for six months and lived in Ely for over 30 years until she died. The then Moderator of the Synod of Wales, John Humphreys, said of her at an act of thanksgiving for her life in 1997:

> She was at home with all ages. Young people gathered in the Manse on Sunday evenings, she'd enjoy them, and they her. Her care for the older members of the community, for vulnerable members of the community, is public knowledge though none of us know the totality of it. Her special love was the Ely Hospital and all its people. How many people lodged with her, from how many countries? Who knows! How many received hospitality from her, how many pots of marmalade and much else has she made for others?...
>
> Mary also understood that serving people also meant serving on committees. She was generous in her contributions to District, Province and the wider church. She was generous in her ecumenical commitment. She was generous with people who were reluctant to accept women ministers. She worked on community and local authority committees – and particularly contributed to Youth and Education within Cardiff City Council. It's hard to know where to draw the line; and I know full well that each of us feel this or that moment deserves special mention – the Ely Holiday club, the Saintwell Luncheon Club, the Women's Conference, her preaching and teaching.[72]

A woman minister may well be invited into the domestic heart of a household in a way a male minister would not expect. In the 1920s the visiting style of Baptist minister Edith Gates included friendly chats while her women parishioners stood at their wash-tubs. Automatic washing machines put paid to that possibility. However a conversation over the washing up or some other chore can help to build relationships and may be seen as more natural for a woman minister than her male colleagues. Hilda Pettman put great energy into church extension during her ministry and had her share of surprises when visiting families unannounced:

Once, when I was doing my first visiting, I encountered an emergency at the front door. A woman opened to my knock, thrust a messy baby into my arms and said, 'Here, take this,' then turned to attend to a child being sick all over the hall. When the worst was over she took the baby from me, muttered 'Green apples again,' and then exclaimed fervently: 'Thank God you wasn't the curate!'[73]

Constance Coltman advocated women's particular gifts as spiritual confessors. In a 1921 article she asked how many 'motherly Christian women' had heard unofficial confessions from women who then said they could never have shared these things with a man. A woman confessor would have a wholesome influence:

> She would often, though not always, be more effective in dealing with the spiritual problems raised by the young girl's protest against potential motherhood, her elder sister's revolt against enforced spinsterhood, the mysterious rhythms of hope and fear in pregnancy, of self-sacrifice and self-centredness in motherhood, the aching longing of the barren wife, the piercing pain of the widow mourning her only son, and that crowning sorrow, which surpasses even the Dolours of Mary, that only the mother of a Judas knows. And though many men confessors are wonderfully patient with their women penitents, they rarely quite understand even the ordinary difficulties of the interior life for a woman. Most women have to work out their vocation within a narrower circle and with a different balance and emphasis than most men.[74]

She did not suggest that women should always go to a woman confessor and even conceded that some men might prefer a woman too. The important thing was that the Church should offer both men and women to fulfil this role so that everyone could find the person they needed.

There are many interesting questions about gender and leadership style in ministry, most of which focus on whether women are naturally less hierarchical and more collaborative than men, or whether they work this way because it is less threatening to others than an assertive approach. It has always been unusual for a woman to be in sole charge of a large congregation, since they more often become assistants to a male minister or take leadership in a smaller church. In the 1920s a profile of Euphemia Mackintosh, minister of Central Congregational Church, Johannesburg commented:

> Mrs Mackintosh is the only ordained woman in South Africa, and her ministerial position is somewhat unique. She is neither assistant nor co-pastor, but has the congregation's full sanction for taking services or part-services at any time.[75]

Some of the women whose stories have been gathered by this project developed their leadership in team settings, with varying results in terms of equality and recognition. Gillian Bobbett's ministries in Chelmsford, Swindon and Teeside all involved teamwork, which she strongly advocates:

> Thus I have almost 20 years of experience of teamwork – all of the non-hierarchical, collaborative style, which I would strongly defend. (There's something here about stereotyped male and female ways of doing things.)[76]

Sometimes, however, women find themselves doing the jobs within a team that nobody else will do while those around them may take notice and justify this for rather questionable reasons. In a 1975 interview Margaret Lawson spoke of her treatment by her male colleagues. Then the article gave a male Moderator's view of women's ministry. First, her views:

> Some are inclined to be patronising. There are humble men and big-heads. I frequently find myself being the one taking on the donkey-work – slave girl idea. But, on the whole, we have a good working relationship.

> The Revd John Buckingham (a United Reformed Church Moderator who had a number of women ministers under his charge) admits: 'A woman is often called upon to do chores within the pastoral round which a man is not expected to undertake. But this can be an advantage. It brings her more closely into the homes of the neighbourhood. This is one reason why women so often do better work than men in building up "new area" pastorates'.[77]

Betty Williams looked back on a number of events in her ministry which highlighted problems of recognition for her leadership and authority. Her story illustrates the way in which support from the clergy of other denominations can help to build the self-confidence of a woman minister:

> In my first church I learned that the Senior Deacon had agreed to my call because he thought a woman would be 'biddable'. In my second, one lady asked the Moderator, 'Can we send her back if we don't like her?' Both later became my staunch allies in the work. Because I was the first woman minister in my county I was eyed askance by many people in my own and other denominations. On various occasions members of the congregation, including one of my old school teachers and a local vicar, walked out when I stood up to preach. One lady even had a codicil written into her will to the effect that she must never be 'buried by a woman'. Conversely some people came to church just for the novelty of seeing an ordained woman.

There was also some prejudice from fellow Congregational ministers some of whom had a tendency metaphorically to 'pat me on the head' for being such a clever girl and others who just ignored my existence and spoke disparagingly in my presence of women's abilities and characteristics. But generally I was accepted on equal terms by other Church leaders, being very fortunate in having both Bishops and Rural Deans in Dorset who supported the idea of women ministers, which greatly assisted relationships. In fact, once I had settled into ministry I was well-accepted and warmly supported overall.[78]

Women ministers develop different tactics and approaches for dealing with those who find their presence challenging or strange. Margaret Laurie, who trained at St Paul's House and had over 30 years' experience of pastoral charge, commented that she had found:

> ... no prejudice from those accepting me and those who do not keep out of my way so they are not a problem either. When it comes to making tea etc. in predominantly male company I usually just sit back and wait! Over the years male behaviour has changed, but very slightly. Maybe it was an advantage to have been in an equal pay and status situation alongside men before I entered the ministry.

> Mostly in my ministry encouragement and opposition have come together because of some controversial issue in preaching or writing ...nice for people to notice me whatever their reaction![79]

Florence Frost-Mee was also in favour of being noticed in order to advocate women's ministry, and of identifying herself with other women, as she revealed in a 1975 interview:

> During her ministry at Charlton from 1951-67, Mrs Frost-Mee was asked to go to France to be 'looked over' when the French Reformed Church was considering the ordination of women – 'I was very relieved when they decided to have them.' She took part in an ABC TV series on Women in Society and represented the (Cong'l) denomination in the formation of Radio London.

> At Ilford, before the United Reformed Church, she joined two congregations. 'Special commendation to the ex-Presbys who took the larger step and accepted the Congregational building and me.' She was chaplain to a conference of the International Association of Women Ministers in America, and, as vice-president, arranged a similar one here in 1974. 'I get mad with women ministers who won't join single-sex groups, when they're needed'.[80]

For some women in ordained leadership, however, the idea of being pigeonholed as a 'woman minister' as opposed to a minister is the last thing they want. Frances Chambers observed:

First of all, I do not think of myself in terms of a woman in ministry, nor do I think in terms of the distinctive contribution of women, perhaps because I have little experience of women colleagues, and have never been a part of a "holy huddle" of women discussing such issues. This is probably my loss...[81]

When for a short time she had been a member of the all-women Soroptimists organisation, Frances Chambers had felt similarly uncomfortable. She had also made it a rule in her ministry not to accept invitations to take part in discussions about women priests in the Church of England. In her view this was a domestic issue for that Church, which anyway had a radically different understanding of priesthood from that of ordained ministry in the Congregational tradition.

Another woman minister who did have positive experience of working alongside other ordained women was Sheila Sanderson whose pastoral ministry in Leeds spanned the years from 1956 to 1983:

We were fortunate in Leeds to have a fine proportion of women ministers all springing from the Congregational Church – Revd Margaret Fullerton, Revd Constance Clark, Revd Edna Forster, Revd Marjorie Ayton and Revd Alice Platts – and more whose names I cannot remember who only served in Leeds for a short while.

The ministry at Woodsley Church was a lay one – continued with full time teaching – during which the area round about was affected by wholesale demolition, some churches pulled down and new ones built, a Methodist and Catholic one. As clergy we got together and tackled the Council after which we had a regular Ministers Fraternal here in my flat. We had joint services in each other's churches – in the Catholic Church after Vatican Two. From this a Community Association was founded, and the first Activity School in Leeds for the long Summer Holiday. On Good Friday all the clergy processed round the area led by the Anglican Processional Cross! They were great days, especially when my good Congregationalists joined the 'Stations of the Cross', and watched their Minister flanked by altar boys with candles doing some of the readings. One said reflectively: 'Mrs Sanderson, did you realise we said the Lord's Prayer fourteen times!' [82]

One unifying theme in all these stories is the fact that individual women have always needed to find their own strategies for dealing with issues related to gender, identity and a religious vocation. Being educated at a time when girls are encouraged to succeed academically as much boys, and can grow up with some awareness of feminism, does not automatically guard a woman from the same expectations and traps that have always lain in wait. Kirsty Thorpe reflected on some of the changes of outlook she had undergone during her 30s, as she tried to come to terms with motherhood, divorce, Christian feminism and how to resurrect her lapsed training for ministry:

> At the same time as I was beginning to develop a new, critical approach to the story told about women in the Church I was going through my own story of loss and re-emergence. I was the product of a proud, competitive, highly academic girls-only school where I had learned some valuable tools for operating in a male-dominated world but had few analytical techniques to help me survive when things went wrong in that environment. I had been conditioned to deal with my failures by simply trying harder, but I'd never really questioned whether the odds were subtly stacked against women in the first place. It took motherhood and domesticity to open my eyes to the identity loss and intellectual despair so many women undergo. Discovering Ignatian spirituality and doing a theology degree gave me some ways to re-enter the world from a new starting place.[83]

You are what you wear

As the history of women's ordained ministry in Britain approaches the end of its first century one issue which has consistently attracted almost as much comment as the topic of what women do in church is that of what they wear. During the First World War, when Maude Royden made national newspaper headlines with her preaching, plenty of attention was also given to her clothes and in particular her headgear. Judging by the photographs of the time, the first generation of women ministers quite often covered their heads to lead worship, wearing either a mortar board or a softer, four-cornered version of an academic cap. At a time when many women wore hats to attend worship this no doubt looked appropriate. It would be fascinating to know, however, if any lingering need to forestall criticism based on Paul's injunction to the women at Corinth about not praying with uncovered heads was also involved.

It was not until very late in the twentieth century that any clerical outfitters started making garments expressly for women. Before that women ministers had to make their own decisions about style of dress for work. In 1957 the *Illustrated News* produced a picture feature article on Jean Wilkinson as the first woman minister to have pastoral charge in Wales. Noting that the 'town-girl' minister would need to wear gumboots to visit her scattered flock around the valley the article said:

As Jean Wilkinson walks through Mountain Ash with a woollen coat over her pleated skirt and sweater, there is nothing that marks her as different from any other young woman. For she wears no distinguishing sign comparable with the male clergyman's 'dog-collar'.[84]

During the same period, Janet Webber made a definite decision to wear a cassock, preaching bands and gown to lead worship. The significance of clothing as regards attitudes towards women ministers is evident from her account:

> This was not done in the 1950s – most women wore a tacitly agreed uniform of black suit and white blouse. The blouse could be frilly if you were a frilly person, and some wore preaching gowns on top, and older women tended to wear something like a choir cap as well. I found some kind of round-necked blouse to wear under the cassock, which was fine on Sundays, though my little congregation thought I was bit a popish. I wasn't helped by the curate from the Parish Church who used to come past my church just as I was shaking hands with my flock after morning service, and delighted in calling out in a loud voice across the width of the street 'Good morning, Reverend Mother!'

> But on weekdays it was another story. At District meetings my church secretary or one of the deacons would introduce me – 'This is our *Lady Minister*'. I was not their Lady Minister, I was their Minister, and I totally rejected this sense of a peculiar species, so what was I going to do about it? I needed to wear something in the week that said I was a Minister. I enlisted the help of a fashion-conscious lady in my congregation and off we went into Bristol to search for an outfit that would say 'minister' *and* be feminine. We tried all kinds of garments and frills, but nothing worked. In the end we went to SPCK and bought a man's clerical shirt and dog collar – unthinkable! Next was the question, where do I first appear in this garb? This was my first real act of diplomacy, I think! We had an ecumenical Bible study group and I decided that was the place to try it out – my members wouldn't be able to gasp with amazement, and the Anglicans wouldn't be able to say anything. Overnight, transformation! It was amazing! I was no longer their Lady Minister. Now they had a sense of identity, they'd got a Minister, a proper Minister, not this kind of substitute creature.[85]

Janet Sowerbutts relates that when in 1990, she became the first woman provincial Moderator in the United Reformed Church, Thames North province agreed to buy her a new cassock. She duly went to Wippells, the ecclesiastical outfitters, and was shown the cassocks, which had all been made for men. 'What do you do about women's cassocks?' she asked. 'Put darts in them, madam,' came the answer. When the garment duly arrived by post the darts were just above the waist, nowhere near bust level. She sent the cassock straight back!

Mature ministry

Just as marriage and parenthood mean different things for women and for men, so ministry in one's mature years can be a different experience for a woman as opposed to her male colleagues. Male ministers nearing or in retirement are often regarded as sources of wisdom and insight, and are expected to bring special gifts to difficult or demanding problems, but women may be left to discern within themselves the advantages of experience and age rather than having these acknowledged for them.

Janet Webber recounts her own recognition, towards the end of her ministerial career, that her wide experience was of value to her colleagues and the Church as a whole. She moved to Swansea in 1992:

> Now at last I was able to accept my seniority. That might sound as if I was desiring to assert myself, but that is not the point – what is important is accepting other people's need to look up to me and rely on me, as I needed to do in my earlier years (and still do!). It may be that there is something here about being a woman, despite all I have written, and that I can only now begin to see this. Certainly it was the affirmation given me by four 40-year-old male colleagues in South Wales that enabled me to move enjoyably into such a role. Now I'm happy to see myself in this way. I don't have to hang back and prove my value....
>
> As I moved, at 63, into the last District I would serve as a stipendiary minister, I was aware that I had much to give. I didn't need to wait backstage like a new girl, but could offer my insights straight away. Is it being a woman that has held me back? Or is it to do with my parents' obsession that my sister and I should not be show-offs in any way? I don't know – but it's very pleasant now that it doesn't worry me any more![86]

One aspect of ministry that can be enjoyed well into retirement is that of continuing to lead worship on Sundays. For someone like Mary Evans, the whole concept of retirement was a non-starter, and she remained active in all aspects of church work until her death. She officially retired from Ely, Cardiff in 1986, though in reality she never stopped being involved with the life of the Church on the estate. For two years from 1988-91 she worked in Bettws, Newport and then from 1991 to 1995 in Minster Road, Cardiff. At an act of thanksgiving for her life the then Moderator of the Synod of Wales, John Humphreys, said:

> But truth be known, Mary never retired and probably never will. She has a passion for service, a passion for justice, a passion for people, and a passion for the presence of God. Mary was ordained to the Ministry of Word and

Sacrament in 1966 but ministry was her way, her being, not a role, or status, and certainly never a job or a chore, nor something to separate her from people. Being Mary was living! And living was never in the small world of church.[87]

Some women have had full careers in other work and given lengthy service to the Church as lay pastors, often continuing well past normal retirement age. Mary Carpenter, a teacher, became a lay pastor in the Congregational Union of England and Wales before retiring from education. Her obituary declared:

> At the age of 67 she was invited to the pastorate of Hatfield Road Church, Ipswich, where she remained for 10 years. The only church building was a dilapidated corrugated iron structure and the regular congregation was rarely more than 12. When she left in 1965, the fellowship worshipped in a pleasant modern and debt-free building, and had purpose-built halls well on the way to being paid for.[88]

In 1977 a special resolution was passed at the United Reformed Church's General Assembly, ordaining Phyllis Cordon, a lay preacher who had completed a career as a welfare assistant in child health clinics seven years earlier. This was in recognition of her work for the church in Long Eaton and then in Painswick, a ministry which lasted from 1972 to 1982.[89]

Gwynith Chalmers, a United Reformed Church laywoman, represented Bournemouth Free Church Women's Council on the National Free Church Women's Council for many years and was on the government's Women's National Commission in the 1990s, before and after the 1995 United Nations conference on women in Beijing. She explained her reasons for keeping busy in terms that might ring bells with others who keep ministering in later life: 'Jobs just seem to come my way and since I am on my own I feel that as long as I am able to do thing that need doing it is better than sitting at home and becoming a "cabbage"'.[90]

Ministry in other ways

Being an ordained minister is not simply about learning how to love self and neighbours through pastoral care of a congregation. Women have fulfilled their ministry in other places too, principally through being appointed as chaplains, either in addition to local pastoral work or instead of it. This has often drawn wider publicity, since the secular world has been slow to catch up with the fact of women's ordained ministry, and has tended to notice the phenomenon only when women ministers appear beyond the confines of the Church, taking part in civic events for instance.

In 1968, minister and minister's wife Dorothy Spence was pictured in *The Congregational Monthly* as the chaplain of the newly elected Mayor of Scunthorpe, Councillor Mrs Alice Irene Cropper. The picture caption noted: 'Mrs Spence, mother of an 18-month-old baby girl, took part in the civic service and walked in procession to the church'.[91] According to the *Congregational Year Book*, Dorothy Spence was not in pastoral charge at the time, having completed her ministry at Failsworth in 1965. This illustrates yet again how much ministry by women has taken place without formal recognition in the annals of the Church.

Hospital chaplaincy has also given women ministers an opportunity to offer their gifts to the world at large, even if it can be just as daunting to speak truth to power in a medical institution as within the Church. During the Second World War, while in ministry at Northampton, Hilda Pettman encountered resistance to her ministry from an Anglican clergyman within a hospital.

> She went into the hospital chapel to find the clergy-stall, reading-desk and kneeling-stool barred to her by an Anglican chaplain. Her fellow-ministers refused to let her resign to save a fuss and said that, if she did, they would withdraw from all hospital chaplaincies in the area.[92]

This gesture of solidarity persuaded her to stay, in the event the Anglican chaplain gave up his behaviour, and what stayed with Hilda Pettman was her sense of pleasure at having been supported by her fellow (male) ministers. That mattered far more to her than the fact that the Anglican chaplain had given in, as was still evident when she talked to Yvonne Tomes about the incident years later.

The ministry of Mary Evans in Ely Hospital, Cardiff was unique in several ways, not least because of the long period of more than 30 years during which she was associated with its life. The large hospital, which has since closed, was just over the road from her manse. She recalled her appointment there as Free Church Chaplain:

> There was a short break in this ministry but I went back when I retired and am still there. My claim to fame – at one period I was told that I was the only woman chaplain to a mentally handicapped hospital. I was never aware that the fact I was a woman hindered my work or my relationship with hospital staff at all levels. This has given me a depth of experience, but today it is difficult, because of the new attitudes to care, which too often are influenced by profit.[93]

Kate McIlhagga's experience of hospital chaplaincy in the 1980s gave her a sense of entering several communities under one roof. Keeping track of where patients were was one challenge and she learned how to 'loiter with intent', ready to be called on when needed if she had earned the trust of staff:

On one or two occasions I had the privilege of becoming involved in the life of patients or staff. I learned a great deal from the experience. Giving people permission to talk at a deeper level when they were ready was important. Making the time to listen, hearing what was said, not making assumptions, being used as a reconciler and asking before praying were all part of the learning curve. I made a lot of mistakes and many friends. Hospitals now see ecumenical teams working alongside medical teams. The chaplain is a highly professional member of staff with skills to offer alongside those of the social workers, nurses, doctors and even consultants. Regarded in the past as 'gods in white coats', doctors' training has allowed them to become much more people-friendly while still maintaining a professional objectivity when needed. Ministers also need to know about boundaries. For us this is much more difficult and we often cross them, slip over them or are tempted to transgress them. Ministers, it may surprise you to hear, are human.[94]

In 1992 Rose Barrett moved from work in a local congregation to hospital chaplaincy at the North Middlesex Hospital, establishing regular Sunday worship with the support of a network of helpers from local churches to transport patients:

We have seen this Sunday service as an opportunity for both befriending patients, and seed-sowing of the Gospel. Because of the rather ecumenical nature of my post, I celebrate Holy Communion on alternate Sundays, with an open invitation to all present who 'love the Lord' to receive. This may on occasion include Anglican and Roman Catholic patients receiving, but don't tell the bishops that! Through the on-going ministry of these services and ward-visiting I have known patients with no formal church or religious background, who have gradually come to faith in Christ and have experienced God's gift of healing and wholeness, and yes, although we don't talk too much about them in United Reformed Church circles, I have seen miracles happen![95]

She described conducting a wedding for a desperately ill patient on a ward, baptising the children of staff members and leading services of remembrance when babies had died in miscarriage or been still-born: 'Although I now have closer involvement with death, funerals and bereaved relatives than in local church ministry, there are some celebratory occasions too'.

Connie Holmes, a lay preacher from Sutton Coldfield, developed her ministry as a lay chaplain in homes for the elderly. Things began when she was invited to lead worship in several homes, from which opportunities opened up to visit sick residents, and give support to relatives and staff. She wondered if this kind of work could be a way for lay preachers to offer their services outside the walls of the church building. Homeowner Alan Pearce said of her ministry:

Admitting that you can no longer care adequately for someone you love is a very difficult thing, and often gives rise to feelings of guilt and inadequacy. It is a time of great trauma all round, or it can be. Mrs Holmes willingly makes herself available to relatives as a 'listening ear' and is seen by them as someone that they can talk to in confidence and who will offer advice if required, but most of all help them through any feelings of guilt which they might have.[96]

Being a chaplain in the workplace is another way in which women's ministry has gained a new profile. Susan Armitage felt ready for any opportunity that might occur when she and her family moved to Potters Bar in 1971, following three years on the ministerial team of a new housing estate. She explained to an interviewer that she then learned of the great possibilities in industrial mission, and felt this was where she could make her contribution.

As she had to be church-based she became assistant minister at Hatfield United Reformed Church, taking two services a month, as well as being industrial chaplain at Hawker Siddeley alongside a male Anglican colleague. In a 1975 article in *Reform* Susan Armitage talked of her work in the factory. Despite the lack of a chaplains' office any shop floor conversations could be completely private as you had to get close to people to overcome the noise. Her role was to ask questions about the future of the work and issues to do with impending nationalisation:

> I question them hard. What *kind* is it to be? Challenge is not all one way. A group of young West Indians came out with 'Hey, we were talking in the pub last night, how can God be at the same time three and one?'[97]

Hazel Barkham worked for two years in the 1980s as an industrial chaplain in a Chesterfield glass factory, with 950 employees. She, too, found it a valuable ministry:

> I tried to learn more about the glass industry and be a Christian presence within it. A maintenance engineer hid from me, but when I found him eating his sandwiches, I wasn't so frightening as he'd expected. Workers appreciated having a chaplain to reflect with them on issues arising from their work and their faith. Terry in the machine shop didn't want anything to do with a tool of the establishment which he presumed I must be. As I got nearer he spotted my Christian CND badge and from then on we had plenty to talk about.[98]

When Hazel Barkham was active in the women's peace demonstrations at Greenham Common, she found people in the factory were interested to hear about the vigils, and the police activities, while her church members were not so keen to hear she had been arrested.

Forces chaplaincy is another form of community-based ministry and one that particularly suited the gifts and temperament of Jackie Petrie. Having worked for 20 years as a Church of Scotland deaconess, most of that time in the Royal Air Force, she decided to seek ordination but was put off when told by her denomination she would need to begin again with a six-year ordination course. The United Reformed Church accepted her on condition that she did one academic year at Westminster College, Cambridge. At the end of that, in 1989, the Secretary of State changed the rules and to her surprise Jackie Petrie found herself being commissioned as the first woman chaplain in any of Her Majesty's Forces.

Profiled by *Reform* in 1997, she professed herself reluctant to be featured, as she feared she did not fit the stereotype of a military chaplain. Rather than being concerned about the minutiae of military equipment at a base like RAF Brize Norton, she was more interested in the 3,500 enlisted personnel, their families and the 400 civilian employees making up the community. She commented:

> Most of them begin conversations with 'I don't come to church padre but...' and I say 'you and 99.9% of this community, so don't worry about that, and I'm not here to get you in church. I'm here to be for you whatever I can be.' We can work on any situation that a person finds themselves in, from 'I want to grow as a human being' to 'my relationships always go pear shaped' to 'I want to learn how to control my anger' to 'I think I might be homosexual'... absolutely anything that a person wants to begin considering – 'I don't want to be in the Air Force anymore', anything at all.[99]

For Jackie Petrie the role of the chaplain, far from making her an outsider, actually put her in the middle of things, wearing the same uniform as those flying the aircraft and caught up in the same concerns. On leaving forces chaplaincy she expected to miss the sense of being at the heart of a community. Still, recognition and appreciation had not always been readily granted. Her first station commander had not wanted a woman chaplain, agreed to her posting only under duress, and told her at their first meeting that he was not convinced she would be an asset:

> However, having said that, we have an annual confidential report. The station commander writes it and they have to do a de-briefing. He read the narrative, which began 'I didn't want this Chaplain to come on my unit, I realise now having worked alongside her for a year that I was quite wrong, she's one of the best Chaplains I've ever had to deal with.' And I thought, for him to actually write that *and* read it to me, he really went up in my estimation.[100]

One thing not mentioned in that interview was how Jackie Petrie's pioneering role related to the service of Elsie Chamberlain as a Royal Air Force chaplain. In March 1946, the young Congregational minister was given the rank of squadron officer in the WAAF and her name appeared as a 'Woman Chaplain' in the RAF's appointment list.[101] She worked first in the RAF staff college at Cranwell, near Lincoln, where she found leading parade ground prayers a terrifying experience. However, the men in the rear ranks said they could hear her as they had never heard anyone before. Soon she was posted to RAF St Athan in South Wales, where her health broke down in months with a severe attack of arthritis. Invalided out of the RAF after failing her medical board, she continued to receive a disability pension until June 1951. Her daughter comments:

> Despite her illness and short appointment, Elsie was very proud of her position as first woman chaplain in the Forces. Until her death, in 1991, she often wore her RAF stole at very special services and occasions.[102]

Elsie Chamberlain's status may not have been the direct equivalent of that enjoyed by Jackie Petrie 40 years later but there is no doubt that in her own mind, and that of many other people, she was the first woman Forces chaplain. Areas of confusion in women's history often arise about who was the real pioneer to enter a new area. This is because, as this project has frequently shown, stories of earlier advances get easily lost and a continuous female presence is hard to maintain.

Another form of community-based ministry, apart from Forces chaplaincy, is that of a Church Related Community Worker (CRCW) in the United Reformed Church. This is a role unique to the denomination, which it has been pioneering since 1981, and it was recognised by the General Assembly in 1987. Gwen Smithies has trained as a CRCW and works in community projects attached to St James' and Shiregreen United Reformed Churches in Sheffield. She reflects on her strengths and weaknesses as a result of her work there, on her earlier teaching experience in adult education, and her new training:

> I know I have a strong tendency to organise and solve problems. Whilst this in some aspects of my life is one of my strong points – as project co-ordinator I am employed to plan, prepare and organise a running programme – I have come to realise that this is not always helpful to the enabling side of my role. I can only facilitate a situation, which might lead and help others to solve their own difficulties. I also expect others to share in my excitement and enthusiasm at what might interest me – I have many very varied interests but have come to recognise that not everyone gets a buzz when they're up to their elbows in clay or watching with amazement the vivid paints blending together and absorbing as if by magic onto silk or trekking up a mountain side craving peace and tranquillity. I personally recognise how difficult it is to share enthusiastically the abilities of computer software. I am also a very transparent person – my eyes, my facial expression, my bodily posture are always dead giveaways of my feelings. Sometimes I still look on certain of these as weaknesses but have come to recognise they can be strengths also.

> I know and recognise that my body language can suggest a deep willingness
> to be involved in a situation and my eyes can be highly expressive of a diverse
> range of feelings leaving little need to communicate verbally. A concern for
> me has been that others seem to think I am more able than I am. But perhaps
> I do have the skills and knowledge that other people recognise in me but I
> sometimes lack self-confidence.[103]

Foreign parts

This project has mainly concentrated on the stories of women who stayed in Britain to fulfil
their ministries but the nineteenth and twentieth centuries also saw many opportunities
for women to serve the Church all parts of the world. In the 1950s many of the women
who returned from work with the London Missionary Society sought ordination and one
of these was Doris Leyshon. She had served in India from 1944, first as the principal of
a girls' boarding school in Kaurapukur, and had encountered resistance from the men in
the local village because of what they saw as the freedom enjoyed by female staff members.
She refused to lay down the law as the village men wanted nor would she assert her
authority as her female teachers desired. Instead she challenged them:

> I said to these women: 'You have to make your views in discussions. If you
> marry a Hindu what about your children and your Christian faith?' I heard
> afterwards that one of the teachers did marry a Hindu.[104]

On her next term abroad she worked from 1951 to 1957 in the centre of Calcutta,
in a school kindergarten and two churches, and much enjoyed chairing the education
committee of the YWCA. The secretary of the Calcutta YWCA was Ivy Khan, who left
in 1957 to become secretary of the YWCA India. Doris Leyshon considered she owed a
tremendous debt to the leadership of this young, vivacious and gifted colleague.

Later pastoral work in Wales was nothing like the visiting she had done in the
slums of Calcutta. She recalled:

> Back at the theological college in Brecon and Swansea from 1958 to 1961 I was
> the only woman – and not allowed to live in! There were two conservative
> evangelical students who disapproved of women in the ministry. After 1961
> one of them invited me for a weekend to his home and to take the services
> on the Sunday at the church where he was minister. I had served with the
> LMS for 14 years so my experience was acknowledged. On the rare occasions
> when some concern needed to be discussed with the Principal and staff I was
> one of a small group designated to meet with staff. It was a very happy time.

I started my ministry in 1961 at the Congregational Church, Ogmore Vale. In a terraced road I heard the remark: 'Mrs Brown, the minister's wife is at your door.' I remember Alice who was a member of the Congregational Church in this mining valley. Her husband died before their first child was born. There was no Income Support. She survived by gardening, taking in washing, knitting – finding anything in which she could earn enough to keep her and her child. In the 1960s she was the instigator of forming a group to care for the housebound in the valley. Every fortnight the housebound were collected, given a tea followed by a homely entertainment. The group still exists.[105]

Many returning woman missionaries made the transition to church leadership at home, though not all of them were ordained as ministers. Cecilia Downward's service in China and Malaysia was chronicled by her home church under the headline 'Brassey Street's Own Missionary' when the history of Trinity with Palm Grove (URC-Methodist) congregation, Wirral, was written in 1988. The article told of her arduous escape from the Japanese in 1944, her ejectment from South China by the Communists in 1949 and her retirement, with the caption beneath her picture stating:

Miss Cecilia Downward who has helped to preach the Gospel at Brassey Street, at Swatow and Wukingfu, in Malaysia, and (after retirement) at Lymm in Cheshire, and whose life epitomises the way in which new doors have opened as old ones closed.[106]

The greater ease of foreign employment opened up by the advent of the European Union provides another way in which contemporary women can exercise their ministry outside Britain. Jane Stranz trained at Mansfield College and was ordained in 1991 for service overseas, as her husband was then working in the European Parliament. She has served the Eglise Reformée de France through pastorates in Dunkirk and just over the Swiss border from Geneva. One of her first challenges was to learn the right sort of French with which to lead worship:

The French I'd learned was very much oral French – the French of the bistro – rather than literary French or the French of the pulpit! So I would come out with what I thought was a dignified turn of phrase but people would think that I'd spoken very much like a teenager, saying things like 'that's great' in a slang sort of way.[107]

A special challenge for a Protestant minister working in a predominantly Catholic country is the geographical size of each pastorate. It would be impossible for Jane Stranz to maintain close ecumenical relationships with her Catholic colleagues because there are up to 15 priests within her 'patch'. Asked how the French cope with a Protestant minister who is English, and a woman, she remarked:

I think they think it's quite fun. When I was in Dunkirk, I was invited to preach at the big mass during the week of prayer for Christian Unity. We have an exchange of pulpits, and 500 people were there and I thought 'Grief, what are they going to think?' but the other side of it is French Catholicism is very open and liberal, for the most part, and they sort of coped with it reasonably well, certainly the younger Catholic priests did. Probably it is just as difficult for Protestants to cope with a young woman English minister, I suppose.[108]

Even though she has never served as an ordained minister in the United Reformed Church, Jane Stranz insists strongly she is still a part of the denomination. She sees herself as a link, both in small practical ways such as trying to find au pair girls and in terms of representing another part of the Reformed tradition to the United Reformed Church. The Eglise Reformée de France, for instance, celebrates communion in the round and shares a common cup.

Receiving women ministers from other parts of the world to work in the United Reformed Church can be another way of creating links and gaining insights. Cheryl Dibeela and her husband, Prince, are both ordained ministers of the United Congregational Church of Southern Africa who came to Britain in 1998. He was mission enabler for East Midlands Synod from 1998 and she did research at Selly Oak. After several years in Britain she looked back on her ministry in Botswana with different eyes, especially the pastoral issues she had faced there of women undergoing mental and physical abuse, being harassed at work and suffering within families. At a women's gathering in January 2001 she reflected on her experience in Southern Africa:

Being a woman minister in a predominantly male dominated institution did not help much in liberating these women because I was caught up with my own concerns. When I spoke about my difficulties in the ministry, the expectations of my congregation etc., I was constantly reminded by my male colleagues that I was too 'soft' in my approach. I needed to show that I was in control, 'be more authoritative,' they would say. I guess they meant well but little did they know that I could not be authoritative, it was not in my character, or perhaps it was obvious but they felt I needed to change, to be more like them. I felt distressed because I did not have the necessary support and knowledge on how to deal with these feelings of uncertainty.[109]

Cheryl Dibeela's conclusion, having had space and distance within which to consider what had been happening in her ministry, was that a need existed for a special ministry to women in Botswana. She could help women to reclaim their lost spirit through Bible studies, conferences and women's groups. In that way they could reach down to the unhappiness inside themselves, find their purpose in life, build their confidence, and grow in dignity and self worth.

A ministry to children

Women's ministry, both lay and ordained, has often been associated with a special care for children but this has been a trap for some. The cause may have been the widely held assumption that women, whether married or not, have a natural affinity for young people. Margaret Knee, looking back on her early ministry from retirement, thought she had been wrongly typecast in 1958:

> I moved into ministry after nearly twenty years of teaching in schools and colleges. It was this experience that accounts for me being drafted into the organisation of Children's Work for the CUEW – although I never felt enthusiastic about it. Nor did I have any bright ideas on it! I did, however, enjoy meeting Sunday School teachers in various parts of the country and discussing the problems 'on the ground'. [110]

Dorothy Wilson (see chapters 4 and 5) was someone with special gifts for religious education and the training of young people whose ministry remained involved with this area of work. She began her pilgrimage with a Sunday School course at Westhill College, returning to run the Sunday School of her home congregation of the Presbyterian Church of England. Even in her eighty-sixth year Janet Chisholm could remember how Dorothy Wilson had taught her at Sunday School in Trinity, Claughton, Presbyterian Church, Birkenhead:

> When I first went to Sunday School in 1913 all ages met together in a big hall. Shortly after that Miss Dorothy Wilson introduced the graded system and we were called 'The Beginners'. We met in rooms over the road from the church. We had little chairs and sandtrays & other interesting things. The next stage was 'The Primary'. And her sister, Miss Catherine Wilson took that.[111]

Later in the First World War, Dorothy Wilson became the denomination's Young People's Secretary. Early in her career she contributed lessons to Sunday School periodicals and wrote the Junior Department Handbook of the National Sunday School Union, as well as books of stories. Later, while training for ministry at Mansfield College, she wrote her B. Litt. thesis on 'Child Psychology and Religious Education', and during the 1930s was Director of Religious Education at Mills College, California where she was awarded an M.A. degree. She never married and her career was cut short by ill health.[112]

Elsie Jones was another key figure in the growth of children's work who clearly felt drawn to that ministry and comfortable with it. A laywoman, she served for eight years from 1940 on the education department of the LMS and was then appointed Pilot Officer of the CUEW, in charge of this church-based youth organisation. On her retirement in 1968 *The Congregational Monthly* wrote that she had devoted herself for 20 years to the care and training of children in Congregational Churches:

She introduced the National Pilot Camp and from 1948 ran these training holiday courses. During this period she was a working and writing member of the Children's Group associated with the Conference of British Missionary Societies, producing programme material for the member churches. Through this same group Miss Jones gathered children of many denominations in a series of Unity Camps which were appreciated by children and leaders alike.

In addition to promoting mid-week activities for children, she has since 1952 organized the Children's Rallies at the May Assembly; and the sight of Westminster Chapel filled with singing children has encouraged many a Junior Church teacher and given a sense of belonging to the Great Church to succeeding generations of children. The appreciation expressed at the Council for Miss Jones' outstanding service will be echoed heartily in churches up and down the country.[113]

And many more besides

It would be impossible to do full justice to all the types of ministry where women have left their mark both in the United Reformed Church and its parent traditions. This survey has concentrated on ordained women, partly because relatively little has been told of their stories up to now and partly because it takes even more work to uncover the contribution of so many unsung laywomen. Even so much more remains to be said about women's work in chaplaincy and special category ministries, about women lay workers, deaconesses and Church Related Community Workers but this project represents a start.

The contribution of women to multi-faith work is another area to be covered in the future, as is their involvement in the broad enriching of worship in all its forms. Think of an inspiring and challenging contemporary liturgist and the name of United Reformed Church minister Kate Compston is likely to come up. Consider the output of contemporary hymn writers and exponents of new music in worship and Congregational minister Janet Wootton's name cannot be overlooked. Search for someone with a ministry of creative art through embroidery, wall hanging, stole or picture and the gifts of Pamela Pavitt, wife of a retired United Reformed Church minister, spring to mind at once.

One aim of this project has been the raising of the collective profile of women's ministry. In the process some hurts have surfaced and silences still remain. When interviewed in 1975, Christine Collin summed up the pros and cons of ordained ministry in clear terms:

> What helps a minister most, always, is to be considered as a person like anyone else. There are Sundays when the longing to sit in the pew and be fed and led in prayer is a physical pain.[114]

Kate McIlhagga concluded her contribution to a book on women's ministry with this reflection:

> From an Edinburgh teashop to a Franciscan refectory is a far cry. From learning to write on a slate to producing this on computer is a major leap. From a city park to a Fenland village, a housing estate to a new community, a market town to a rural fishing village is quite a pilgrimage. All has been ministry: all has been part of the ministry of the whole people of God. God is present in every blessed thing and place; present in friend and stranger; present in the voids, the absences and the silent terrors of the night. Going on pilgrimage certainly changes the pilgrim. Setting out in faith is never easy, but for richer and for poorer, in sickness and in health still holds for ministry as it does for marriage.[115]

For Kathleen Hendry, who celebrated her 70th anniversary of ordination in 2001, the changed role of women in the Church had been highlighted at a service in 1989. A new associate minister was being inducted to Purley United Reformed Church and three ministers stood behind the communion table – the chairman of Croydon District, the pastoral studies tutor of Westminster College, Cambridge and the newly-inducted minister – all three of them women. As to her own reasons for ministry, she professed to still being as baffled as anyone else.

> If there had been no Church I would never have learned the Bible's understanding of life. Because of it a teenage girl cheekily critical of the Church came to spend 60 years as an ordained minister. Don't ask me why.[116]

Chapter 10

How this story has been told

A small article appeared in *The Christian Commonwealth* on 18 September 1917, entitled: 'Another Woman Minister'. The heading referred to the wide coverage some religious journals had given to the growth in women's ministry and leadership in the Church during the First World War. *The Christian Commonwealth*, subtitled 'The Organ of the Progressive Movement in Religion and Social Ethics', reported approvingly:

> A particularly interesting ceremony took place at the King's Weigh House Church last Monday, when Miss Constance Todd, BD, and Mr Claud Coltman, MA, were ordained to the Congregational ministry. The officiating ministers were Revds Dr Orchard, Leyton Richards, MA, G Stanley Russell, MA, and G E Darlaston, MA. In the course of his address Mr Russell said that the ordination of a man and a woman together was a sign of the beginning of a new era, when woman would no longer be considered the subordinate of man. On Tuesday Mr Coltman and Miss Todd were married. They have been appointed to the assistant ministry of the King's Weigh House Church, and will take charge of the East End Mission in Darby Street. Mrs Coltman was educated at Somerville and Mansfield; she was the first woman student at the latter college. She has great hopes of the future of women in the ministry.[1]

This report can be judged at face value as a factually accurate and faithful record. However a closer look at the events surrounding this ordination, and the development of women's ordained ministry in Congregationalism and the United Reformed Church, reveals more going on than meets the eye. Applying a feminist hermeneutic of suspicion to this story and using discourse analysis on the way it has been written about allows examination of the silences within it and helps to explain the delay in Mr Russell's 'new era'. Thus the traditional view of Congregationalism as brave, enlightened pioneer of women's ordination can be revised more honestly for the twenty-first century.

One grey area in reports of the 1917 ordination involved the people present. *The Christian Commonwealth* correctly stated that four Congregational ministers took part. The Revd W E Orchard, minister of the King's Weigh House Church and an outspoken pacifist, presided. A 'feminist by the understanding of his time',[2] Orchard was a committed ecumenist with High Church views and later became a Roman Catholic priest. Stanley Russell was minister of Grafton Square Congregational Church and G E Darlaston was at Park Chapel, Crouch End. The fourth minister, Leyton Richards, was another staunch peace campaigner later dubbed 'one of the choicest spirits amongst Congregationalists'.[3]

His role as secretary of the Fellowship of Reconciliation (1916 to 1918) had resulted in his leaving pastoral charge and temporarily joining King's Weigh House Church.

However the *Congregational Year Book 1918* stated: 'Coltman (Mrs) Constance, Mary BD London. Ministers ordaining Revds Dr Selbie, R J Evans M A and others'.[4] The apparent conflict between this official yet misleading version of events and the accurate newspaper report requires investigation. In October *The Christian World* reported that the Revd W B Selbie had originally planned to attend the ordination as Principal of Mansfield College, Oxford, where Constance and Claud Coltman had trained. He withdrew because of concerns about whether proper procedures had been followed.

> Mrs Coltman, on the testimony of Principal Selbie, had passed through with great distinction the full theological course at Mansfield College. Dr Selbie had promised to take part in her ordination, but on finding that the rules with regard to consultation and arrangement with the London Congregational Union had not been complied with, he felt bound, in loyalty to the Union, to withdraw his promise.[5]

There might be a straightforward printing deadline explanation as to why the denomination's official record gave inaccurate details about who ordained the first woman minister in the United Kingdom. Alternatively the entry may have been written later in 1917, to include a theological college principal and the long-standing secretary of the London Congregational Union, whose presence gave an air of authority and correctness to a new departure. By linking the names Selbie and Evans to the ordination the *Congregational Year Book* may have prevented the raising of some eyebrows at this event. Simply mentioning the involvement of four London ministers, including two outspoken pacifists, at the height of the First World War might well have raised questions. Perhaps an editorial decision was taken to give them a low profile in the 'others' category.

At this stage the Congregational Union of England and Wales had no standard procedure about who conducted ordinations. It was not until 1919, with the appointment of provincial Moderators, that a degree of centralised order began to be brought to the system of ministerial settlements and removals. The minutes of some central committees at the time reveal a tension between the central administration's attempts to impose uniformity and a confusing amount of diversity at local level. It is clear that regulations were not always being followed.

In view of this background one might speculate as to whether the year book entry was a re-writing of history to regularise an extraordinary event. If Constance Coltman's ordination took place without the prior approval of the London Congregational Union, then to name the four ordaining ministers could have highlighted the absence of anyone representing the County Union or her college. By glossing over the September ceremony the entry concentrated on the second stage of Constance Coltman's entry to ministry, an induction service at Darby Street mission in December 1917. Dr Selbie and Mr Evans had been present on this occasion to give official though retrospective blessing to women's ordained ministry.

The official version gave no hint of the procedural debates that took place in central denominational circles once the events of 17 September were known. Mr Evans hinted at these when he spoke for the London Congregational Union at Constance Coltman's December induction service however. Under the heading 'Recognition of Rev Constance Coltman', *The Christian World* reported him to have said:

> ... when Mrs Coltman applied for recognition as a minister he felt this was
> a new venture, and that being so, the matter was dealt with slowly and
> deliberately. He felt that if women were to be received into full ministerial
> membership they should not slip in by a back door, but that it should be done
> by the church with its eyes open and by the exercise of its best judgment.
> Therefore, although there had been some difficulty in the way, he was now
> in the happy position of being able to say that Mrs Coltman was received
> into full ministerial membership of the London Congregational Union of the
> Congregational Union for England and Wales.[6]

Mr Evans gave no public details about what procedural stages had been gone through between the September ordination and the December induction. In fact he had written to the CUEW's General Purposes Committee less than ten days after the ceremony at the King's Weigh House Church, on behalf of the ministerial committee of the London Congregational Board. That letter reported that at their meeting on 25 September the Board had received an application from Mrs Coltman BD for full ministerial membership:

> Mrs Coltman has taken the full theological course at Mansfield College
> and has the full leaving certificate. She has also been duly called to the
> Assistant-Pastorate of the King's Weigh House Church. Consideration of her
> application was adjourned, and I was instructed to write to you to know what
> the view of the Congregational Union of England and Wales is on the general
> question of the reception of women as fully accredited ministers provided
> they have fulfilled the conditions which apply to men. We felt that this was
> of very great importance, not only for the Union, but for all the Unions and
> for the Denomination, and that any County Union considering any particular
> application ought to know first of all what the view of your Union was. We
> shall be glad to know what the position is as soon as possible.[7]

This letter failed to say that a service claiming the status of an ordination had already taken place prior to County Union approval. The General Purposes Committee agreed to recommend to the Council of the Congregational Union that 'the Rules as at present framed do not prohibit recognition of women who have fulfilled the regulations'. Women's ordination was not so much being endorsed as not being ruled out. The *British Weekly* reported that the autumn Council meeting discussed the matter for some time:

> While the discussion was waging between the pros and cons of the principle, Mr Gerard Ford suddenly remembered that some years ago the Union had adopted a resolution in favour of the admission of women into the full work of the ministry, although, he naively added, no one thought at that time that advantage would be taken of such a decision. Therefore it was decided to dispatch a special messenger to Memorial Hall for the minute book. On its arrival, it was found that Mr Ford's recollections were strictly accurate, for the records showed that the resolution in favour of the admission of women as accredited ministers was adopted by the Assembly eight years ago. And so the discussion on 'the barrier of sex' instantly subsided.[8]

In fact Mr Ford's memory of events was not so accurate after all. The General Purposes Committee had been approached in 1909 by J I Rhys, secretary of the East Glamorgan Congregational Association, about ordination for a Miss Clarice Smith. A joint General Purposes and Settlements and Removals committee process on women's ordination was set up in response. It recommended, by a majority of 14 to 10, that women should be accredited as ministers provided they met the same conditions of admission as men.[9] When the Council of the CUEW discussed that recommendation, in October 1909, it had not made the positive response Mr Ford later remembered. The Minutes state: 'After a lengthy discussion it was agreed to proceed to the next business, the representatives of the Press being asked not to report the discussion'. [10] The *British Weekly's* diary column at the Council reported:

> The talk was that the Council of the Union is steadily growing more business-like and effective, that it seems idle to pretend that its proceedings can be secret, that a proposal to recognize women ministers provoked strong opposition and was shelved at the Council, that the suffragettes are rousing reactions in unexpected quarters.[11]

Mr Ford was refreshingly honest in admitting at the 1917 Council that few involved in the discussions eight years before had realistically expected they might soon have to consider a potential woman candidate for ordination, who met the training requirements and had received a call from a congregation of the CUEW. This sense of surprise may explain the London Congregational Board's concern about the ordination at the King's Weigh House Church in September 1917. It could also account for the confusion at the October 1917 Council meeting and the version of events in the 1918 Year Book entry.

Whatever the truth behind the official version, the story told by Mr Evans at the induction and reflected in the *Congregational Year Book* totally omitted the problems which the first woman had met in gaining full recognition. One might wonder whether the irregular ordination service was intended to force the pace with the London Congregational Board or to spike the guns of those who might create procedural difficulties.

One effect of Congregationalism's official version of the events was that the obstacles encountered by Constance Coltman went unrecorded. Her name appeared alongside those of her male colleagues in the alphabetical list of ordained ministers yet the process of establishing her in ministry had not been straightforward despite her excellent qualifications. Even Constance Coltman's obituary did not correct things but rather created more confusion. This version suggested she gained recognition at her ordination, omitted the later induction service and downplayed the significance of being ordained one day and married the next:

> After a little hesitation her application to the Congregational Union of England and Wales for recognition and ordination as a Congregational Minister was granted on September 17, 1917. She and Claud Coltman were ordained at the Weigh House, and they married soon afterwards.[12]

Until recently men have been the main recorders of historical events, which may explain the failure to chart the uneven pathway of the first ordained woman. Modern feminism sees empowerment as beginning when women tell their own story of struggle. An article on women's history observes: 'Historians' neglect of women has been a function of their ideas about historical significance'.[13] Congregationalism may have accorded some historical significance to a few women on entry to the all-male ministerial leadership group. It did not recognise or remove the resistance these women met or notice how many women were excluded from exploring a vocation by poor education or low income.

Ironing out the wrinkles in the historical narrative conceals the conflict and difficulties faced by the first woman ministers. It also prevents the asking of awkward questions or the apportioning of responsibility, so that the reasons why one group encountered problems in entering a sphere dominated by another group remain hidden. To hear someone else's story of earlier difficulty and struggle can be a source of strength for those who come later and realise their experience is not unique. There may be reasons why generations of women ministers said little publicly about their individual difficulties until late in the twentieth century. Once inside the male preserve of ministry they may have decided against making waves by naming the problems they faced. Their energies may have been so absorbed by work that there was no time to protest anyway. Perhaps they decided to avoid anything that could be interpreted as a sign of weakness or proof that ministry was too much for them. The male-dominated leadership culture of the time may have 'co-opted' them so powerfully that they never asked why some of the issues they faced did not trouble their male colleagues.

An example of how the simplified story of women's ordination has affected wider studies in Church history is found in Adrian Hastings' *A History of English Christianity 1920-1990*. Reproducing the story Congregationalism has liked to tell he perpetuated the impression that this matter was cut and dried in 1917. Close to the eve of women's suffrage, while many Anglicans ridiculed women's ordination, Hastings suggested the Free Churches were already comfortable with women ministers:

> Baptists and Congregationalists had accepted the ordination of women. In 1917 Constance Todd was ordained to be Dr Orchard's assistant at King's Weigh House.[14]

Referring later in his book to the 1970s debate about women's ordination in the Church of England, Hastings noted the social and pastoral arguments in favour of this which emerged from Protestant churches that already ordained women. However he conceded that the actual experience of women ministers made the arguments less conclusive.[15] Perhaps Hastings sensed the worrying gap between the rosy received version of Free Church women's ordination and the difficult reality of women's ministry on the ground.

The obstacles to women's leadership in the Church were in the forefront of Constance Coltman's mind when she was asked by Maude Royden to write on Post Reformation women in the Free Churches for her friend's book, *The Church and Woman*:

> Far more women possess an unfulfilled vocation to the ministry than the outside world imagines. Limited financial and educational equipment often prove an almost insuperable barrier to the obtaining of the prolonged theological training which is required from the modern Nonconformist minister. Even could the training be obtained, there is the difficulty whether the Nonconformist ministry can be regarded as an economic livelihood for women....Where women are officially or otherwise exercising pastoral charge, it is usually as leaders of small causes, which are glad to get such help, but can hardly pay a living wage.[16]

It was not simply the issues of training, educational demands and low stipends that held back Congregational women's ordained ministry in the 1920s. Even stronger than these, in Constance Coltman's view, was the prejudice against women ministers amongst many church members. This was a powerful and pervasive influence, and one she considered had grown worse in certain quarters since the end of the First World War.[17] It was significant because Congregationalism's way of calling ministers depended on votes at Church Meeting and one or two articulate opponents could nearly always prevent a woman from becoming minister of a particular church.

Another little-mentioned obstacle to women's ordination was the marriage of women ministers. At this time women were expected to give up paid employment upon marriage. Constance Coltman had made plain her own attitude by being ordained one day and married the next. In her article she declared that Protestant history demonstrated that women's ministry need not be incompatible with marriage. Women outnumbered men by 2 million in post-war Britain and the large proportion of unmarried women who had to support themselves had priority for getting work. The question of work after marriage was never clearly resolved with relation to the first generations of women ministers. Constance Coltman answered the problem by sharing one wage with her husband and drawing on her private family income.

Further light on the phenomenon of women ministers came in a 1929 booklet *Women Free Church Ministers.*[18] This profiled three Baptist, ten Congregationalist and nine Unitarian women ministers. Of these 13 served congregations in England, one in Scotland, two in Wales, one in Australia, Canada, New Zealand, Papua and South Africa respectively while one woman held a national denominational post. The photographs and biographies showed their determination and energy. Maude Royden's forceful preface declared:

> It is because the fundamental principles of the Christian faith transcend racial, class and sex barriers, that the Church, in the name of Christ, admitted the Gentile, abolished slavery and raised the status of women: it is because we are slow to bear such amazing teaching that there is still much racial exclusiveness, much class and sex contempt, even in Christian countries.[19]

Meanwhile the Moderators of the Congregational Union of England and Wales had been preoccupied throughout the 1920s with the lack of trained ministers, the hardship caused by low stipends and difficulty in moving ministers. A 1934 Commission of Inquiry recommended among other things:

> ... it is a principle in our Denomination that women are on entirely the same footing as men as regards admission to our Ministry and their position within it.... There are women already among our recognised Ministers, and they are doing good service, but their number is very small. When we have regard to the great part taken by women in the life of our Churches, and the greatness of the contribution which it is in their power to make to the teaching and pastoral care of our people, we cannot be satisfied with the present state of affairs. It seems clear that our Churches are not often disposed to invite women to undertake the duties of the regular pastorate. It may be that there are reasons for this which ought to be overcome. It may be that we ought to discover other forms of ministerial service for women, prepared for perhaps by other kinds of training than that now given to men in our Colleges, through which we might more effectively employ their powers for leadership in our Churches.[20]

This was probably the first expression of denominational concern about the problems faced by women in over 15 years of ordained ministry. The report suggested two more Commissions, one on 'Ministry of Women in our Churches' and another on the colleges. After the Women's Guild committee objected to the 'highly unsatisfactory' choice of eight men and one woman to consider women's ministry [21] two women were added.

The findings of the Commission on the Ministry of Women, reported to the CUEW Assembly in 1936, were disappointing and women ministers only figured in the last three pages of the ten-page report.[22] Constance Coltman's critique and the challenge of the earlier Commission to discover the obstacles to women's ministry in local churches were sidestepped. Instead the document focussed on finding new forms of ministerial service for women. It recommended that qualified women should train other women as leaders especially for 'experimental evangelistic work among non-church going women'.[23] The report proposed a trained Order of Deaconesses and paid tribute to women missionaries despite their high 'leakage' through marriage or retirement. If they married other missionaries at least their service and experience were not lost.

The women ordained since 1917 (17, of whom 13 were in pastoral charge) had spoken positively of their experiences by letter and interview, so the Commission was reassured that 'on the whole the experience of these women has been a happy one, and that their ministry has proved effective and valuable'.[24] All talked of the 'friendly and helpful' relations they had with male ministers, deacons and church members, though sometimes other women had been reluctant to support their call to a church. While some had found difficulty in securing a pastorate others had been called by a congregation before leaving college. Despite the common assumption at the time that women were best suited to pastoral work these women stressed their love of preaching and commitment to continue doing it.

Most of the women had received very favourable reports for their work in pastoral charge, and at least two failing congregations had been revived, but:

> there is considerable testimony to a widespread and strong unwillingness among the churches to consider a woman as candidate in a vacancy, so that much greater difficulty in settling a woman is experienced by the Colleges unless she is of exceptional ability, and that in several cases women have received calls because the church was in financial difficulties and could not offer an adequate salary to a man.[25]

This led the members to six convictions. Firstly, the measure of success enjoyed by most of the women ministers excluded even suggesting that their eligibility for ministry in the Congregational churches should be challenged. Secondly, (with no detectable hint of irony) the difficulties and disappointments they would encounter in the churches forbade any general encouragement of women to enter ministry. If women of exceptional ability, certain of their vocation, were willing to run all risks then they should be helped not obstructed. Attitudes might change as congregations saw women ministers prove their distinctive worth. It could help to encourage woman into any future groupings of churches served by two or three ministers, another proposal then under consideration in the CUEW. Thirdly, though trained like the men, women should all be in one college.[26]

Next, the report considered the stipends offered to women ministers and politely passed no judgment on the way churches offered women a smaller salary than would seem proper for a man. It deplored the idea of this becoming the general rule or churches thinking they could always call a woman for a lower stipend. Both County Unions and colleges must seriously consider whether they encouraged this tendency, allowing for special cases. On pensions, the Commission questioned whether women should be admitted to the Superannuation Fund on the same terms as men, since it was 'at least doubtful' whether they could physically sustain the strain of ministry to the same age as a man. Finally the Commission thought it undesirable for a woman to continue in a pastorate after marriage. The claims of a pastorate would not allow her to fulfil the duties expected of a wife and mother but she might continue to preach.

Thoughtful and sincere though this Report was its findings read more like a collection of good intentions than a strategy for the future. Questions such as the relationship between ordained women and the proposal for trained laywomen and deaconesses were not addressed. One searches in vain for evidence that the colleges, County Unions or Committees of the Union implemented any of these proposals. It was significant that a denominational report had valued women ministers and mentioned some of the obstacles they met in the Church. Even so the reluctance of the Commission members to apportion any blame for some of these problems seriously weakened the impact of the report. The later verdict of a history of the Women's Committee in the CUEW was:

> The value to the Union of this report is not easy to assess. Of great potential importance was the unequivocal endorsement of the principle that women should be debarred from no kind of service or leadership within the life of the church which they are able to and qualified to give. Subsequent events would seem to show acceptance, albeit tentative and un-enthusiastic, of the principle.[27]

During the 1930s Congregationalism began to share the story of women's ministry with the world at large. In 1939 the CUEW Council received a report of talks between the Church of England and the Free Churches on the 'Outline of a Reunion Scheme' that had grown from the 1920 Lambeth Conference. Seven eminent Congregational men were appointed to review the report on behalf of the denomination. Their findings firmly stressed the importance of women's ministry within Congregationalism:

Having proved the value of women in the ministry, and convinced that difference of sex should not be regarded as a barrier, where the vocation is recognised, we desire the continuance of the ministry of women whom God has called on equal terms with men.[28]

This gave a clear message to the other denominations in the discussions. Some would have considered women's ordination impossible while others would have had no theological objection, although not actually undertaking it. The impression was given that pioneering Congregationalists had no doubts about women ministers and had demonstrated their worth. No mention was made of lower stipends, of problems entering theological colleges or of grassroots resistance to women. The alternative suggestion, that women be trained for a supportive role rather than as leaders alongside men, was also omitted. Ecumenical talks were then halted by the outbreak of the Second World War.

By 1939 the account of women's ministry in Congregationalism as a public success story was in marked contrast to the reality of the challenges women faced in local churches. The Second World War caused irreversible changes in the role and status of British women as the First World War had not done. Twenty years after 1918 the British labour market had returned to being the virtual male preserve it was in 1914. Permanent changes in attitudes towards women in paid work resulted from the 1941 enforced registration of all women between the ages of 19 and 40 (later 50) for war work and these were destined to affect the Church as well as other parts of society.

The post-war period saw a slow increase in numbers of women ministerial candidates, swelled in part by the return of women missionaries, against a background of new ecumenical moves. A memorable sermon by Archbishop Fisher in 1946 appealed to the Free Churches to adopt episcopacy as a step towards full communion. In response Mansfield College Principal Nathaniel Micklem wrote a pamphlet on *Congregationalism and Episcopacy* in 1951 outlining the elements of agreement that might lead to greater unity. He also aired his views on women's ordination, an 'experiment' that could be more troublesome to Church unity than the historic stumbling block of episcopacy:

Has our experiment proved successful? I feel sure that it has, in the sense that a few women ministers have done useful and faithful and acceptable service in our ministry. On the other hand, as College Principals know only too well, there is in our churches little demand for women ministers, and it is only with the utmost difficulty that they can come to receive a call. My own view, for what is it worth, is this – that wherever there is a small group of ministers working together, at least one of them should be a woman. I believe there is room for a woman minister in every sizeable parish, but I am very doubtful whether, except in a very few cases, there is an opening for women ministers or a desire for them in our ministry as it now is.[29]

In 1958 the denomination told a far more positive version of the story of women's ordination to the World Council of Churches. The WCC's department on the Co-operation of Men and Women issued a list of facts from its member churches in 1958. The Congregational Union of England and Wales said:

> Women are admitted to the full ministry. There is no separate legislation concerning women Ministers. Women have been fully ordained since 1917. The denomination gives full recognition and status to its women Ministers, and there are now 24 women in full pastoral charge of churches, and an average of 2 women students a year are taken into theological colleges: these colleges will not accept them unless they have an alternate profession to which they can turn. (From a letter dated 10 January 1958, from the Secretary of the International Congregational Council).[30]

Nothing in the statement explained why, if women truly received full recognition and status throughout the denomination, they needed other possible ways to earn their living.

As 1962 approached the Congregational Union commissioned two histories to commemorate the tercentenary of the birth of Nonconformity in 1662. Erik Routley's *The Story of Congregationalism* was aimed at the popular market. He considered the new respect granted to women in Congregational ministry during the twentieth century to be an historic change, though many people now saw it as the settled order of things. Nothing in the historic documents of Congregationalism opposed women's ordination yet Routley was almost certain the seventeenth century authors of the Savoy Declaration would never have thought of such a suggestion. Of Constance Coltman's ordination he wrote:

> The ordination of women came as a practical proposition only after the First World War had produced that revolution in public opinion about women's status which is familiar now but which the Suffragists of Edwardian days found it so difficult to establish.[31]

Routley spoke of the small, steady stream of women who had enriched Congregational ministry since 1917 and had trained alongside men in colleges founded with men primarily in mind. Since 1945, with the establishment of St Paul's House in Liverpool, women had gained access to special training 'not overloaded with theological lore, but intensely practical and alert in its ethos'.[32] They were prepared for short ministries, founding new churches or reviving decaying ones, and Routley dubbed the venture one of the historic acts of modern Congregationalism.

What Routley omitted was that the women at St Paul's House were not ordained but part of a community of 'Home Missionaries'. Nor did he say that the community had been initiated by Muriel Paulden, was not under the direction of the CUEW, and had met some obstacles in gaining recognition.[33] Though expected to preach, give pastoral care and administer the sacraments these women were not accorded the same status or pay as their mainly male, ministerial colleagues. No doubt some people approved of St Paul's House because its women missionaries seemed to offer no direct threat to the male-dominated ordained ranks. A feminist reading of this might conclude that in exchange for lower income and status, the St Paul's House women were being freed to minister where men would not have gone, so gaining valuable if poorly-publicised experience.

In his other 1962 work, *Congregationalists and Unity*, Routley again praised the work of St Paul's House and stressed that women's ordination was a break with ancient practice. 'The puritan tradition is very far from feminist',[34] he wrote and confessed doubts about the propriety of women's ordination. Since most women did not serve long in pastoral charge this hampered the resourceful and appropriate use of the denomination's womanpower. It would be better to concentrate on the Home Missionaries of St Paul's House, who could give full-time consecrated service to the church, as happened with women's orders in the Methodist, Anglican and Roman communions. He concluded by hinting he wished to see a stop to women's ordination: 'We must be ready to learn from more ancient traditions, even where they appear to us somewhat levitical in their prohibitions'.[35]

Routley's misgivings contrast with the more favourable account of women's ministry in R Tudur Jones' scholarly work *Congregationalism in England 1662-1962*, the other official tercentenary history.   The book's index referred to over 40 women in the 300-year history of Congregationalism, a significant proportion of them benefactresses. Tudur Jones considered one of the most striking features of the period from 1916 to 1960 had been the increasing part played by women in the life of the Congregational Union of England and Wales. However, like Routley, he failed to advance any theological argument for women's ordination and explained it largely in terms of social forces:

> The emancipation of women in the early years of the twentieth century had opened up the possibility that some of them would be moved to offer themselves for Christian ministry. The first woman to be ordained to the Congregational ministry was Mrs Constance Mary Coltman, MA, BD, who was ordained from Mansfield College in 1917 as an Assistant to Dr W E Orchard at King's Weigh House. Many years passed before a woman became Chairman of the Congregational Union, the first being the Revd Elsie D Chamberlain in 1956-57.[36]

Tudur Jones referred to the 1936 Commission on the Ministry of Women but made no mention of its findings on low stipends for women. Instead he highlighted the Commission's findings on the role of deaconesses and the failure to implement these. Though generally supportive his account of women's ministry conveyed no indication of the difficulties encountered by women seeking ordination.

Congregationalism had to update and deepen its story of women's ministry when, in the 1960s, the CUEW again responded to the World Council of Churches initiative, 'The Co-operation of Men and Women in the Church'. This study, covering the Church, the family and society, asked denominations to consider how the women they employed were being used. A group of four ordained men and two laywomen was set up to undertake this task for the CUEW, sending questionnaires to women in ministry, to 100 churches which had women ministers, and to more than 200 other churches which were asked to give information on women's contribution to church life. The initial findings went to the CUEW Council in November 1964 but were referred back for more work with the suggestion that a woman minister should be on the group.[37] Eventually the Revd Florence Frost-Mee joined the group and their revised report acknowledged its debt to her.

The report found a striking difference between the experience of women in ministry during the 1930s and those in the 1960s, who were finding entry to college and getting a church were easier. Some clergy still refused to accept ordained women, and an Anglican rector had objected to a woman minister burying the dead in his churchyard,[38] but in other cases women had been invited to preach in denominations that did not ordain women. A number of congregations spoke of growing to accept women's ministry, though they may originally have called a woman only because there was no other candidate or they did not have a Manse to house her in.

The women ministers themselves encountered two main problems: finding time to do domestic work and the loneliness of the job. Most of them had been praised for their very sensitive pastoral work. Women ministers were mostly serving small churches and only 11 of them had churches with memberships over 100 according to the *Congregational Year Book*. The report saw some lessening of prejudice, although acknowledging it would probably be many years before women were accepted into the full ministry of the church as easily as men. It recommended that to promote the full co-operation of men and women in ministry, women ministers needed adequate domestic help to free them for work. A friend or relative keeping house for them might prevent the loneliness that could otherwise hurt them physically and spiritually. Some women might work better in group ministries, another recurring idea from the 1936 Commission report. Finally:

> ... churches need to be reminded that there is nothing inherent in her sex to prevent a woman from having a vocation for the ministry, or from being endowed with the necessary gifts and ability.[39]

In 1972 most English-speaking Congregational Churches in England and Wales joined with the Presbyterian Church of England to form the United Reformed Church. As the first Moderator of the new church's General Assembly, Kenneth Slack was asked to write a profile of it for a series on Christian denominations. The self-confident tone of his book conveyed no sense that the two traditions might still be coming to terms with the full implications of women's ordination at local level. Since inclusive language was not yet an issue the book used the male pronoun throughout to indicate both women and men. In parentheses to a statement about church government Dr Slack wrote firmly:

> (I use 'he' for convenience: all offices in the new Church, as in the two Churches that united, are open without any distinction to men and women. This includes the ordained ministry.)[40]

There was a similarly confident tone in the United Reformed Church's contribution to a book for the 1986 *'Not Strangers but Pilgrims'* process of the British Council of Churches. One section of its ten-page contribution, under the heading 'Church Order', stated:

> Our experience is that God calls both women and men to every ministry of the church. Through our Congregational roots this experience extends for 70 years.[41]

Limitation of space may explain this very brief account of the longest tradition of women's ordination in the United Kingdom. The unsuspecting reader might form the impression that equal recognition of women's ministry alongside men had come without a struggle in this part of the Church, even though during the 1980s the subject of Anglican women's priesthood was a matter of hot debate.[42]

Ignorance and confusion about the history of women's ordination has persisted in many places, not least within the denomination itself. This has partly been because Congregationalism made so little of the subject until interest in women's history and women's ordination grew in the later twentieth century. Telling a smoothed out version of events, which gave little sense of the struggle, pain and adventurousness of the early pioneers, also perpetuated a lack of understanding. When American scholar Edward C Lehman Jr published his research into traditional gender roles in the Churches of the United States and the United Kingdom he demonstrated a lamentable lack of knowledge about the early history of women's ministry in the United Kingdom. He said the first woman in Congregational ministry was 'Maude Warden', who candidated in 1913, trained at Mansfield College, Oxford and was ordained in 1917.[43] Lehman probably made this mistake by conflating a mis-hearing of Maude Royden's name with the details of Constance Coltman's story. He would not be alone in thinking lifelong Anglican, Maude Royden, was the first woman minister in the CUEW for that misapprehension still persists in some United Reformed Church circles even amongst people who might be expected to know better. Elsewhere Lehman made more errors in his account of Maude Royden's 1917 work at 'a Congregational church in London' (presumably the City Temple) including the misleading statement that she had become its pastor.[44]

He explored the relationship between levels of receptivity to women ministers and the length of time for which a denomination had been ordaining them. Though he concluded there could be a link between the two he warned that differences in 'religious sexism' only make sense when seen in social and cultural context. From his study of resistance factors to women's ordination in Baptist Churches, the Church of England, the Methodist Church and the United Reformed Church he wrote:

> Members inclined to accept women as ordained clergy are most likely to be younger Methodists or United Reformed members from relatively high status families. They tend not to be highly involved in traditional forms of religious life. They don't pray at home very much. They don't place much importance on traditional evangelism. Instead, they think the churches should be involved in social reform efforts. Their congregations tend to be small struggling bodies whose numbers have been declining recently and whose coffers are getting slimmer. Although they acknowledge that the clergywoman issue is a controversial one, they tend not to be overly concerned about it.[45]

It is hard to accord much weight to Lehman's findings in the light of the inaccuracy of his historical research. The tendency of some academics to advance major theories on the basis of limited evidence was further illustrated by Kenneth Brown's study *A Social History of the Nonconformist Ministry in England and Wales 1800-1930.* Describing a severe ministerial recruitment crisis that hit all three leading nonconformist denominations at the end of the nineteenth century, which was compounded by the effects of the First World War, Brown declared that Baptists and Congregationalists had tackled this in a novel way:

> Another outcome of declining recruitment was the attempt made by some denominations to widen the potential pool of recruits by admitting women to the ministry.... Mrs C M Coltman was the first woman in the Congregational ministry in 1917 but there was a lot of prejudice to overcome, not only within nonconformity itself but sometimes from within the families of aspiring female ministry.[46]

It might have surprised those at the CUEW Council in 1917 to discover that they would later be said by one historian to have decided in favour of women's ordination as a way of solving a manpower shortage, which had been worsened by the War. Had this been a deliberate policy decision, as Brown claims, one might have expected more encouragement and support for the trickle of women candidates during the inter-war years.

There have been as many different views about women's ministry expressed from within the United Reformed Church as from outside it. In 1989 the then General Secretary, Bernard Thorogood, wrote about the causes of division in ecumenism:

The gap becomes very evident when the ordination of women is debated, as it must be throughout the world church. In my own tradition the debate was concluded seventy years ago when the first woman was ordained to the ministry of the word and sacraments, for no theological question has since been raised on this issue among us.[47]

Edmund Banyard's twentieth birthday book for the denomination, *Straws in the Wind*, at least hinted that the reality for women ministers on the ground could be a little more complex than this *fait accompli* version of events. With a blend of self-congratulation and humility he stated:

All ministries within the Church are equally open to women and men. That does not mean that we have yet achieved a proper balance in using the people God has given to us, but many churches would be lost without their women Elders and today far fewer committees are male dominated. We have reason to be grateful for the women who are currently Departmental Convenors. In 1989 Jackie Petrie made history by becoming the first woman to be commissioned to chaplaincy in the Services since the 1939-45 war; in Thames North Province we have our first woman Provincial Moderator, and during 1992/3 we shall have our second woman Moderator of the General Assembly.[48]

Other voices in the United Reformed Church have acknowledged the gap between the rhetoric of a smooth transition to women's ordained ministry and the reality of a painful, continuing process. In his Moderatorial address to the 1989 General Assembly of the United Reformed Church, the Revd Keith Forecast tempered a sense of achievement about women's ordination with acknowledgement that more must be done:

Nor should we forget that for 70 years we have recognised that women have an equal place with men in ministry among us at every level. Once again, we have a long way to go before that equality is fully recognised and universally practised, but we can take some legitimate satisfaction in the fact that the Churches of our order have led the way. And as other denominations get themselves involved in hesitant, agonising and sometimes divisive moves in similar directions, we can claim to have as much experience as anyone to share.[49]

As a result of the growth in women's studies as a field of academic work, and the surge of interest in women's history, the 1990s saw a number of personal accounts of women's ministry. Kathleen Hendry's 1991 autobiography, *Don't Ask Me Why – Sixty Years a Woman Minister* covered her training in the 1920s, and her ministry between the Great Depression and retirement in the 1980s. It contained much personal reflection on being a pioneer of a new role in the Church. An anecdote about a 1974 visit to the General Assembly of the Church of Scotland is typical of the book's no-nonsense tone:

We four United Reformed Church representatives...stayed in the same hotel, and as I came last one morning to the breakfast table the Revd Howard Williams stood up; embarrassed I asked him please to sit down. He said he always stood up for a lady, whereupon the Revd Arthur Macarthur exclaimed, 'But Kathleen isn't a lady. She's one of our ministers.' I liked that.[50]

Janette Williams' biography of her mother Elsie Chamberlain, *First Lady of the Pulpit*, chronicles the setbacks and obstacles her mother overcame in ministry and its tone is understandably adulatory in parts. She quotes *The Christian World* from May 1955:

First woman chairman of the Union, first woman RAF chaplain, first ordained woman on the staff of the BBC, first Congregational minister to be a vicar's wife. With all these first-class accomplishments we must expect a first-class year of chairmanship in which we know we will not be disappointed.[51]

In 1994 Lavinia Byrne produced a book, *Women in the Church*, in her role as secretary for the Community of Women and Men in the Church at the Council of Churches for Britain and Ireland. This time the United Reformed Church's contribution showed new awareness that the ordination of women had far-reaching implications, which the Church was still struggling with. Replying to the question 'What is the principal contribution women make to the life of your Church?' the denomination's statement had a hint of penitence about it:

There is no principal contribution. It is our belief that women and men, created equal in God's image, should equally contribute to the life of the Church. Yet we recognise that we have not always enabled this to happen and that old ways still linger on. However, we are committed to furthering this equality and developing a true community of women and men in the church.[52]

The following year, on the first anniversary of the Church of England's vote to ordain women as priests, Congregational minister Janet Wootton wrote an article for a journal of feminist theology about the ministry of Free Church women. Her paper bristled with frustration at the lack of general recognition for women's work and leadership, as well as the scanty knowledge of their history. She spared her own tradition no rightful criticism and warned of the danger that ministry could become another a low-paid and female-dominated preserve.

A year ago today, the historic decision by the Synod of the Church of England was greeted by the British Press as if there had been no ordained women in Britain or in the Anglican Communion ever before. We in the free churches have a long and proud tradition of the full participation of women in the ministry of our denominations. But we cannot be complacent. The statistics from the year books show that there is still work to be done.[53]

Another book was issued to mark the United Reformed Church's quarter century in 1997, *From Streams to Oceans*, but it made few references to women's ministry. As staff secretary of the Doctrine, Prayer and Worship Committee, the United Reformed Church deputy general secretary John Waller wrote about a liturgy that had provoked national headlines. One minister, Fleur Houston, had conducted a service to release a woman from her vows after the ending of her marriage. The question as to whether sensitivity to this sort of pastoral need might be something that occurred more naturally to a woman minister than to a male colleague was not mentioned in the report. Perhaps the Committee was wary of being dubbed 'politically incorrect', a jibe that now stifles much potential analysis of gender issues inside and outside the Church. Elsewhere in the book the Revd Sheila Maxey, then Secretary for Ecumenical Relations, gave a list of things she admired about the denomination:

> Acceptance of Women in Leadership. Although the United Reformed Church
> is a relatively small church, I am not aware of an 'old boy network'. The calibre
> of women in national leadership positions is clear.[54]

Some would agree about high quality women but disagree about the lack of an 'old boy network'. Attending a General Assembly theological college lunch soon dispels any idea that whom a minister trained with or whom they know makes no difference in the United Reformed Church.

In 1998, *Under God's Good Hand* surveyed the history of the three traditions which would later form the United Reformed Church, from the early fifteenth to the late twentieth century. Its author David Cornick, then principal of Westminster College, Cambridge and now General Secretary, concluded that one discernible 'contour' on a future map of the denomination could be its attempts to honour the gifts of all God's people, women included. He wrote:

> The role of women in the church is slowly and painstakingly being recovered
> by historians. When that work is complete, histories such as this will need
> re-writing.[55]

The urgency of that re-writing was evident during the 1990s debate on the ordination as ministers of practising homosexuals. Speakers on both sides quoted Constance Coltman's ordination to support or oppose their propositions but very few had a full grasp of the precedent they were referring to. Daughters of Dissent may correct that ignorance by replacing the telling of a simplified story with a more complex and honest '*her*story' that allows contemporary women and men in the Church to make sense of the reality they encounter.

Chapter 11

Recurring Patterns in the Ministry of Women

> For many months he has been puddling and muddling in the midst of certain insane jargonings of hysterical women, and crack-brained enthusiasts, who start up from time to time in public companies, and utter confused stuff.[1]

With these words the essayist Carlyle wrote dismissively to his mother about the minister Edward Irving and the 'Prophetesses' who spoke in tongues during worship at Irving's Catholic Apostolic Church in London during the 1830s. Irving was forced out of his post as minister of Regent Square Scotch Presbyterian Church, London in 1832 on grounds of heresy and established another congregation in Newman Street, off Oxford Street.[2] The main message of the Catholic Apostolic Church he founded was that contemporary Christians, both men and women, had access to the same apostolic gifts as people in the Early Church had done. Four orders of ministry were recognised, namely apostles, evangelists, pastors and prophets, with the latter speaking in tongues and prophesying. Irving taught that provided it was rightly governed, in every way, the contemporary Church would experience a repetition of all the phenomena of Christianity's earliest years.[3]

Women had a high profile in Irving's short-lived movement, as often happens when part of the Church is swept by a wave of evangelical or Pentecostal fervour allowing women to exercise equal authority to men by the power of the Holy Spirit. Later in the nineteenth century, the Evangelical Revival of 1859-60 reached England and Wales from America via Ulster, and brought a fresh flowering of women's leadership in the form of widespread female preaching. *The Revival*, a newspaper first published in 1859 giving information about evangelical gatherings, gave notices of a steady flow of meetings with women preachers. These occasions were outside the normal structures of formal worship, however, and usually open to women only. For this reason they did not allow female speakers to make the transition from inspired revivalist orators to a fuller, more lasting role as authorised and legitimated leaders within the mainstream structure of the Church.

These two examples are indicative of the way that throughout Church history women have faced a major problem in claiming a role and using their talents for public leadership. They have been recognised as saints, martyrs, nuns, mothers, wives, ministers' wives, Sunday School teachers, pastoral carers, fund raisers, tea makers, cleaners, hymn writers, musicians and choir members, but rarely as those who preach, preside at Holy Communion or do theology. Though times of religious ferment have given women a platform for leadership they have usually found themselves forced out of the pulpits and reduced to silence in mixed company once more when the excitement has died down. Sectarian groupings that emerge from an outpouring of religious fervour, as Irving's did, usually fade out and so only allow women a short-lived platform. If they do not falter and fail, new movements usually establish organisational structures that prevent women from being able to continue their equal participation in leadership and teaching, once the 'early days' are over. Christian feminist scholars Rosemary Radford Ruether and Eleanor McLaughlin note:

> It is characteristic of the leadership roles in Christianity claimed by women that they derive their authority from personal charism rather than from office. This is so, not because, as men have supposed, women are more disposed toward the emotive and intuitive, but because it reflects the sociological fact that women for the most part were not allowed to claim authority of office. So it was in those areas where roles based on the 'gifts of the Spirit' were recognised that there was likely to be space for women.[4]

This is one of several recurring patterns which emerge from the story of women's ministry. Another is the way that, over the centuries of Church history, accounts of women's brief adventures in leadership have barely been recorded or have vanished between the lines of the male-dominated versions of events written by male historians. There is also a pattern whereby social upheavals, including war, have produced temporary conditions of social flux that favoured women's ministry. It is noticeable however that even when new opportunities have been opened up for women, they have been taken up very slowly, and sometimes fallen into disuse again. A further pattern is the extra strain, outweighing that faced by their male colleagues, borne by women seeking leadership roles in the Church. Damagingly self-sacrificial ways of working often seem to have been an unavoidable accompaniment of women's ministry, coupled until very recently with lower pay.

A pattern of resistance to women within training institutions is also revealed, which frequently prevented them from developing the skills needed by fully equipped leaders or deterred them from even candidating. The search for freedom to move, for institutional space within which to be themselves, is another pattern of women's story in the Church. In the Middle Ages women could find space within convents, all-women centres of learning, but post-Reformation Protestant women have had little chance to carve out space for themselves until the beginnings of feminism in the nineteenth century. All these patterns need examining, for it is only as contemporary Christians explore the way gender relations have operated in the Church's past that new ways of working together in mutuality and partnership can begin to be established.

Contemporary Roman Catholic feminist scholar Elisabeth Schüssler Fiorenza sees the first pattern identified here, of women being allowed temporary teaching and leadership roles in times of religious change, as having its origins at the very start of the Christian Church. She focuses on the way women were active and important disciples of Jesus during his lifetime, and highlights the influence of women missionaries and community leaders in the Early Church. Yet within a few generations women's ministry had been severely restricted, as Fiorenza acknowledges. By the time the Church became an institution of the Roman Empire, during the fourth century, women's leadership had been effectively sidelined. Fiorenza writes: 'Much of women's "her-story" in early Christianity is lost. The few references which survived in the New Testament records are like the tip of an iceberg indicating what we have lost. Yet at the same time they show how great the influence of women was in the early Christian movement'.[5] Students of women's history encounter a depressing number of 'icebergs', a recurring pattern which marks the way women have exercised public ministry during times of change and then lost ground, with little record of their achievements left to show for it.

Another illustration of this emerged in nineteenth century Methodism, a tradition bearing some similarities to those strands of Nonconformity which later formed the United Reformed Church, while also being quite distinct from them. Assessing and evaluating events from the history of one tradition can be a valuable way to shed new light on things taking place at the same time elsewhere in the Church. While Irving's Catholic Apostolic Church was allowing women a limited chance to speak in religious services under the name of 'prophecy', there were different examples of women's leadership emerging in Methodism. Within Wesleyan Methodism, the early nineteenth century saw a closing down of the avenues for women to continue the public preaching ministry they had exercised in the earlier, less formal years of the movement. John Wesley, though initially hostile to the idea of women preachers, had later endorsed their ministry 'in extraordinary cases'. Following his death the Wesleyan Conference of 1803 significantly reduced the opportunities for any woman who experienced such an extraordinary call from God to exercise her gifts. She should speak, in general, to other women only and must seek strict permission from the Circuit and the Superintendent Minister in advance. Being able to convince those within the male power structures that one had authority to preach from the Holy Spirit was no longer enough.[6]

Things were different for a time within those strands of Methodism that emerged, in the late eighteenth and early nineteenth centuries, at the other end of the church polity and organisational scale from Wesleyan Methodism. In 1797 the Methodist New Connexion was formed, urging a stronger voice for the laity and greater democracy in chapel affairs. William Clowes and Hugh Bourne were forced out of their circuits for their refusal to obey Conference strictures on open-air revivalist meetings and established the Primitive Methodists in 1811. The Bible Christians were founded in 1815, parting company with Wesleyan Methodism like the other secessionist groups over their opposition to central control, their dislike of the growing power of ministers, and the desire to preserve the spontaneity and freedom which had previously characterised chapel life. All these secessionist groups were initially formed to preserve the greater freedoms of the original movement and included in these was the right of women to preach.

Even within the Bible Christian movement, however, women preachers still encountered institutional opposition.[7] They played a significant role in the growth of the Bible Christians but their names were not used on advance publicity for meetings, nor could they be put in charge of male colleagues. From a peak of 27 women itinerant preachers and 62 men listed by the Bible Christian annual conference minutes in 1827, the women's numbers fell steadily throughout the rest of the century. Jacqueline Field-Bibb has suggested the high fall-out rate among women itinerants could have resulted from the hard conditions they faced on the road. Almost half (31) of the 75 women Bible Christian preachers named in membership records between 1819 and 1907 served for just three years or less.[8]

The 1820 Bible Christian conference gave advice on health to male and female preachers: 'Let all, both male and female; take care of their health; beware of taking too long journies, and of remaining with wet clothes on; and also beware of going out after preaching at night; and of sleeping in damp beds, it being so very injurious to health'.[9] When a questioner at conference asked about the fate of 'worn out preachers' it was agreed that women itinerants no longer working on grounds of ill health should be paid as before, provided they maintained a 'becoming character', and either stayed single or married a male travelling preacher. The nineteenth century witnessed a gradual decline in the number of Bible Christian women itinerant preachers until the low point of 1894 when only four women were named in the minutes of conference. Like their male counterparts, these women were subject to annual renewal by their local circuits on the basis of their preaching standards. Unlike their male colleagues, they were not allowed to vote at District Meetings, though they were expected to attend and take part in the business done.

In 1907 the last in the line of women Bible Christian itinerant preachers, Lillie Edwards, saw her vocation sacrificed to the greater cause of Church unity when the Bible Christians joined with the United Methodist Free Churches and Methodist New Connexion to form the United Methodist Church. The new Church decided that despite Miss Edwards' 13 years of ministerial service and experience her position there would be 'anomalous', presumably because of the lack of female colleagues. She was obliged to retire, received £135 in lieu of pension rights, and was appointed to the role of 'female special agent' in the Hastings Mission for a year.[10] So ended the longest period of women's leadership within Methodism, from 1819 to 1907. The story was only resumed in 1974 when the Methodist Church, formed by union in 1932, finally ordained its first women ministers.

A number of recurring patterns emerge from this brief account of women's ministry in one era of Free Church history. The ministry of women itinerants was never exercised in complete equality with their male colleagues. Although their vocations and gifts were valued, their contribution was always limited by rules within the wider Church community, which prevented them from exercising too much power. When women preachers found it hard to sustain ministry for more than a few years, there is little evidence of anything having been done within the male power structures to find out why, or suggest changes to stem the loss of trained and gifted women.

It is also significant that the relatively brief flowering of women's ministry within secessionist nineteenth century Methodism arose where certain conditions coincided. These were an itinerant ministry, low social standing for ministers, working class congregations with limited financial resources and low ministerial stipends. The Primitive Methodists, who had women itinerants between 1819 and 1862, fixed the annual salary of travelling female preachers from the outset at half that of a single man, which in 1819 amounted to £8.[11] Primitive Methodist stipends were less than those of Wesleyan Methodists. In 1851 a Primitive Methodist minister with three children received £71 per annum, compared to the annual stipend of £120 which a Wesleyan minister would have received in the 1860s.[12] The stipends of Bible Christian ministers were generally lower still, so William Mason and his preacher wife Mary lived on £30 a year in 1840, plus a small family allowance for their eight chidren.[13] At that time the idea of equal pay for women would have been virtually unthinkable, yet the half wages given to female preachers illustrate a pattern of low rewards that women have repeatedly encountered. When given a chance to exercise their ministry, women have often done so in sacrificial circumstances with limited financial recognition, and the subsequent strain on their health has taken its toll in sickness and premature retirement.

The story of the Bible Christian itinerant women preachers highlights a further recurring pattern, whereby women's ministry has fallen victim to the superior demands of ecumenism, as viewed by the Church authorities. Lillie Edwards is one of a long line of women who have been told their ministerial aspirations are of lesser significance than the need to advance inter-church relationships. How many potential women priests and their supporters suffered from the argument, frequently voiced in the twentieth century Church of England, that to ordain them might do damage to Anglican relations with Rome? Monica Furlong identified the use of the ecumenical argument against women's leadership in her 1984 book *Feminine in the Church*. Following the founding of MOW (the Movement for the Ordination of Women) in 1979 opponents of women in the priesthood had voiced a number of new views:

> It was also pointed out that the rise of ecumenism had made the goal of the ordination of women more remote. Neither the Roman Catholic Church nor the Orthodox Church was noted for an enlightened attitude toward women, but 'unity' with them was seen as a more desirable and urgent goal than revising our own theory and practice about the ministry of women.[14]

The question arises as to how much priority had been accorded to ecumenism with Roman Catholic and Orthodox Christians *before* the issue of women's ordination to the priesthood rose high on the agenda of the Church of England. A Free Church observer might also wonder how often the balancing argument, from the other side of the ecumenical dialogue, was advanced within Anglican circles. It could just as legitimately be said that the Church of England's reluctance to acknowledge and value women's ministry was damaging its ecumenical relations with those Free Churches that ordained women in the 1980s. While the women's ordination debate was spreading in the Church of England, women ministers were already significant members of the ordained clergy in the United Reformed Church, Methodist Church, Baptist and other denominations.

The existence of Free Church women ministers in local ecumenical partnerships with the Church of England sometimes advanced the cause of women's ordination and gave positive models of women in leadership to Anglican people. Women ministers might be hailed as living proof of how little Anglicans needed to fear women priests. Elsewhere the ministry of Free Church women provoked awkwardness and caused hurt on both sides. Some Anglican women, who had progressed finally during this period from being deaconesses to ordination to the permanent diaconate, found it difficult to work alongside fully ordained women of another tradition. At times the Free Church women ministers were left feeling they were invisible or unacceptable in the eyes of certain Anglicans.

When the Church of England, Methodist Church, Moravian Church and United Reformed Church considered a National Covenant in the early 1980s, United Reformed Church minister Kate Compston was concerned that the position of ordained women had not been sufficiently safeguarded in the proposals:

> The issue of episcopacy is non-negotiable. By contrast, if the Covenant is accepted members of the Anglican Church may exercise their conscientious reservations about the cherished principle that the ordained woman has as valid and complete a ministry as the ordained man.
>
> It is enough to be told that, as nonconformist ministers, we will not be 'true' presbyters until we have been episcopally blessed (and in the case of our successors episcopally ordained). It is more than enough for many women ministers to be informed that whilst our male colleagues would graciously be accepted after Covenanting, we might still be unrecognised by some of our Anglican friends.[15]

There is one powerful, practical counter argument to the view that the ordination of women in some parts of the Church presents a barrier to church unity and this has been exemplified by Christian women of all denominations, lay and ordained. When they meet at social, representative or training events, women frequently find their shared experiences are more unifying than the denominational differences dividing them. The history of one ecumenical body, the World Council of Churches, suggests that far from being obstacles to ecumenism, women in the Church have been some of its greatest exponents. An example of this would be Madeline Barot, a Frenchwoman, who was the first director of the WCC's Department on the Co-operation of Men and Women in the Church from 1953 to 1966. A history of the ecumenical movement called her 'an extraordinary figure in the history of modern ecumenism'.[16] Many of the pioneers of women's ordination were also ecumenical in the way they crossed denominational boundaries to gain ordination (see chapter on 'Ecumenism'). Similarly in the late twentieth century some Anglican women from Britain were ordained as priests in other parts of the Anglican communion, such as the Episcopal Church of the United States, before the General Synod decision of 1992 made this open to them within the Church of England.

Issues of ecumenism and of women's ordained leadership grow increasingly complex. In 2002 the General Assembly of the United Reformed Church debated a plan for an Ecumenical Bishop in Cardiff East. One of four denominations involved, the Church in Wales, could only approve a man as first post holder. Some women urged General Assembly to support the venture and others agreed on a once-only basis, provided the restriction would be lifted after the first appointment. For the United Reformed Church to participate in a ministry closed to women meant limited suspension of the denomination's founding document, the Basis of Union. In autumn 2002 the proposal fell anyway for lack of support in the Church in Wales's Governing Body.

Meanwhile debate is deepening in the Church of England about the possibility of women becoming bishops and of rescinding the 1993 Act of Synod by which 'two integrities' were established as a way of accommodating opponents of women's priesthood in communion. In 1998, Methodist women ministers expressed deep concern about these two issues within Anglicanism at Methodist Conference.[17] Issues of women's leadership remain a possible stumbling block as the Methodist Church and Church of England gradually implement the Covenant they agreed on in 2003. The Methodist Church has stated: 'an episcopate in the Methodist Church would be open to women as well as to men'.[18] Both traditions say: 'The only issue of principle that divides the Methodist Church and the Church of England over the historic episcopate is the question of the ordination or consecration of women to the episcopate'.[19] It will be interesting to see if women in leadership are once again seen as obstacles to ecumenism before this particular process is complete.

Feminist scholars have recently begun to identify the rise and fall of women's fortunes within the Church. They have called their retrieval of forgotten stories '*her*story' to emphasise the difference between the hunt for evidence of women's activities and the accounts of male-dominated *his*tory. Mainstream Church history usually refers to women only within limited parameters and 'acceptable roles' such as wife, mother or fundraiser. A substantial nineteenth century work entitled *Lancashire Nonconformity* [20] mentions women solely as minor characters in congregational life. They are ministers' wives, benefactresses, church founder members or fundraisers but nothing more. To become a victim also qualified a woman for honourable mention, as when the unfortunate wife of an incoming minister was fatally injured en route to a new pastorate:

The journey on horseback ... was attended with a serious accident, which eventually resulted in Mrs Harrison's death. Thus the new minister entered upon his duties amidst the gloom of family affliction, the discouragements of 'a weak and declining church', and with the prospect of an income 'small and insufficient for the support of a minister in any tolerable degree of respectability and comfort.' Amongst those of his people who showed great kindness is named Jeremiah Fielding of Hartshead, whose sister attended Mrs Harrison until her death, and afterward married the bereaved husband.[21]

Another way for a woman to be immortalised in mainstream Church history and find her place in the record of events is to be dubbed a 'saint' or an 'angel'. For this to happen a woman has to perform a difficult balancing act between giving highly self-sacrificial service whilst simultaneously presenting no direct personal challenge to the male organisational hierarchy of the Church. A typical example of someone the twentieth century regarded as a 'saint' was Gladys Aylward, a former London parlour maid whose work in China before and during the Second World War was given the Hollywood treatment in the film 'The Inn of the Sixth Happiness'. [22] Her suitability for 'sainthood' was helped by her short stature and the fact she was no academic threat, having failed to get the right qualifications to be sent to China by a missionary society. Though her work in enforcing the Chinese government ban on foot binding for rural women would now be seen as radically feminist, Gladys Aylward typified the sort of women's service with which the Church feels comfortable, as she did not rock the boat.

Commenting on the phenomenon of written lives of women saints, and the way these have been used, feminist theologian Elizabeth Stuart remarks:

> We must be careful here, because hagiography may not reflect the reality of individuals' lives. But it was written for a variety of purposes, one of which was to encourage people to behave in a certain way, so even if hagiography may actually exaggerate the behaviour of certain historical women, it does send a message to all other women about what is expected of them.[23]

Instances of women ministers being described as 'angels' raise questions as to where deserved praise ends and hagiography begins. Retired doctor Derek Watson wrote a distinctly hagiographical biography of Muriel Paulden, *Angel of Jesus, Muriel Paulden of Liverpool 8*. Identifying her spiritual gifts in terms of the fruits of the Holy Spirit, as described by Paul, Watson listed Muriel Paulden's love, joy, peace, patience, kindness, goodness, faithfulness, gentleness and self-control. In terms of peace she had never been restless or over-active but shared the burdens of others by shelving her own and offering their troubles to the Lord. As for gentleness: 'She had strong views against the Church's negative attitude to the ministry of women, but did not think this could be changed by a confrontational stance. She was content to further this cause by a gentle and more indirect approach.' [24]

Though parts of his book portrayed Muriel Paulden's courage and determination, Watson still described her as an 'angel'. When retired minister Alice Platts wrote to Daughters of Dissent, however, she made indirect reference to this by firmly stating her former colleague Muriel Paulden was: 'No Angel. Rather pioneer, rebel, a great teacher, a great Christian'.[25] Watson's work had described the weekly regime of St Paul's House, the unique female training centre Muriel Paulden founded and ran, but his biography failed to explain where the energy and vision for her powerful and very individual ministry came from. Echoes of this sort of response to women's ministry can also be heard in the obituary of another early woman minister, Margaret Fullerton (née Hardy), which noted she was known in Leeds as 'the angel of Marshall Street'.[26]

When powerful women are given the public image of saints or angels, this enables the Church to put them on a pedestal, and in a paradoxical way reduces their potential as role models. By focusing simply on the good deeds which earned women a place in the records, Church historians avoid asking why these women acted as they did, how this might have been affected by their gender, and whether there were differences between their public persona and their private views.

In contrast with the field of Church history, '*her*story' traces the story of women's leadership in the Church from the Bible right through the millennia of the Judaeo-Christian tradition. Analysis of their stories helps to explain why advances in women's ministry have been hard to safeguard and easily forgotten by following generations, leaving each new group of women to reclaim their past and discover their place in the tradition of women's leadership. Rosemary Radford Ruether and Eleanor McLaughlin's 1979 book, *Women of Spirit: Female Leadership in the Jewish and Christian Traditions*, is an example of such scholarship. Identifying the way in which the issue of women's ordination surfaced in America during the nineteenth century, Ruether and McLaughlin comment:

> This occurred among those groups whose evangelical understanding of preaching as prophetic ministry led them to affirm women's equal right to be a vehicle of the Spirit. At the first ordination of a woman, that of American Congregationalist Antoinette Brown in 1853, we find this view of ministry. The evangelist, Luther Lee, who preached her ordination sermon, justified the break with tradition by declaring, 'every Gospel minister is a prophet, and every prophet under the new dispensation is a Gospel minister'.[27]

Brown stayed in pastoral charge for less than a year before asking to leave her post. She cited among the reasons her refusal to preach eternal damnation or to ostracise an unmarried girl whose baby had died. After her resignation she married, raised a family, wrote on religious and women's rights issues, and on her husband's death eventually returned to ministry in 1901 as a Unitarian.[28]

Stories about Brown and others like her have often been lost, have become submerged within mainstream 'male' history, or else have been interpreted misleadingly by those with no sensitivity to issues of gender difference and inequality. One product of the recent major growth of women's history has been to reveal those recurring patterns that have defined and limited women's participation in the Church. Previously hidden parallels have emerged in the ways in which women, at different times and in different places, have been systematically excluded from Church structures. When women in the Early Church were gradually edged out of their missionary roles, as the hierarchy became more organised, a damaging precedent was established. As time elapsed after the initial, pioneering work of charismatic women and men in founding new congregations during the apostolic age, it became harder for women to resist the establishment of a male-dominated clerical structure. Once Church and state became closely identified, as the Roman Empire adopted Christianity to be the state religion, effective resistance to the results of male-domination (or 'patriarchy' as feminism terms it) grew almost impossible. 'Herstory' reveals how recurring patterns of obstructive attitudes towards women's ministry appear with striking regularity across the centuries as well as denominational and cultural boundaries. The same arguments against women's leadership continue to be voiced, and similar mechanisms put in place to restrict their freedom in using whatever gifts they consider the Holy Spirit to have given them for the benefit of the whole Church.

Even when doors for women's advancement have opened, '*her*story' suggests these have often remained poorly publicised and underused. The history of Bristol Baptist College records that it was decided in 1919 to admit women as students but the first to arrive, Gwenyth Hubble, did not enter the college until 1937. By 1960 she had only been followed by one other woman student.[29] In 1921 the Presbyterian Church of England declared there was no theological bar to women's ordained ministry, yet it was not until 1956 that their first woman minister, Ella Gordon, was ordained. Between 1956 and 1966 only three further women ministers were ordained in the Presbyterian Church of England, (see the chapter 3 on Structures for more details of this story).

Another recurring pattern of women's leadership in the Church is that entry into a new role does not automatically bring with it recognition (financial or personal) and acceptance. Although the Congregational Union of England and Wales opened its doors to women's ordination in 1917, before any other tradition in Britain, the slow ordination rate of one woman a year in the inter war period was only just enough to keep the access open. Once inside the Church structures these women ministers encountered a range of further challenges, so much so that by the outbreak of war in 1939 serious questions might have been raised as to how much the resistance to women's leadership at all levels of the Church had been overcome. Those women ordained within the CUEW from 1917 onwards faced an uphill struggle to convince others of their call, to get suitable theological training, and then to find pastorates willing and able to pay them a living stipend. Congregational churches not only paid women lower stipends than their male counterparts, in line with employment practices at the time, but they also allowed some women ministers to adopt a highly self-sacrificial model of ministry at great risk to their personal health and well-being. Identification of the phenomenon of 'ministerial burnout' came later in the twentieth century but the obituaries of some early women Congregational ministers echo the stories of those nineteenth century Methodist women itinerant preachers whose health had given out in less than three years on the road.

The recurring pattern of obstacles placed in the path of women seeking ordained Congregational ministry in the 1920s and 30s, and after the Second World War, was in clear contrast to the confident view of the future which had been voiced at the ordination of the first woman minister in the Congregational Union of England and Wales, Miss Constance Todd. When she and her fiancée Mr Claud Coltman, were ordained at the King's Weigh House Church, London, in September 1917 one of the four ordaining ministers, the Revd G Stanley Russell, declared that this was 'the beginning of a new era, when woman would no longer be considered the subordinate of man'.[30] The fact that this new era has been a long time dawning, and is only partially realised even now, suggests that Congregationalism's professed pioneering role in advancing women's ministry needs to be reassessed. (see chapter 10 on 'How this story has been told')

The Equal Pay Act of 1970 (though the legislation exempted churches) made it unacceptable for employers to pay women less than men for the same work yet issues of lower financial recognition for women's ministry have persisted even since the United Reformed Church came into existence in 1972. By paying nationally set stipends from central funds the United Reformed Church has introduced equality of ministerial pay for men and women, irrespective of the resources of the particular church(es) where they are based. Inequalities persist in terms of benefits in kind, hidden extras like new carpets for the minister's manse, and payment or otherwise of fixed car allowances. All these may have more to do with local resources than the gender of the minister. This is a vast improvement on the system in the Congregational Union of England and Wales where individual churches negotiated a stipend with their minister and might totally undercut the recommended amount. It is hard to quantify whether women are still less likely than men to be introduced to pastorates with a larger number of members in one congregation, a high percentage of economically active, well-educated members and expectations of academic learning and a certain social standing from their minister. A CUEW study, submitted in 1965 as part of a World Council of Churches project on the Co-operation of Men and Women in the Church, Family and Society noted that:

> Most of the churches that call women are small ones. According to the 1964 Year Book, only 11 women have churches with over 100 members. The largest churches prefer to have a man as minister. A woman must be more gifted and better qualified than a man to obtain an opportunity equal with his.[31]

One problem in trying to assess the equality of opportunity open to women seeking pastoral charge within the contemporary United Reformed Church is that some churches are seen as influential preaching stations although their membership numbers may not reflect this. Churches that have a 'name' and significant status do call women ministers now but figures from the 2001 Year Book confirm that women are still a minority in leadership of higher membership congregations, which apparently persist in preferring a male minister. The 22 largest churches in the 2001 Year Book were all being ministered to by men, while churches with women ministers were 23rd, 25th and 27th in terms of membership. Average attendance statistics reveal that men were also leading the 22 churches with the largest numbers in worship, with a woman minister serving the 23rd largest church in terms of attendance.[32] (See chapter 2 on 'Statistics and Storytelling'.)

During the mid 1990s United Reformed Church minister Christine Fowler conducted research into non-stipendiary ministry in the denomination and found it to be dominated by women. This suggested a hidden but continuing pattern of women receiving less financial recognition for ministry than their male colleagues, despite equal pay for stipendiary ministry. The 1995 Year Book showed 44 % of the women ministers listed (that is 103 of the 237) were non-stipendiary, compared with less than 25% of male ministers. Fowler voiced suspicions that women were being deterred from thinking about stipendiary ministry, and were guided by Synod Moderators, ministerial training Assessment Conferences and training boards towards non-stipendiary ministry instead. She wrote: 'Mainly male-dominated selection and assessment boards have a tendency to bring their prejudices and preconceptions of motherhood and ministry to the interview. Research done over the past two years has revealed that many women who are NSMs would have preferred to be stipendiary – whether full or part-time'.[33]

The Year Book lists the pastoral charge and ministerial appointment history of individuals, showing whether they are stipendiary or non-stipendiary. It does not include overall figures on the number of men and women in ministry or any statistics relating gender to stipendiary/non-stipendiary status. Perhaps the argument for not collecting these statistics is that it would be retrograde and unhelpful to record the gender profile of types of ministry, in this age of equal opportunities. In actual fact the United Reformed Church's equal opportunities policy, adopted by General Assembly in 1994, allows for monitoring of women's participation in Church life as well as that of black people and those with disabilities.[34]

The struggles of contemporary United Reformed Church women ministers, and their predecessors, to gain full recognition and acceptance in their ordained role now stretch back over almost a century. The fact this story is part of a wider worldwide pattern came to light during the World Council of Churches Ecumenical Decade of Churches in Solidarity with Women (1988-1998). A WCC periodical headlined in 1991 the struggle of ordained women in Taiwan in terms that ring too many bells for comfort:

In the wake of the controversy generated by the critical article written by a young female minister and published in the Taiwan Church News a seminar to allow female ministers to share their struggles was held at the General Assembly Offices in Taipei last August. Fourteen of the 38 ordained women in the Presbyterian Church of Taiwan were present to share their stories. They said that some teachers and fellow-students at theological seminary tended to be paternalistic or domineering in their relations with female students and that women students are excluded from the 'lottery' which helps to match churches looking for a minister with graduating theologians. Female ministers, they said, tend to receive less pay than their male counterparts, and churches are slower to call a woman to the pulpit. Finally, very few women hold positions of leadership at national level.[35]

It could be argued that another pattern in the story of women's ministry, which gave them temporary legitimisation in times of social ferment during the twentieth century, was the effect of warfare. Constance Todd's ordination at the height of the First World War coincided with a far ranging if short-lived re-evaluation of the potential contribution of women to civil society, precipitated by widespread manpower shortages. She had originally entered ministerial training in 1913 but the social climate as she began looking for a pastorate looked radically different. By 1917, with most active, able bodied, young men away at the front, women were taking on new jobs at all levels of the paid employment and in the voluntary sphere, including fresh opportunities in the Church. The 'Notes by the Way' column of *The Christian World* reported in January 1917 that sources of 'supplies' of new ministers were exhausted:

> Retired ministers are snapped up by churches whose ministers are serving as chaplains to the Forces. With the closing of many theological colleges and the men reduced almost to extinction point in those still open, the student stand-by is no longer available... The church without a minister looks with longing eyes on churches in possession of satisfactory pastors.[36]

Some people made a connection between the shortage of men in ministry and the potential for women to step into the breach. *The Christian World* reported a story from Scotland in March 1917:

> The question of the admission of women to the Theological Hall is raised by the April issue of *The Scottish Congregationalist*. If, it is argued, the arts and medical classes of the university are open to women, why not the Divinity Halls? Already some of the Scottish Union have had female 'pulpit supply' on account of the dearth of preachers.[37]

In June 1917 the same journal reported on the departure from Oxford of a minister's widow, Mrs Stevenson, and her children for work in East London.

> A wallet of Treasury notes added materially to the verbal tributes to her abilities and devotion which were paid by Dr Selbie, the deacons and several lady members. Dr Selbie took occasion to dwell on the wonderful service women are rendering the churches in wartime. He knew of one church where the deacons and all the male Sunday School teachers were gone and the work of the church was carried on by the minister's wife and the wives of some others. They had shown themselves quite as capable as the men.[38]

The phenomenon of women filling the gaps left by men in the Church was also happening in other Protestant communities during the First World War. An article in *The Christian Commonwealth* said:

> French clergy are not exempt from military service, and many of the ministers' wives have courageously stepped into the gaps thus created and have taken up their husbands' work. They preach on Sundays, teach the catechism, visit the sick and even conduct funerals.[39]

It is hard to prove convincingly that the First World War conclusively advanced the cause of women's ordination but it was significant for bringing about special, if temporary, social conditions within which new female role models of women's leadership in Church could emerge. The women who took on lay leadership and began preaching set important precedents by showing their capabilities on the public stage. One woman who rose to national prominence in the Church during the First World War was an Anglican laywoman. In 1917, as Constance Todd was completing her ministerial training, Maude Royden caused national newspaper headlines on becoming pulpit assistant at City Temple, a major London Congregational church. Maude Royden and Constance Todd were lifelong friends and several other early Congregational women ministers cited Maude Royden as an inspiration for their own journey towards ministry (see chapter 5 'On not keeping silent in the churches: women in the pulpit').

Miss Royden the pulpit assistant was just one of the vast number of middle class women who took on new roles as nurses, ambulance drivers, civil servants, Land Army workers or staff in insurance, banks or businesses during the war. At the same time 400,000 female domestic servants left their jobs for factory work.[40] All these women had the chance to gain new skills and, more importantly, to be seen by the general public as competent and reliable workers. Though most were expected to return to domesticity on the return of the men from the Armed Forces, and women's employment fell back to below pre-war levels in the 1920s, the fact that women had entered new areas of work and performed well was not lost on those who wished to promote women's role in society.

A story from the Second World War and another part of the Church lends support to the idea that social change in time of war may be a factor in advancing the cause of women's ordination. Florence Tim Oi Li was ordained as an Anglican priest by Bishop Hall of Hong Kong during the Second World War in 1944, having journeyed to him across Japanese lines, and was the first woman to be a priest in the Anglican communion. Both the 1948 Lambeth Conference and Archbishops Temple and Fisher later rejected her orders. Bishop Hall was censured and Li was told if she continued to work as a priest he would be forced to resign. For many years she did not exercise her ministry, but she always refused to resign her orders, which she considered a permanent gift from God. In 1984, at a thanksgiving service in Westminster Abbey for the fortieth anniversary of her ordination, the Revd Dr Florence Tim Oi Li finally received the recognition for her ministry that had so long been denied.[41]

When in 1948 the newly formed World Council of Churches started gathering material for a report on the life and work of women in the Church, the responses from 50 countries also showed that wartime had opened new opportunities for women (see chapters 7 and 4 on Ecumenism and on Ministry and Theological Education). In her fascinating summary of the findings, *The Service and Status of Women in the Churches*, Dr Kathleen Bliss wrote of the work done in Germany during the Second World War by 'Vikarinen', non-ordained women curates:

> There is no more overpowering answer to the question whether, leaving for the moment on one side the theological issue, women are *able* to exercise the full ministry, if they are given the opportunity, than the account in the German report of the work of a number of Vikarinen in the East of Germany in the last part of the war and since.[42]

These young women had stepped in to lead pastorless churches when all men including ministers had been called up for military service. They had worked in refugee camps, sustained congregations under Russian occupation and ministered to people under severe physical hardship, at great cost to themselves. After the war and the separation of Germany, the West had an excess of male clergy and only two or three women were left in charge of parishes. Meanwhile in the East a shortage of male clergy meant women were still needed to hold pastoral positions in the Church. Kathleen Bliss commented: 'As soon as women were not needed theological arguments against their ministry were strongly voiced in the Church'. [43]

Recurring patterns of limited acceptance and renewed resistance to women's advancement in the Church can be shown to have parallels elsewhere in gender history. It has not been a unique phenomenon of Church life that women should have been paid less for equal work, should have failed to gain positions of lasting authority in decision-making structures forms, should have found their authority to be entirely dependent on their personal qualities and limited to periods when circumstances made their contribution a temporary necessity, or should have had their advancement blocked in the name of some higher cause when the need arose, all factors resulting in a heavy potential cost for their health and well-being. Sometimes the obstacles encountered by women seeking leadership roles, both in Church and society, have been totally mundane yet nonetheless influential for that.

Jacky Smith, a retired woman minister in the United Reformed Church, encountered another pattern of resistance to women's advancement in the form of inadequate plumbing. With a self-deprecating tone shared by many of the female pioneers who wrote to this project she recalled:

> I haven't much of a story to tell. I was very active in a Congregational Church in Patricroft near Eccles, Manchester. My minister was the Revd Ian Wallace who had been trained in Nottingham. He tried a couple of colleges including Nottingham for me and the reply was the now standard rejection of women 'we have no female toilets'. However, I got in at Bristol where there was already a woman, Jessie Halfpenny, now Jessie Clare.[44]

Theological colleges have not been alone in allowing the lack of suitable plumbing to be a disincentive to full access by women. There is an obvious parallel with the previous lack of toilet facilities for women MPs in the palace of Westminster, which was only fully tackled on the arrival of a significant number of women members at the 1997 General Election. The historian Martin Pugh has noted that when elected to the House of Commons in 1919 Lady Astor and the other women pioneers were each given one room and a dressing room: 'in the latter stood a wash stand, a tin basin, a jug of cold water and a bucket.'[45] This lack of appropriate sanitary facilities mirrored what Pugh described as the continuing Parliamentary atmosphere of a gentlemen's club, which meant that facilities remained largely unaltered until there were 41 women MPs in 1987.

A biography of Lady Astor conveys the sense that the new women MPs were not being admitted as *full* members, of equal standing with their male colleagues. The writer approvingly notes that the new MP was careful not to trespass on the privacy of her new male colleagues: 'She did not go into the smoke rooms or the bar nor did she eat in the dining-room except very occasionally. A private room had been placed at her disposal, to be shared with any future women members, where she could sit with her secretaries and attend to her correspondence. The result was that she rarely met members except in the Chamber itself or the lobbies. They were able to enjoy unmolested the amenities of their exclusive political club'.[46]

There were repercussions from the reluctance of some early women MPs to do anything that might be interpreted as challenging the male atmosphere of Westminster. One of these was the persistent confusion caused for later generations of new women members of Parliament by the way in which the men's toilets were marked 'Members Only'. Being members themselves, some women naturally assumed they were free to enter these toilets, whereas in fact the female toilets were marked 'Private, Lady Members Only'. The hidden message behind these differing notices would seem to be that male members of Parliament are the norm and women some form of limited special case. As the then Mrs Shirley Williams, an MP from 1964 to 1979, remarked in a letter to *The Guardian*: 'it tells one quite a lot about the House of Commons'.[47]

In an article on 'Ground Rules and Social Maps', sociologist Shirley Ardener suggests that in order to deal with the challenge represented by women MPs the House of Commons has regarded women as 'fictive men' on their entry into the male-controlled space of Westminster. She writes: 'When rules of separation pertain, many difficulties arise at critical points and various devices are then introduced to cope with them while maintaining the underlying principle of classification. Mechanisms for entering private or exclusive space may be needed'.[48] An institution which is reluctant to acknowledge a group of people, or is blind to their needs, can effectively block them by failing to provide basic services such as toilets that allow their full participation. The lack of public facilities for disabled people in many public buildings is another example of this sort of space guarding. If an institution expects incomers to adopt the behaviour of existing members as their 'norm' then any change resulting from the arrival of new people can be minimised. The whole of this project demonstrates how much such forces of institutional resistance have been at work in the United Reformed Church, and its preceding traditions, with reference to women's ministry both lay and ordained.

Admittedly, the lack of female toilets at Westminster did not hinder women's election to the House Commons but it symbolised a lack of willingness to welcome and embrace women's presence as women rather than as 'fictive' males. There are parallels with the treatment meted out by some theological colleges to generations of women seeking entry to Congregational ministry in that other 'gentlemen's club' the Church. It was easier for college authorities to plead a lack of women's toilets than to acknowledge any reservations they had about the challenge and change represented by the prospect of women students in an all-male institution. The latent fear that women might prove themselves every bit as capable as the men, or even better, could thus be safely avoided.

In common with women entering other new forms of employment in the first half of the twentieth century, those women who felt called to ordained ministry in the Congregational Church had to look for institutional space in which to manoeuvre. They sought out places in the Church where they were not constantly encountering the equivalent of 'Members Only' notices on the door. Constance Todd married the day after her ordination, and went to a poorly paid ministry in the East End alongside her husband, Claud Coltman. Mary Collins, Muriel Paulden, Margaret Hardy and Edith Pyke Lees who were all in pastoral charge during the 1920s also chose inner city ministry, perhaps because they were the only candidates willing to look at churches offering low salaries and bad housing. There were advantages to being on the edges of the institutional Church, however, for the margins give one room within which to move. Other women sought greater freedom within the Church through work in what was termed the 'mission field', many of them returning to Britain after the Second World War to seek the ordination which it had not been possible for them to receive before they went to work abroad. The search for space in which to operate more independently as a woman was not unique to those women who entered ministry. An 1893 publication on 'Ladies at work' reassured those considering a career in medicine overseas that: 'In our eastern colonies there is an illimitable opening for the lady-doctor. She need have no fear that she is encroaching on the rights of the sterner sex. It is a recognised fact that medical aid to the women of India can only be given through women'.[49]

Another pattern, shared by ordained ministry and those other professions opening up to women in the early twentieth century, was the predominance of well-educated, economically independent, women among the first pioneers. It was only after the Second World War that women ministerial candidates with fewer educational qualifications and from working class backgrounds also began to receive a welcome in the CUEW. A number of women were drawn into ordained ministry as widows, in succession to their husbands, and at the invitation of the local congregation concerned. The pattern of succeeding a husband in a role also happened when some of the first generation of women MPs were elected to succeed a husband in his parliamentary seat, either because of his death or his elevation to the House of Lords. Introduction to a woman's qualities through the initial medium of her husband was a safe way to discover the gifts of leadership she might have, and this gave the reassurance that she might do the job just as well as he did.

A different aspect of the self-sacrificial nature of women's ministry was represented by the number of women who trained as ministers in their own right and went on to marry ministers. There is no way of estimating how much these women contributed to the Church through full time, voluntary ministry or by working full time alongside their husbands yet claiming only one stipend. In the words of the familiar supermarket promotional deal, 'two for the price of one' is always attractive, and the Church has never been averse to 'buying one and getting one free'. Responses to this study project from retired women ministers demonstrate that ministerial couples were receiving a single stipend between them well into the 1960s. Recently the picture has changed, as marriages between ministers have become more common, and the widely held assumption that women will work for nothing or for reduced pay has been challenged and reassessed.

Some patterns rest on anecdote or suspicion rather than hard evidence and are very hard to substantiate. For instance, when an all-male committee first begins to have women members, one of these may well find herself appointed secretary. By this method she is given a position of apparent authority but may be confined to taking notes of what others say, so being effectively prevented from speaking a great deal herself.

A pattern of negative response to women in leadership, particularly those who seem forthright and confident, emerged in some quarters in the latter stages of the twentieth century and has undoubtedly had an effect on women in the Church. It is ironic that this reaction against women's authority should have been caused by one of the most visibly successful and powerful women of late twentieth century British society, Baroness Thatcher. Some phrases have entered into popular vocabulary like the 'Curse of the Mummy', a phrase coined to describe the continuing influence of Margaret Thatcher on the Conservative party, or 'being handbagged' as a description of receiving a firm response from a woman on any matter. Any woman who knows her own mind and expresses it, particularly if she has a well-modulated voice and smart suit, is in danger of the accusation she is behaving like Margaret Thatcher. As women ministers become more numerous, and female leadership more common in all parts of Church life, the significance of this reaction against feminism needs to be watched. The writer of a detailed critical study of Margaret Thatcher's way of handling an interview concluded:

> In being powerful, MT projects a style of womanhood which is essentially patriarchal, and which reproduces patriarchal society in the process of appearing to break through it. Paradoxically, then, what looks like a gain for women is a defeat for feminism. Similar things could be said about the limits within which women are advancing into relatively more powerful positions in industry, the professions, the police, and so forth.[50]

The Daughters of Dissent project is about telling forgotten stories of women but it is more than that. It also seeks to address the reasons why women's stories have been lost or undervalued and suggest how this may be changed. Simply to focus on the recovery of lost narratives would not be enough to counteract the backlash against feminism that has been taking place throughout society in recent years. In a 1970s article American feminist writer Sheila Collins outlined how new possibilities emerge as women tell their stories:

> In the process of collective storytelling, we begin to see patterns: networks of oppression connecting women in Harlan, Kentucky, with women in Altoona, Pennsylvania, and upstate New York. If we go far enough, we unravel the skein that leads us back to our great grandmothers, across the country to women in Chicago and on the Cheyenne Indian reservation in Wyoming, to women in the Bantustans of South Africa and women in the countrysides of Puerto Rico and Chile. We begin to ask ourselves: Why these patterns of defeat? Why, after a century of struggle, is our land more devastated than ever; why after the advent of birth control and women's liberation are more thirteen-, fourteen- and fifteen-year-olds having babies than ever before, and why are women in Puerto Rico, New York, on Indian Reservations, and in Appalachia being sterilized in large numbers? Why are women, as a group, losing ground according to every socioeconomic indicator available? [51]

For Collins, the value of asking such painful questions lay in the way it helped women to identify with the systematic repression of the majority of the earth's people. In telling and retelling women's stories of struggle, Collins believed the patterns of steadfastness, salvation and liberation contained within them would gradually emerge, allowing contemporary women of all races and outlooks to reconnect with the traditions buried in their own folk history. Daughters of Dissent seeks to become part of this process of uncovering, re-telling and hence of liberating. Stories of resistance and the challenging of obstacles are retrieved not as an end in themselves, or simply in order to identify patterns from '*her*story', but in order to construct strategies for a better, more tolerant, self-critical, 'equal opportunity' Church in the future.

Chapter 12

Rethinking Gender and the Church[1]

I am very excited by the Daughters of Dissent project and very pleased to have been asked to take a small part within it. So much of the public debate about the place of women within the Church over recent years has been conducted within the rhetoric of other traditions – it is good that we are finding and using again our own distinctive voices.

But having said that, I want to tell a story set in an Anglican church. We once held our annual Elders' Day at the home of an elder who lives in a small village on the edge of Oxford. We wandered at lunch time into the tiny and ancient parish church, one of the oldest in the city. I knew already that the priest there was against the ordination of women, but I discovered something even more extraordinary. Inside the pulpit, visible only to the preacher and hidden from the congregation is a relief representation of a woman saint. It is a wonderful piece of art, the work of the well known artist Eric Gill. What was so striking, and what some of the male elders could not help commenting upon, was the shape of the saint. She is portrayed in this hidden space, with all the delicious curves of a sensuous woman. Such blatant and powerfully female sexuality could not, it seems, be displayed to the congregation, though she could keep the preacher company in the pulpit. Women must be hidden, for safety's sake. Some representations of women are not suitable for church. Beside the debate about women's access to ministry or priesthood, this legend seems more far-reaching, powerful and terrifying.

I am sure it is obvious to all of us now that the question about the ordination of women is only a small part of a much greater and very complex set of issues amd challenges, I would go so far as to say that it is possible to ordain women to the Ministry of Word and Sacrament and change the Church hardly at all. This may well turn out to have been our experience within the Dissenting tradition and if we leave it there then we have failed. However much we may applaud and celebrate the wonderful, courageous and exceptional women who have fought these particular battles for ordination, even apparently major victories reveal how much remains to be done. We need nothing less than a new awareness of and engagement with the whole question of gender. The ordination of women seems a tiny part of this.

When I was actively engaged in Labour politics in Salford in the mid 1980s, I was struck by the powerful parallels between the traditions of Socialism and the traditions of Dissent. Both traditions had loud public discourses about women's rights and liberation. Both sets of institutions proclaimed themselves as front runners in the changing face of gender politics. However, when I went to Labour party meetings (in what was a very 'old Labour' kind of ward), all the talk was about supporting 'the lads' on strike, I found myself one of very few women present and the whole culture of discussion, decision making, leadership and even socialising was profoundly macho and patriarchal. It was hard indeed to see how the rhetoric of equality related to the lived reality. Equally, I was learning that, despite the noble traditions of Dissent in relation to women, my own church culture was decidedly patriarchal. The role models the church offered me as a minister were 'mighty men of God' – admirable, strong, powerful, stirring orators and sometimes politically ruthless – and indisputably men. It seemed to me that the ideal human being of Nonconformist culture was decidedly more macho, with less room for variety, than in some other Christian traditions which seemed, on the face of it, to offer women no access to leadership or ministry. It struck me that there was little real point in ordaining a few women if the lived cuoture of the Church understood gender in such a way, if 'male' was to remain normative and women were to be understood still as alien, derivative and other. The gender politics of straightforward 'equal rights' was just not strong enough to break the old ways of a patriarchal church.

Paul famously declared that 'in Christ there is neither male nor female'. But who was he kidding? If we think about it only for a moment, we can recognise how very fundamental to each of us is the fact that we are one gender or another. It is not (or rarely) a matter of no consequence. Most of us would find it deeply disturbing to find our gender 'wrongly' acknowledged or mistaken. And those who wish to who feel compelled to live their gender in unorthodox ways often find themselves abused or misunderstood. The daughter of a friend of mine decided to become a 'boy' when the family moved house. She cut her hair short, wore trousers and called herself by a boy's name. The girls at school teased her and told her to use the other toilets. My friend is largely unperturbed by her daughter's gender-making, but wants life to be sweet for her nonetheless. Hayley, a transexual character in the popular TV drama Coronation Street, has conveyed some of the pathos and agony of feeling yourself the wrong gender and her story demonstrates the anxiety and fascination this subject creates. Even Enid Blyton's Famous Five enact for us some of the negotiations of gender as girl readers decide whether they are more Anne or George. In or out of Christ, gender issues cannot simply be dismissed. They are fundamental to our selves.

The Church has not taken seriously the many questions about gender which our secular culture is embracing and facing. We run into complex debates about sexuality, but leave gender largely un-thought within the Church. It is time to begin to reflect upon our assumptions, to question and assess the Church's role in shaping gender and to ask wha the future might look like. The changing nature of the relationships between women and men is a striking feature of our culture. What can we say as Christians, or more particularly as Daughters of Dissent? We might find that the time is ripe to dissent from some ways of being daughter, and to create daugherhood, sisterhood or womanhood new.

Some people in the Church will argue that gender goes much less deep than humanity, that women and men have a shared fundamental human nature. This view goes with a liberal, equal rights agenda which had characterised the mainstream of recent Dissent. Others in the Church will emphasize the differences between men and women, arguing either that such differences are innate or essential or that they are socially constructed. Conservative evangelicals and radical feminists may thus find themselves in an odd alliance, because they both believe that gender makes more of a difference than liberal feminists do. These differences illustrate the enormous variety of approach and understanding. Where do we stand?

I belong among those who argue that gender (and even sexuality) are not fixed, given and innate entities. There are not traits or characteristics that are inevitably and eternally 'feminine' or 'masculine'. I want to resist those who say that the genders are complementary – a judgement which always seems to leave women in the secondary place. But equally, it is not all simply 'in the mind' – we do not have anything as simple as a free choice about how we live out our gender (as my friend's child has discovered). We are all born into a culture in which gender is already constructed in particular ways and even as we learn to speak we too are constructed and made. Even our most apparently fundamental experiences – childbirth, sex, illness and death – come to us already mediated through the signs and narratives of our culture. However, it is not true either that we are straighforwardly determined. There is enough variety amongst us to demonstrate that! More than this, we are not only observers of gender, but also its creators. We are constrained, but we may also be active, and gender as an expression of culture is constantly being fought over and re-made. There is room for negotiation, for subversion and for critique. The creation of gender is incomplete. Our personhood is coming into being, but never arrives.

The process of the creation of gender is something in which the Church has already played a significant role. All the signals in the small church in Oxford tell us something of how some traditions of Christianity are creating gender. There are many ways in which our own traditions have engaged in this too. Our understandings of marriage, of the family, of sainthood and discipleship, of the sexual division of labour, of the relationships between spirit and body, reason and feeling – have all contributed to the creation of gender as we have known and experienced it. The question is what we will do in the future. How will our Christian faith participate in the creation of gendered identity in the new millennium? We have some profound storied and resources amongst our traditions and we have our imaginations, our creativity and the guiding of the Holy Spirit. We have the opportunity to use these gifts to encourage values, relationships and ways of speaking that will help us to create a more 'gender inclusive' community.

Ordaining women has been a significant step on the journey, but I suggest that the true significance of the ordination of women can only be judged by its effect on the lives and spirit of *all* women. If nothing else is done, beyond ordaining some exceptional women, women in the Church and women in general may still be left struggling, oppressed and afraid. Unless we are brave enough to think more radically about gender, the fathers will still rule, gender will still be made according to unjust laws and women will still suffer violence and poverty. A much larger task awaits the Daughters of Dissent.

Appendix

Two Responses to the Daughters of Dissent Project
Presented at a Day Conference at Mansfield College
in September 1998 (with later additions)

John Humphreys

My first response is one of gratitude for the privilege of sharing in the Daughters of Dissent conference and of having been given the opportunity of reading the presentations beforehand. The very fact of this conference is an indication of the distance that is yet to be travelled.

Part of the way I approach what I have read comes from my background as one of those people from Wales, about which the Encyclopaedia Britannica used to say, 'see England'. One of the most formative times of my preparation for ministry was in the teaching of Katherine Doob Sakenfeld, particularly in a course she taught entitled 'Teaching the Bible as Liberating Word'. She encouraged the use of mind and heart, no mean achievement in the heady atmosphere of academic discipline. I remember the way she drew from each of us the freedom to talk about how we pictured God. For one assignment she grouped her class. Four of us were asked to work together on Miriam's Song from Exodus. We were from Texas, the Philippines, Singapore and Britain. We were to read Miriam's Song together over a number of weeks, bringing to it our particular histories and the history of our nations. Particularly remembering the background and foreground of colonialism and imperialism. How could these four people read Miriam's Song together? The Song is about the horse and rider being drowned in the sea. How could the oppressors, the dominant ones and the oppressed, the colonised, read scripture together? Who is victim?

The overall feeling that I have is one of being overwhelmed by some of the material presented and of being stunned again by how slow we humans are in expressing the Gospel. Attempts at self justification do immense damage to individuals and communities. The danger of saying that great strides have been made is to de-humanise all those lives lived without the opportunity to receive from the 'great strides', regardless of the discussion of their greatness.

I have a question that is probably a confused question. How is it that we have allowed ourselves to entrap ourselves in world views which distract from our humanness before God? The force of self-preservation that keeps people suspicious, the failure to allow each other to express the depth of our beings, the sense of horror at one's own humanity and delight (therefore) at controlling or denying the humanity of others.

I am intrigued at the way in which Kirsty Thorpe's paper describes the ways in which patterns of reversal of control into the hands of (some) men has been repeated each time there has been the risk of too great a contribution from women. These patterns are seen in the ways in which the Bible has been handled, to make it as tidy as possible for particular minds and people with particular positions in society. A study of material from the post-exilic period, a period wrongly called the restoration, reveals how eclectic was the range of people offering insights into the nature of God and the future of his people. There was a lively interaction between identities which are too easily glossed over because of our need to show how all these fit in with a neat image of Jesus. The Bible is revelatory in its characteristic inability merely to tell one story – look at the many strands in Acts.

We do not explore what makes us tick as human beings. Ruth Clarke will remember that when the Church in Wales was debating whether women could be priested it was pretty easy to look at some of the speakers and know where they were coming from. For all the concentration on sex, there is still so little exploration of sexual and gender identity. Fear of the (unacknowledged) forces inside lead to oppression of those forces rightly or wrongly pweceived in others. There is a desperate need to explore how to escape the 'male dominated clerical structures'. Though not phrased in quite that way several attempts in some of our District Councils have so easily slipped back to the familiar.

Not only is there the historical link that Kirsty Thorpe identifies between women's ministry and low pay, there is also the present link between women's ministry and the 'less desirable situation' (socially/culturally/hierarchically).

I sense that one of the key factors about the Church as an institution that prevents its growth especially amongst teenagers and those in their twenties, thirties and even forties is the way the institution inhibits open dialogue and an acceptance of the particularity of the individual. Elaine Kaye's paper speaks of the way that Dissent became institutionalised; this need to be explored further. Why does the institution favour male dominance? What is it about maleness that prefers control to honesty, monochromism to harmony? How does this tie in with the preoccupation in past centuries with witch hunts and how is this manifested in the present?

To ignore the history of women is to make anonymous, to disenfranchise. It is only over the last twenty years or so that the history of Wales has been taught in Welsh schools; note the swing in the results of the referendums over that same period. Keith Whitelam's book, *The Invention of Ancient Israel: The Silencing of Palestinian History* (London: Routledge, 1996) is a powerful review of how the major Old Testament scholars of Europe and north America of the last 50 years or so, whilst claiming to study the history of Israel, have done so primarily from the view point of the history of the 'western' faith, have in fact de-historicised the Palestinians. They speak of Palestinian land and artefacts but never of Palestinian people.

Language. An Education Commission of three men in the middle of the nineteenth century visited Wales and declared our people would never be civilised so long as we persisted with the Welsh language. A different language from the dominant (imported) language still threatens, and certainly becomes an excuse for ministers not coming to work in the basically English speaking United Reformed Church in Wales!

How carelessly we read the Bible and hear from it cheap confirmation. How exciting when we can listen to others reading it from very different perspectives. The book of Esther does not mention God. It has been one of the 'unimportant' books until recently! From their context South American liberation theologians are recognising in Esther one who liberated herself by liberating others. She remembered her roots, she remembered her true vocation and she remembered her unmentioned God. Kirsten Nielsen introduces her commentary on Ruth[1] with a fascinating discussion on the inter-textual context of particular texts, Ruth belonging 'within an intertextuality of women's stories that deal with infertility and the triumph over it' (p. 13).

Within our present context where the importance of 'my rightness' dominates, the examination of language and history are slow but essential tools for liberating ourselves from the cleft-sticks of the present. This process is not primarily cerebral, nor in fact are we! The church needs the untold story, the unmeasured statistic, the careless language brought into the open.

David Thompson

I was delighted to be invited today; and I emphasise that because you may not respond with equal equanimity to everything that I am going to say. I want to comment first about some underlying principles and issues, then to pick up some of the more detailed points raised in the three papers that we have heard and finally to say something about the Churches of Christ perspective in relation to this discussion.

One of the things that struck me immediately about this project was to ask, What is the agenda, the framework of interpretation? There are various frameworks that can be applied to such studies; themes of oppression and marginalisation are not the only themes which can be pursued, nor need they necessarily be the dominant ones. I am rather sceptical about much of post modernist work and the emphasis on rhetoric, discourse etc. My own view is that it has probably got a shelf life about as long as existentialism had in the 1960s. Nevertheless it does contain some useful insights.

My first introduction to the 'hermeneutics of suspicion' reminded me of the way I had been taught to look at historical texts as a student thirty years ago. No one can assume that the text says everything, because history is constructed out of very partial records. I always tell my medieval history colleagues that they are lucky, because they have all the documents that they can ever need to examine. For me, as a modern historian, there are more documents than I shall ever have time to look at in the whole of my life. This raises very different critical questions, especially methodological questions, about the selection of material. One must always be critical of sources and I heartily endorse the comment that the more versions of the story we have the better. That is one of the advantages of having four gospels and two different source texts within the Pentateuch and the historical books of the Old Testament.

Alarm bells always ring in my mind when people talk about conspiracy theories. Although I love detective stories very much (which may be one reason why I am a historian), I always take the view as a historian that if there is a choice between conspiracy and cock up, cock up is the more likely. It is very easy to lapse into conspiratorial mode in discussing some of these topics and it is not always helpful.

I still think that the marginalisation of working class stories in the Church is more significant than the marginalisation of women's stories. It tells us something about the nature of the Church and its structures, about very many people whose voices in the Church have never been heard and always need to be heard. I can illustrate that with one example from my doctoral work on the churches in Leicestershire. Although it was very difficult to get detailed evidence about membership in churches in the mid-nineteenth century, there were one or two churches with fairly complete membership registers, which I hoped to use for social analysis. This proved to be impossible because more than half the people on those lists were women. If they had an occupation it was not recorded and certainly not traceable. Therefore it was impossible to do any kind of social analysis except one which derived from the occupation of those to whom they were married, who were usually not members.

This is one of the practical reasons why when writing history it is often very difficult to write more than one or two sentences about women; the kind of source material available beyond the oral record is very limited. There is more than we are often aware of, and it is necessary to have the antennae to see that; but it is limited. This is why the oral history projects which have mushroomed since the 1960s are so important; but they only tell us so much.

In relation to the details of the main papers one point that emerges most clearly from this project is our tendency still to write Church history predominantly in terms of ministers. Local church histories are usually organised according to the ministries of successive individuals. In vacancies normally nothing happens. If the church has no ministers then it usually has no history - literally. Anglican or Roman Catholic history nationally can be written in terms of bishops, which is manageable. The Free Churches do not have bishops, so it is necessary to select from the multitude of ministers when writing Free Church or Church of Scotland history. What tends to happen is that historians concentrate on the Moderators, or the Chairmen of the Congregational Union, or the princes of preachers; and often these are the same people.

As for questions of women's ministry, consider the significance of Quaker women, such as Sarah Grubb in the early nineteenth century, gradually battering their way into the Men's Yearly Meeting. In 1896 it was agreed that the most important issues should be discussed at a joint session of the Men's and Women's Yearly Meetings. The recognition given to women ministers by the Society of Friends suggests that it may have been easier to make progress on the fundamental issues of equality where the formal distinction between ministers and people was differently articulated.[2] Twentieth century Quakers eliminated the distinction between ministers and lay from their tradition.

Another issue raised from the earliest years was that of low pay among Bible Christian ministers. That says something about the low standing of the ministry as a whole, as well as about the social composition of the Bible Christians, relative to some other churches. It is very interesting to compare ministers' salaries in the nineteenth century. The arrival of national, as opposed to local, pay scales since the formation of the United Reformed Church has made quite a difference to the way people are treated. Churches of Christ were never a wealthy church with significant remuneration. It is also interesting that in the early twentieth century, as ordination became regarded as more significant, so the significance of ordaining a woman also increased. The to-ing and fro-ing in relation to recognition of Constance Coltman's ordination was related to the diffuse nature of Congregational ministry and questions of national as distinct from local recognition. The issue was only partly, if at all, theological.

Thirdly, I turn to the Churches of Christ perspective. In the nineteenth century they were dominated by biblical literalism, resulting from their belief in the restoration of New Testament Christianity. David King, who dominated the movement in the second half of the nineteenth century, acknowledged that the New Testament provided evidence for deaconesses; hence it was appropriate, almost necessary, for churches to ordain them. Similarly elders had to be men, because the New Testament said that they should be the husband of one wife, and there ought to be a ministry of widows because that was also in the New Testament. King believed that holy women were needed more than anything else in the large churches he knew. [3]

In 1880 (rather more than ten years before a similar meeting at the Congregational Union assembly) nine women at the Annual Meeting in Huddersfield inaugurated a separate Sisters' Conference to discuss the work of women in the churches. The secretary, Sarah Black, was daughter of James Wallis, an original founder of Churches of Christ in Great Britain. Mrs Louise King, wife of David King, presided and Mrs G Y Tickle, wife of the editor of the *Christian Advocate*, was appointed Corresponding Secretary to gather and publicise information from the churches on what their women were doing.[4]

Over the next decade the Sisters' Meetings repeatedly lamented the fact that so few churches sent in reports of what they were doing and in 1885 it was noted that what was reported represented sisters of less than one tenth of the churches in the co-operation.[5] The main work done by women was amongst women so it did not raise the possibility of them taking leadership roles over men. In 1881, at the Sisters Conference in Manchester, Louise King acknowledged the latent power in the churches represented by women, but cautioned: 'We must move gently, engage in no Utopian schemes, nor wait for great occasions, but just lay hold of the work that lies nearest to us, no matter how simple or how humble.' She added that 'woman's star is now somewhat in the ascendant' and listed the many public positions women now held for which they had previously been regarded as incompetent, concluding with a list of eight women in the primitive churches.

Other topics discussed at Sisters' Conference were the salvation of children (1882), cultivating a taste for pure literature among the young (1883), how sisters could attend Sunday morning service without detracting from the comfort of the bread-winner, on what is often the only day which he can entirely spend with his family (1884), the duties, rights and privileges of Christian women, and marrying out of the Church (1885) and correspondence between senior sisters and younger women seeking situations with a Churches of Christ nearby (1888).[6] The Sisters' Conferences promoted a confined view of women's work, even though their language could sound more radical. Sometimes they met opposition, as at Leicester in 1882, when there was an attack on the Sisters' Conference, which was firmly deplored by G Y Tickle.[7]

At the 1889 Conference the young evangelist Sydney Black denounced the view that women should take no public part in the life of the Church, or should only work with women, or only preach to the unconverted but not in the Church.[8] Only two out of seven later speakers supported his position. David King thought that women's share in ministry in the New Testament did not prove that they were public speakers. For several months the Churches' two periodicals were filled with comment, more critical than supportive, but Black defended his position. King reprinted a piece from the American *Christian Quarterly Review* in the *Ecclesiastical Observer* on why Paul's command that women should remain silent was of general rather than particular application.[9] Alexander Brown, who had written a hostile review of the paper in the October *Christian Advocate*, wrote an article in December about women in the New Testament. Women should not speak in church, teach men and or have the same liberty in prayer as men. However he advocated sisters' meetings, women's evangelistic meetings, and systematic visitation of women by women, very much as the Sisters' Conference had been advocating for a decade.[10]

While some of the more conservative spirits still lived, perhaps Louise King's approach was more likely to make progress than Black's directness. She out-lived her husband from 1894 until her death in 1913, editing his biography as well as the magazine, *The Old Paths*, which he had edited for many years. By the time of her death, there had been further changes in the position of women. In 1903 Miss L K Dawson was the first woman to be elected to a standing committee, the General Sunday School Committee; a second followed in 1906. In 1910 the size of the Foreign Missions Committee was increased by two so that two women could be elected.[11] When the Temperance and Social Questions Committee became a full committee of the Conference in 1920, a woman was elected, and by 1922 there were four. By contrast the Sisters' Committee did not become a full committee of the Conference until 1937. In 1912 Mrs Cranfield was employed as a Home Missions Sister, working among women in Glasgow. [12] Their numbers grew during the First World War.

I would like to have seen more in the project on the significance of missionaries. The first Churches of Christ women to be recognised in a quasi-ministerial role were missionaries overseas. Churches of Christ began overseas missionary work in 1892, when three missionaries went to Burma, and in 1902 the work was extended to Siam.[13] Although the work done by the women was acknowledged in the annual reports of the Foreign Missions Committee, it was clear initially that the principal work was that of the men. In 1909, however, the Annual Conference accepted the offer of Percy Pittman and his wife from Melbourne, Australia, to go to the new mission at Daltonganj in India, and it also assumed responsibility for the mission in Nyasaland.[14] In 1910 two women joined the Foreign Missions Committee. That year's report noted the special work among women being done in Siam by Mary Clark. The committee had been gratified but also embarrassed by 'the number of brethren and sisters who have offered themselves for work on foreign fields', since they lacked the funds to support their training.[15]

The first reference to single women missionaries was in 1911, when Miss Allan came to Daltonganj at her own expense from South Australia to assist Mrs Pittman, particularly in zenana work (with secluded high caste women). Mary Bannister, a trained nurse from Burnley who had been waiting three years for an opening overseas, went to Nyasaland in 1912. In the same year Esther Halliday began work in the schools in Siam, thereby releasing Mary Clark for other women's work.[16] Significantly the 1913 Foreign Missions Report stated, 'the Missions over the Seas, where our brothers and sisters are holding forth the word of life, have during the past year shown development and growth'. Esther Halliday was now in charge of the Girls School, and Mary Bannister was said to be as enthusiastic and hard-working as ever, doing much needed dispensary work and having a helpful influence among the women.[17]

Mary Bannister and Esther Halliday illustrate the change that had subtly taken place in Churches of Christ missionary work, not least because their backgrounds were so different. Mary Bannister, an orphan, was baptised in March 1893 in Burnley Church of Christ. Inspired a decade later by the preaching of Percy Clark, on furlough from Siam, she offered herself for missionary work and served in Glasgow before arriving in Nyasaland nine years on. Her work was interrupted by the Government's suspension of the mission in 1915, but she argued strongly for the Churches of Christ to return. When this happened in 1928, she took charge of the girls school at the Gowa mission. Forced to retire in 1935 because of ill health, she returned to England, and died in July 1940. 'Mary gave her life for Africa', wrote a former colleague, Henry Philpott, Secretary of the Missionary Committee.[18]

Esther Halliday was born in 1891, the elder daughter of Dr Robert Halliday one of the first missionaries to Burma. In 1909 she went to Siam, as a trained teacher, serving the mission school in Nakon Pathom for the rest of her career and taking charge of it from 1920. It was estimated that 1,300 students went through the school while she was in charge. During the Second World War she was interned by the Japanese. She retired in 1952 and returned to Scotland. Annual Conference passed a resolution of appreciation for her work over 42 years in 1953. She was loved as a teacher, as a colleague, and for her good works as an ambassador of Christ. Her un-selfseeking spirit won her the affection of both the Siamese and Chinese people. Esther Halliday died in March 1978,[19] after 25 years in retirement, by which time the profile of the work in Thailand was very much lower because it had been handed over to the Disciples of Christ in the USA.

Once there were single women missionaries the Reports of the Missionary Committee gave more space to the work of the missionary wives. They were always expected to have skills, usually medical, which would be of use in missionary work. Mary Clark and her husband Percy worked in Thailand until 1952 and then retired there. She was born in 1880, the daughter of a successful Birmingham businessman, and met Percy Clark in 1899 when he came to Birmingham to train for missionary work. In 1905 she left England to marry him and they served at Nakon Pathom, the centre of British Churches of Christ missionary work in Siam. Mary did medical, educational and evangelistic work, using her midwifery skills to lecture to nurses in training in Bangkok during the First World War. Her command of the Thai language was a great asset, and for many years she travelled long distances by pony or bullock cart to be the midwife for many complicated pregnancies. In 1931 she wrote Stories from Pagoda Land, published by the Foreign Missions Committee. Its frontispiece is a picture of her and her helpers, all women.[20] A second book, Nothing is Impossible, describes the history of the mission during the Second World War and epitomises her outlook. After her death Henry Philpott wrote that she had been referred to 'as somewhat of a legend among us'; and added, 'Maybe, but she lives in the hearts of very many, especially the women who, through her, were led to a living Lord and to true peace'.[21]

Significantly all the Churches of Christ women missionaries were from accepted female occupations, such as nurses or teachers. There was no woman doctor among them, even though several in effect performed the work of doctors in the mission situation. As missionary activity declined in the mid twentieth century this focused the issue of women's place in the churches in Britain much more sharply than before. I remember a friend of mine going out as a Churches of Christ missionary in the early 1960s, who said to me, 'Of course the reason I am going now is that I can't get ordained at home'. I was surprised and baffled at the time; and I think this project needs to take account of that kind of situation.

Footnotes

Introduction

1   *The Christian Commonwealth*, 18 September 1917.

2   Women's Research Project, by Keran Olm-Stoelting, published by the United Reformed Church, Summer 1992.

3   Elaine Kaye: 'Constance Coltman: A Forgotten Pioneer' in *The Journal of the United Reformed Church History Society* IV/2 (1988).

4   The Re-formed Association of the Churches of Christ united with the United Reformed Church in 1981.

5   The Congregational Union of Scotland joined with the United Reformed Church to form a new church in 2000.

Chapter 1

1   Constance Whitehorn, *Women's Share in the Life and Work of the Church with Special Reference to English Presbyterianism* (London: Presbyterian Historical Society of England, 1958), p. 16.

2   A significant number of Congregational churches elected to remain outside the United Reformed Church; most of them are now part of the Congregational Federation. They too inherit the Congregational tradition.

3   See K Thomas, 'Women in the Civil War Sects' in *Past and Present* No 13, April 1958, pp. 42-62, and the chapter on 'Women in Seventeenth Century Baptist Churches' in B R White, *The English Baptists of the Seventeenth Century* (Didcot: Baptist Historical Society, 2nd edn., 1996). For the active involvement of women in earlier separatist groups see R Greaves, 'The Role of Women in Early English Nonconformity' in *Church History* 52 (1983), pp. 299-311.

4   See *DNB: Missing Persons*.

5   Jane Addams, Katharine Lee Bates, Harriet Beecher Stowe and Julia Clifford Lathrop.

6   Clive D Field, 'Adam and Eve: Gender in the English Free Church Constituency' in *Journal of Ecclesiastical History* 44 (January 1993), pp. 63-79.

7   See Marjorie Reeves, *Pursuing the Muses: Female Education and Nonconformist Culture 1700-1900* (London: Leicester University Press, 1997).

8   See the chapter on 'The Theology of Subordination' in Sean Gill, *Women and the Church of England* (London: SPCK, 1994).

9   For recent biographies of the Countess of Huntingdon, see Edwin Welch, *Spiritual Pilgrim: A Re-assessment of the Life of the Countess of Huntingdon*, (Cardiff: University of Wales Press, 1995), and Faith Cook, *Selina, Countess of Huntingdon*, (Edinburgh: Banner of Truth Trust, 2001).

10 See Anne Summers, 'Common sense about separate spheres' in *Female Lives, Moral States* (Newbury: Threshold Press, 2000).

11 The reluctance to limit the hours of working class women in factories reveals that these attitudes were not extended to all sections of society.

12 Sarah Ellis, *Daughters of England* (London: Fisher, Son & Co, 1842), p. 3. Her intended readership presumably included the social groups to be found in urban Congregational churches in the south of England.

13 J A James, *Female Piety: Or the Young Woman's Friend and Guide Through Life to Immortality* (London: Hamilton, Adams & Co, 1852), p. 55.

14 James, p. 17.

15 James, p. 18.

16 James, p. 62.

17 Details of these bazaars are preserved in the Northern College Archive in the John Rylands University Library, Manchester, Box R/32.

18 See Brian Harrison, *Drink and the Victorians: The Temperance Question in England 1815-72* (London: Faber and Faber, 1971).

19 James Sherman, *The Pastor's Wife: A Memoir of Mrs Sherman of Surrey Chapel* (London: Charles Gilpin, 1848).

20 The 1851 Census was interpreted as revealing a surplus of 1,129,000 women over men within the age range 20 and 42, in England and Wales. The disparity in numbers actually increased towards the end of the century.

21 See Sean Gill, *Women and the Church of England* (London: SPCK, 1994) for an account of these institutions.

22 See Crystal Harrison, *History of Ebley Chapel* (Stroud: privately printed, 1997). The chapel was founded as a church of the Countess of Huntingdon's Connexion, but had some affiliation with other Congregational churches.

23 See Elaine Kaye, 'Benjamin Parsons of Ebley Chapel', in JURCHS VI/9 (2001) pp. 673-681.

24 The second edition in 1850 was entitled *Education, the Natural Want and Birthright of Every Human Being*; there were at least two further editions.

25 *The Mental and Moral Dignity of Woman* (London: John Snow, 1842), p. 19.

26 John Sibree (1795-1877) was minister at Vicar Lane, Coventry 1820-58. See *Congregational Year Book 1878*, pp. 350-52.

27 Recent biographies of George Eliot include Rosemary Ashton, *George Eliot: A Life* (London: Hamish Hamilton, 1996) and Kathryn Hughes, *George Eliot: The Last Victorian* (London: Fourth Estate, 1998).

28 See Pam Hirsch, *Barbara Leigh Smith Bodichon*, (London: Pimlico, 1999).

29 The bill was presented to Parliament in 1857 but failed to become law. Two Married Women's Property Acts were however passed in 1870 and 1882.

30 See Kathryn Gleadle, *The Early Feminists: Radical Unitarians and the Emergence of the Women's Rights Movement 1831-51* (Basingstoke: Macmillan, 1995) for a discussion of the contribution of women Unitarians to the women's rights movement.

31 See Ray Strachey, *The Cause* (London: Bell & Sons, 1928), p. 32.

32 See Richard Symonds, *Inside the Citadel: Men and the Emancipation of Women 1850-1920* (Basingstoke: Macmillan, 1999).

33 The management of Queen's was entirely in the hands of men until the end of the century, while that of Bedford was in the hands of both men and women from the beginning. See Elaine Kaye, *History of Queen's College, London* (London: Chatto and Windus, 1972), and Margaret Tuke, *A History of Bedford College for Women 1849-1937* (London: Oxford University Press, 1939).

34 Women were finally admitted to degrees in Oxford in 1920.

35 See Clyde Binfield, *Belmont's Portias: Victorian Nonconformists and Middle-class Education for Girls* (London: Friends of Dr Williams's Library,1981).

36 Her daughter, Mrs Pye Smith, and granddaughter, Miss Pye Smith, were both closely connected with the school in succeeding years.

37 See E Pike and C E Curryer, *The Story of Walthamstow Hall* (Sevenoaks: Longmore Press, 1973).

38 The first American college offering higher education to women was Oberlin, founded in the 1830s.

39 Entry for 13 February 1871, Minutes of the Milton Mount College Management Committee, Dr Williams's Library.

40 Little is known of her early life and background, except that she was born in London, and spent her early adult life teaching in private schools in London and in Great Malvern.

41 For the history of the school, see Hilda Harwood, *The History of Milton Mount College* (London: Independent Press, 1959). The early minute books at Dr Williams's Library reveal some of the difficulties which arose between the headmistress and the founder, William Guest.

42 In a paper read to the Oxford Conference of the Headmistresses' Association in 1886 Selina Hadland listed eight categories of employment suitable for women apart from teaching – invention, administration, medical, literary, artistic, clerical, domestic and commercial pursuits – adding, 'Time fails me to refer to Bible women or missionaries, to Authors or Lecturers, or to the growing demand for women's work in the colonies.'

43 See *Congregational Year Book 1893*, p. 18.

44 The school closed in 1965. See Binfield, *Belmont's Portias*.

45 Thomas Binney, 'Middle-Class Female Education', Dr Williams's Library 3079 A.10 (14).

46 See Richard Symonds, pp. 125-130.

47 For a detailed account of the first women missionaries of the LMS see Rosemary Seton, '"Open Doors for Female Labourers": Women Candidates of the London Missionary Society 1875-1914' in R A Bickers and R Seton (ed), *Missionary Encounters: Sources and Issues* (Richmond: Curzon Press, 1996). See also F Bowie, D Kirkwood and S Ardener, *Women and Missions: Past and Present* (Oxford: Berg, 1993) and Rhonda Anne Semple, *Missionary Women: Gender, Professionalism and the Victorian Idea of Christian Mission* (Woodbridge: Boydell Press, 2003).

48 See Cecil Northcott, *Glorious Company: 150 Years Life and Work of the London Missionary Society 1795-1945* (London: Livingstone Press, 1945), p. 37.

49 Norman Goodall, *A History of the London Missionary Society 1895-1945* (London: Oxford University Press, 1954), p. 13.

50 Northcott, p. 36.

51 See Valentine Cunningham, 'God and Nature Intended You for a Missionary's Wife: Mary Hill, Jane Eyre and Other Missionary Women in the 1840s' in Bowie, *Women and Missions*, pp. 85-105.

52 See J Sibree, *London Missionary Society: A Register of Missionaries, Deputations etc from 1796 to 1923* (London, 1923).

53 See Hugh Martin, *Fifty Years of Carey Hall 1912-62* (Birmingham: Council of Carey Hall, 1962).

54 By 1945 54 of the 345 members of the Board were women. The first woman to be elected chairman, in 1941, was Mrs Marion Chaffey.

55 See David M Thompson, *Let Sects and Parties Fall*, (Birmingham: Berean Press, 1980), pp. 94-99.

56 Catherine Maria Ricketts (b.1841) founded the Brighton YWCA and was the first woman to be appointed to any School Board in England.

57 The early officers of the WMA were always known by the names of their husbands.

58 *The Presbyterian Messenger and Missionary Record* from 1880 onwards provides reports of the WMA. The Association began its own journal, *Our Sisters in Other Lands* in 1879.

59 See Helen Barrett Montgomery, *Western Women in Eastern Lands* (New York 1910) for an account of women's missionary activity in the United States.

60 For the early history of the WMA see *Jubilee History of the Women's Missionary Association 1878-1928* (London: 1928).

61 See W H Chaloner, *Crewe Congregational Church 1841-1947* (Crewe Congregational Centenary Committee, 1947), p. 19.

62 See P Kenschaft, 'Charlotte Angas Scott' in L S Grinstein and P J Campbell, *Women of Mathematics: A Bibliographic Source Book* (New York and London: Greenwood, 1987).

63 See K L Parry (ed.), *Companion to Congregational Praise* (London: Independent Press, 1953), pp. 341-42. Hymn writing was an important and accepted contribution by women, though there were no outstanding Congregational or Presbyterian women hymn writers. Most of the hymns by Congregational women which survived into *Congregational Praise* in 1951 were originally written for Sunday School events. One of the best known hymn writers in her time was Jane Crewdson (née Fox) of Manchester.

64 Clyde Binfield, *So down to Prayers* (London: Dent, 1977), p. 222.

65 See *DNB: Missing Persons*.

66 See 'Settlement Houses: A Community Ideal for the Poor' in Martha Vicinus, *Independent Women: Work and Community for Single Women 1850-1920* (London: Virago, 1985).

67 She remained in this post for 25 years. She was the sole woman representative in her own right from England and Wales to attend the International Congregational Council in Boston in 1891.

68 The activities of the settlement are recorded in some detail in the *Mansfield House Magazine*.

69 The rule was changed in 1914. The process by which women gained a greater share in the assemblies of the Church of England is described in Brian Heeney, *The Women's Movement in the Church of England 1850-1920* (Oxford: Oxford University Press, 1988).

70 See R W Dale, *Manual of Congregational Principles* (London: Congregational Union of England and Wales, 1884), p. 173.

71 See A H Driver, *Carrs Lane Church, Birmingham 1748-1948* (Birmingham: Swan Press, 1948), p.45.

72 See Albert Peel, *These Hundred Years* (London: Congregational Union of England and Wales, 1931), p. 328.

73 Both Albert Spicer (1847-1934; he was made a baronet in 1906) and his wife, Jessie Stewart Dykes Spicer (she also died in 1934) were active in many religious organisations. They had eight daughters and three sons. Albert Spicer educated his daughters to be capable of earning their own living, but was then extremely reluctant to allow them to do so, preferring them to do voluntary work. See *Albert Spicer 1847-1934: A Man of his Time* by one of his family (London: S Marshall, 1938). His daughter Eva Dykes Spicer, who spent a year at Mansfield College, Oxford after taking a degree course at Somerville College, was a missionary with the London Missionary Society in China and Nigeria for 30 years.

74 See *Congregational Year Book 1894*, p. 35.

75 Rebecca Cheetham had also attended the Boston meetings, as a delegate in her own right.

76 Deacons (who were not ordained) in the Congregational tradition were lay people who assisted the minister in the administration and pastoral care of the local church.

77 Anon, *Trinity Congregational Church, Walthamstow* (Walthamstow: privately printed, c.1960).

78 *Free Church Suffrage Times*, June 1913.

79 In the Presbyterian tradition, and now in the United Reformed Church, an elder is a lay person

(although set apart by ordination) who assists the minister in the government and pastoral care of the local church.

80 See David M Thompson, *Let Sects and Parties Fall*, pp. 72-73.

81 Sarah Ellis, *The Daughters of England* (London: Fisher, Son & Co, 1842), p. 64.

82 V D Davis, *A History of Manchester College from its Foundation in Manchester to its Establishment in Oxford* (London: George Allen and Unwin, 1932), p. 195.

83 See A Whigham Price, *The Ladies of Castlebrae* (London: Headline, 1985).

84 Margaret Gibson died in 1920, Agnes Lewis in 1926.

85 Shaw Congregational Church reprinted 'Patchwork on Miss Betty Hall', by Frederic Platt, in 1958. See also Kathleen Hendry, *Don't Ask Me Why: Sixty Years a Woman Minister* (London: United Reformed Church, 1991), pp. 25-28.

86 Information supplied by Mrs Mary Fleming of Burnage.

87 *Transactions of the Congregational Historical Society, 1909-10*, pp. 27-8.

88 See Hilda Martindale, *From One Generation to Another* (London: Allen and Unwin, 1944) and Olive Banks, *Biographical Dictionary of British Feminists*, vol. 2 (Brighton: Wheatsheaf, 1990). Mrs Martindale's two surviving daughters each gained professional distinction, Louisa Martindale (1871-1966) as a surgeon, and Hilda Martindale (1875-1952) as a factory inspector.

89 See Symonds, pp. 130-35.

90 See Keith Gilley, 'Gertrud von Petzold – The Pioneer Woman Minister' in *Transactions of the Unitarian Historical Society* XXI/3, 1997, pp. 157-72.

91 *The Suffragette*, 19 December 1913.

92 This speech was reported in the *Free Church Suffrage Times* in November 1913.

93 See Sheila Fletcher, *Maude Royden: A Life* (Oxford: Basil Blackwell, 1989).

94 Her husband, Claud Coltman, was listed as a probationer minister of the Baptist Union until 1923, when he appeared on the roll of Congregational ministers alongside his wife. The *Baptist Handbook* for 1920 refers to his having been a student at the Midland Baptist College before entering Mansfield College.

95 General Purposes Committee Minute Book 1893-1910, entry for 7 September 1909, and Council Minute Book, entry for 12 October 1909. Congregational Library at Dr Williams's Library.

96 See Elaine Kaye, 'Constance Coltman – a forgotten pioneer' in the *Journal of the United Reformed Church History Society* IV/2 (1988), pp. 134-46, for a more detailed account. See also chapter 4, and chapter 10 for a fuller discussion of the circumstances of her ordination.

97 See J Briggs, 'She-Preachers, Widows and other Women: The Feminine Dimension in Baptist Life since 1600' in the *Baptist Quarterly* XXXI (1985), pp. 337-352, and Ruth M B Gouldbourne, *Re-inventing the Wheel: Women and Ministry in English Baptist Life* (Oxford: Whitley Publications, 1997).

Chapter 2

1 In this paper the term 'ministry' is used to denote any form of service by which Christ is made known. It is therefore not confined to ordained ministry and nor is the Daughters of Dissent project.

2 Norman Fairclough, *Language and Power* (London: Longman, 1989), p. 22.

3 The conversational analysis method of interpreting conversations concentrates on the turns taken in a conversation, and how these work, rather than on what is said.

4   Norman Fairclough, *Language and Power* (Longman: London, 1989), p. 49.

5   *'Hermeneutics of suspicion'* is a term used by Elizabeth Schüssler Fiorenza, and other feminist biblical scholars, derived from the work of Paul Ricoeur.

6   Women in Ministries Newtwork (WIMN) is an informal network open to all women who define themselves as 'ministers' in the United Reformed Church.

7   See chapter 8 for a discussion of statistics and race in the United Reformed Church.

8   *Walk my Sister: The Ordination of Women, Reformed Perspectives* (Geneva: WARC, 1993), Annex 1, p. 170.

9   'Numbers game' authors Kirsty Thorpe and Martin Smith. Thanks to Martin Smith for his work compiling the statistical tables on which the findings in this section are based.

10 David Bebbington 'Introduction' in Linda Wilson, *Constrained by Zeal, Female Spirituality among Nonconformists 1825-1875*, (Paternoster Press: Carlisle 2000), p. xiv.

11 Janet Lees: *Interpreting the Bible with People with Communication Difficulties.* Unpublished Master of Theology Thesis, The University of Natal, Pietermaritzburg, South Africa, 1997.

12 *'Hermeneutics in society'* is a postmodern idea that everything in society is open to interpretation; meaning therefore depends on the method(s) of analysis used.

13 Elizabeth Schüssler Fiorenza, *But She Said* (Boston: Beacon Press Ltd, 1992).

14 Elaine Kaye, 'One Hundred Ministers Ordained between 1917 and 1972 in England and Wales', in *The Journal of the United Reformed Church History Society*, Volume 6 No 10 July 2002.

15 Dorothea McEwan, 'The Future of Christian Feminist Theologies – As I Sense It: Musings on the Effects of Historiography and Space' in *Feminist Theology*, 1999 vol. 22, p. 79.

16 William David Ffrench born in 1881, died in 1961. His Congregational Year Book obituary in 1962 fails to mention that his daughter was an ordained minister (Congregational Year Book 1962, p. 458).

17 Minutes of the CUEW Special Committee, 30 April 1953.

18 Mr E Wightman, letter to Daughters of Dissent project.

19 'We are never alone' by Sallie Ffrench, *Congregational Monthly*, June 1968, p. 10.

20 Norman Fairclough, *Language and Power* (London: Longman, 1989), p. 102.

21 Kathleen Hendry, *Don't Ask Me Why - Sixty Years a Woman Minister,* (London: United Reformed Church, 1991).

22 Jane Shaw, 'Women, Rationality and Theology', in Daphne Hampson (ed.), *Swallowing a fishbone? Feminist Theologians Debate Christianity* (London: SPCK, 1996), p. 65.

23 A conversational analysis method like that described by E H Stokoe 'Talking about gender: the conversational construction of gender categories in academic discourse' in *Discourse and Society*, 9 (2), 1998, pp. 217-240, could be used.

24 Letter from the Revd D English in DoD Archive

25 Letter in the DoD Archive

26 From a survey of 100 former students of Girton College, Cambridge, chosen at random from each decade since 1920, reported in *Guardian Higher*, 30 June 1998.

27 From letters in the DoD Archive.

28 Nancy J Ramsay, 'Truth, Power and Love: Challenges for Clergywomen across the life span', in *'In Her Own Time'*, edited by Jeanne Stevenson-Moessner (Minneapolis: Fortress Press, 2000) p. 274.

29 Adrienne Rich is quoted by Savina J Teubal in *Ancient Sisterhood: the lost traditions of Hagar and Sarah* (Ohio University Press: Athens, Ohio 1990), p. xix.

30 Dorothea McEwan, 'The Future of Christian Feminist Theologies - As I Sense It: Musings on the Effects of Historiography and Space' in *Feminist Theology*, 1999 vol. 22, p. 79.

Chapter 3

1 See *Yorkshire Congregational Year Book* 1926.

2 The contributors, apart from Zoë Fairfield, were C M Ady, Clara E Collet, Una Saunders and William Temple.

3 The Quaker understanding of ministry does not include a special ordained ministry. In the Salvation Army from the outset women were eligible for any office equally with men. See G K Horridge, *The Salvation Army: Origins and Early Days 1865-1900* (Godalming: Ammonite Books, 1993).

4 *The Lambeth Conferences 1867-1948* (London: SPCK, 1948), p. 90.

5 *Congregational Year Book 1921*, p. 20.

6 Catherine Buchanan Alderton JP was the daughter of the Revd Thomas Robinson, minister of Lion Walk Congregational Church, Colchester 1884-1900. She was first elected to Colchester Town Council in 1918.

7 Margaret Wintringham (1879-1955) was the second woman MP to take her seat in the House of Commons. She succeeded her late husband as MP for Louth in 1921 and served until 1924.

8 See Margaret Bondfield, *A Life's Work*, (London: Hutchinson, 1948), M A Hamilton, *Margaret Bondfield*, (London: L Parson, 1924) and *DNB*. See also chapter 6.

9 See *Congregational Year Book 1937*, pp. 84-93. See also chapter 10.

10 Australia and New Zealand, South Africa, British Guiana, Jamaica. The Women's Fellowship of the International Congregational Council was formed in 1954.

11 *Towards Co-operation: A Record of the Service of the Women's Committee to the Congregational Union of England and Wales* (London: Independent Press, 1966). This section is much indebted to Marion Chaffey's account.

12 Elsie Dorothea Chamberlain (1910-91) had worked as assistant to Muriel Paulden in Liverpool before ministries in Friern Barnet and Richmond as well as a chaplaincy in the WAAF. She and her husband, John Garrington, and Anglican priest, had had to overcome many obstacles before their marriage in 1947. She joined the BBC Religious Department in 1950. She was President of the Congregational Federation 1973-5. See Janette Williams, *First Lady of the Pulpit: Elsie Chamberlain* (Lewes: The Book Guild, 1993) and Alan Argent's articles on Elsie Chamberlain in the *Congregational History Circle Magazine*, vol. 4 (1999-2002).

13 Williams, p. 79.

14 The emergence of modern feminist theology is usually dated from 1960, when Valerie Saiving published a ground-breaking article, 'The Human Situation: A Feminine View' in the *Journal of Religion* 40 (1960), pp. 100-12.

15 The Methodist Conference finally voted to ordain women in 1973, and the first women were ordained to the Methodist ministry in the following year.

16 Of the two Baptist women ministers and one probationer minister listed in the *Baptist Handbook* for 1964, only one – Violet Hedger – was in pastoral charge. The other two, Gwenyth Hubble and Marie Elizabeth Isaacs, were working for ecumenical organisations.

17 Of these three were doctors, 30 nurses, 25 teachers and 21 church workers.

18 The first was Mrs Marion Chaffey in 1940. In the 1950s Mrs I M H MacAdam of Leeds, and Mrs G Rider Smith of London were each elected to the chair.

19 The annual national meeting was known as the Synod until 1920, when it became known as the General Assembly.

20 Presbyterian Church of England (PCE), *Synod Reports, 1913,* (London: Presbyterian Church of England, 1913), p. 512.

21 PCE, *Synod Minutes 1920,* p. 571.

22 PCE, *Assembly Minutes 1921,* pp. 900-902.

23 PCE, *Assembly Minutes 1922,* pp. 201-6.

24 The committee reported divided opinion among presbyteries, and recorded the votes of 72 sessions as follows: 15 in favour, 54 against, and 3 doubtful. PCE, *Assembly Minutes 1923,* p. 569.

25 PCE, *Assembly Minutes 1923,* p. 407.

26 Dorothy Frances Wilson (1893-1956). See *Mansfield College Magazine* (Jan 1957) pp. 325-6.

27 Marjorie Basilia McLachlan (1885-1952). She worked in Birmingham, Carlisle, Manchester and Saltdean.

28 D P Thomson (ed), *Women as Elders: The Verdict of Experience* (Crieff: St Ninian's, 1965)

29 PCE, *Assembly Minutes 1935,* pp. 566-7.

30 Annie Isabella Gordon (1909-99). For an appreciation, see Arthur Macarthur, 'Ella Gordon 1909-99' in *JURCHS* VI/6, July 1999, pp. 294-8.

31 In 1961 she moved to Rankin Memorial Church in Liverpool, where her ministry was greatly appreciated. Five years later she moved to teach in St Andrew's College in Selly Oak, but ill-health forced her to retire in 1968. Thirty-one years of retirement were then spent in Scotland.

32 Arthur Macarthur, pp. 297-8.

33 The records of both the WHCA and the WMA are in the United Reformed Church History Society's Library at Westminster College, Cambridge.

34 She chaired the Home Church Committee in the 1950s, and the Maintenance of Minstry Committee in the 1960s.

35 This section is greatly indebted to an account prepared by Mary Barr, and to conversations with both her and May Segain.

36 These figures are taken from David Thompson, *Let Sects and Parties Fall* (Birmingham: Berean Press, 1980), pp. 202-205.

37 Among the church sisters in the early part of the century were Miss E B Crawford, Lydia Hunt and Etta Proctor.

38 Appendix to *Churches of Christ Year Book 1954.*

39 *Churches of Christ Year Book 1954,* p. 30.

40 *Churches of Christ Year Book 1954,* p. 23.

41 'The Place of Women in the Ministry of the Church: a report for study prepared by ministers in the Barnes Close Convention 1965' (typescript), p. 16.

42 She later became an auxiliary minister (now a non-stipendiary minister) of the United Reformed Church. She is the sister of May Segain.

43 May Segain was previously secretary of the National Fellowship of Youth. As secretary of the CWF she was sometimes invited to preach at the more open-minded churches. She is now a non-stipendiary minister of the United Reformed Church.

[44] The Re-formed Association included all those churches which favoured union with the URC. Those who did not wish to join the United Reformed Church formed the Fellowship of the Churches of Christ.

[45] See Margaret Stansgate, *My Exit Visa* (London: Hutchinson, 1992).

[46] United Reformed Church First General Assembly – *Agenda and Reports*, p. 18.

[47] Her father, William Griffith-Jones, had been Chairman of the Congregational Union 1958-9. Rosalind Goodfellow has had a distinguished public career in education, in the URC, in the Free Church Federal Council and the British Council of Churches, and as a magistrate.

[48] A resolution the following year to revise the Basis of Union in inclusive language did not get the necessary two-thirds majority.

[49] This inevitably faced the committee which produced the new hymn book, *Rejoice and Sing* in 1991 with many difficult problems.

[50] This took place in 1981.

[51] Ruth Clarke was for many years a headteacher of a London comprehensive school and a magistrate in south London, before spending a few years of her early retirement as honorary assistant warden at the Windermere Centre.

[52] *Women's Research Project 1992.* The researcher was Keran Olm-Stoelting.

[53] A voluntary partnership between the Scottish Congregational Church (formed from those members of the former Congregational Union of Scotland who wanted to unite with the URC), the Women's Union and the Scottish Open College.

[54] Vera Mary Muir Kenmure, 1904-73.

[55] Catherine M Robertson 1959-60, the Revd Jean Thomson 1972-3, Christine Durrant 1978-9, Joyce M Gray 1983-4, and Sheena Paul 1993-4.

Chapter 4

[1] Christine Irvine 1912-33, Catherine Mackinnon 1933-45, Gwenyth Hubble 1945-60 and Agnes Piggott from 1960 until the amalgamation with St Andrew's Hall. See Hugh Martin, *Fifty Years of Carey Hall 1912-62* (Birmingham: Council of Carey Hall, 1962).

[2] In 1906 the Archbishop of Canterbury instituted Lambeth Diplomas, theological qualifications of degree standard, which were often taken by women who wished to teach 'Scripture' in schools.

[3] She put this skill to good use later by translating the books of Ruth, Jonah and Obadiah into colloquial English for a series published by the National Adult School Union. It is worth noting that a remarkable number of early women ministers expressed a deep interest in and love for Hebrew.

[4] Dorothy Wilson in *Mansfield College Magazine*, June 1932.

[5] Their pastorates were at the Darby Street Mission of the King's Weigh House, Greville Place, Kilburn, Cowley Road, Oxford, Wolverton, Old Independent, Haverhill, and finally at the King's Weigh House in the aftermath of the Second World War.

[6] Society for the Ministry of Women, report of a conference on 'Women in the Church of Tomorrow', January 1939, p. 25, Women's Library.

[7] Mary Osborn (1909-2003)

[8] See chapter 9.

[9] The first was Miss Harriet Byles in 1927.

[10] See *Congregational Year Book 1937*, pp. 84-93.

[11] By 'a democratic constitution' she meant one in which the decision to call a minister was made by deacons and church meeting at the local level, rather than by any higher authority.

[12] Written narrative by Beryl Bennett, DoD Archive.

[13] Unlike Beryl Russell, Doreen Speck had to withdraw in 1948 when she married a fellow student, Malcolm Rogers.

[14] Florence Frost-Mee (1915-2003)

[15] Written narrative by Janet Webber, DoD Archive.

[16] I am grateful to the Revd Ioan Wynn-Griffiths for this information. A life of Susannah Rankin by Laurel Grey, *Sinabada: Woman Among Warriors*, was published in Australia in 1988 by the Melbourne Board of Christian Education..

[17] A Congregational Union report to the World Council of Churches stated that by 1963 73 women had been ordained to the Congregational ministry. 48 of these were college trained.

[18] Derek Watson has written a short biography of her, *Angel of Jesus: The Life and Work in Liverpool 8 of the Revd Muriel Olympia Paulden* (Wimborne: Minster Press, 1994).

[19] Margaret Laurie, a former student of St Paul's has written a short unpublished history of St Paul's, and we are very grateful to her for allowing us to read and quote from it.

[20] During the years 1947-65 St Paul's members served 14 churches on new housing estates, 11 in down-town and 20 in rural areas. See Alice Platts, 'Experiment in Fellowship', *The Congregational Monthly* August 1965.

[21] See Jacqueline Field-Bibb, 'Women and Ministry: the Presbyterian Church of England' in *Heythrop Journal 31* (1990), pp. 150-164.

[22] At the end of her course Doris Nix married a fellow student and did not go forward for ordination.

[23] Margaret Boaden, Ella Gordon, Elizabeth Nash and Margaret Taylor.

[24] *The Modern Churchman 32*, 1990, pp. 1-31.

Chapter 5

[1] The Revd Betty Williams, letter 18 July 1996, DoD Archive.

[2] I Corinthians 14: 34.

[3] Sheila Fletcher, *Maude Royden: A Life* (Oxford: Basil Blackwell, 1989), p. 174.

[4] Erik Routley, *English Religious Dissent* (Cambridge: Cambridge University Press, 1960), p. 169.

[5] A recent exception is Susan Durber and Heather Walton (eds.), *Silence in Heaven: A Book of Women's Preaching* (London: SCM Press, 1994).

[6] *The Christian Commonwealth*, 28 March 1917 in an article entitled 'Women's Kingdom'. Her mother's name is not given.

[7] Susan Thorne, *Congregational Missions and the Making of an Imperial Culture in Nineteenth Century England*, (California: Stanford University Press, 1999) p. 101.

[8] Sheila Fletcher, *Maude Royden: A Life* (Oxford: Basil Blackwell, 1989) pp. 147-149.

[9] Jacqueline de Vries, 'Transforming the Pulpit: Preaching and Prophecy in the British Women's Suffrage Movement' in B M Kienzle and P J Walker, *Women Preachers and Prophets through Two Millennia of Christianity* (Berkeley: University of California Press, 1998) p. 328.

[10] *The Christian Commonwealth*, 28 March 1917.

[11] de Vries, p. 320.

[12] Albert Clare, *The City Temple 1640-1940* (London: Independent Press, 1940) p. 173.

[13] *The Christian World*, 22 March 1917 p. 3.

14 *The Christian Commonwealth*, 21 March 1917 p. 303.

15 *The Christian Commonwealth*, 4 April 1917 p. 331.

16 *The Christian World*, 12 July 1917 p. 3.

17 Albert Clare, *The City Temple 1640-1940* (London: Independent Press, 1940) pp. 191-192.

18 Constance Coltman, 'Post Reformation: The Free Churches' in Maude Royden, *The Church and Woman* (London: J Clarke & Co, 1924) p. 112.

19 Constance Coltman 'Post Reformation: The Free Churches' pp.123-124.

20 D M Northcroft, *Women Free Church Ministers* (London: Edgar G Dunstan & Co, 1929) p. 8.

21 D M Northcroft, p. 10.

22 Kathleen Hendry, *Don't Ask Me Why* (London: United Reformed Church, 1991) p. 21.

23 *Congregational Year Book 1937*, p. 92.

24 D M Northcroft, p. 20.

25 *Congregational Year Book 1963-4*, p. 436.

26 *Congregational Year Book 1963-4*, p. 436.

27 *Congregational Year Book 1963-4*, p. 436.

28 *Congregational Year Book 1933*, p. 251.

29 D M Northcroft, p. 23.

30 *Congregational Year Book 1988-9*, p. 202.

31 *Congregational Year Book 1966-7*, p. 468.

32 Laurel Gray, *Sinabada: Woman Among Warriors. A Biography of the Rev Sue Rankin* (Melbourne: Joint Board of Christian Education, 1989), p. 8.

33 Sue Rankin quoted in Laurel Gray, p. 10.

34 Laurel Gray, p. 146.

35 Mary Barr narrative, DoD Archive

36 Mary Barr narrative, DoD Archive.

37 *The Free Church Chronicle*, Spring 1997 p. 14.

38 Rosemary Radford Ruether, 'The Preacher and the Priest: Two Typologies of Ministry and the Ordination of Women' in Constance F Parvey (ed.), *Ordination of Women in Ecumenical Perspective* (Geneva: World Council of Churches, 1980), pp. 71-72.

39 D M Northcroft, p. 12.

40 Susan Durber and Heather Walton (eds.), *Silence in Heaven: A Book of Women's Preaching* (London: SCM Press, 1994) pp. xi-xii.

41 Susan Durber and Heather Walton, p. 46.

42 D Havergal Shaw, 'What we want is a woman minister', *Women Speaking*, January to March 1971

43 Kate McIlhagga 'Voices in my head' in Lesley Orr MacDonald (ed.), *In Good Company* (Glasgow: Wild Goose Publications, 1999) p. 94.

44 'Britain's best-known woman minister retires from the BBC', *Congregational Monthly*, February 1927, pp. 1-2.

45 *Congregational Monthly*, February 1967, pp. 1-2.

46 *Congregational Monthly*, May 1965,in an article 'Let us once again be adventurers in spiritual things', pp. 9-10.

47 Hazel Barkham narrative, DoD Archive.

48 Janet Webber narrative, DoD Archive

49 Margaret Laurie letter, 16 October 1995, DoD Archive.

50 Doris Leyshon interview, 6 October 1996, DoD archive.

51 *Congregational Year Book 1969-70*, p. 431.

52 Rachel Storr letter, 16 September 1995, DoD Archive. Rachel Storr died in 2002.

Chapter 6

1 Two recent works which help to recover much of this history are Jill Liddington, *The Long Road to Greenham: Anti-Militarism in Britain since 1820* (London: Virago, 1989) and Anne Wiltsher, *Most Dangerous Women: Feminist Peace Campaigners of the Great War* (London: Pandora, 1985).

2 Henry Richard (1812-88). He was Chairman of the Congregational Union in 1877. For 20 years he was an MP. See *DNB*.

3 Jane Addams (1860-1935). See Margaret Tims, *Jane Addams of Hull House* (London: Allen and Unwin, 1961), John C Farrell, *Beloved Lady: A History of Jane Addams' Ideas on Reform and Peace* (Baltimore: John Hopkins Press, 1967) and Jane Addams, *Twenty Years at Hull House* (New York, 1910).

4 See Sheila Fletcher, *Maude Royden: A Life* (Oxford: Basil Blackwell, 1989), pp 29, 87 and 244.

5 See Jill Wallis, *Valiant FOR Peace: A History of the Fellowship of Reconciliation 1914 to 1989* (London: FOR. 1991).

6 See Fletcher, pp. 130-32.

7 Elizabeth Charles was President of the Federation of Congregational Women in the 1960s. She was twice President of the Women's Council of the Free Church Federal Council, in 1963-4 and 1978-9. Her husband, Maurice Charles, was principal of Paton College in Nottingham from 1948 until his death in 1964, after which Elizabeth Charles was appointed Lecturer in Education at University College, Swansea.

8 See Margaret Bondfield, *A Life's Work* (London: Hutchinson, 1948), M A Hamilton, *Margaret Bondfield* (London: L Parsons, 1924) and *DNB 1951-60*.

9 Bondfield, p. 354.

10 Bondfield, pp. 358-9.

11 He was successively a Liberal and Labour MP, and twice a Labour cabinet minister.

12 In the Expositor's Bible Series (London: Hodder and Stoughton, 1996-98).

13 Margaret Stansgate, *My Exit Visa* (London: Hutchinson, 1992), p. 231.

14 Her autobiography, *My Exit Visa*, was not completed in her lifetime, and therefore while it provides a fascinating account of her life and travels with her husband, it gives only a rather sketchy account of her later years.

15 Ruby Mary Webster. See *Congregational Year Book 1969-70*, p. 442. The account here is indebted to an unpublished account by Dame Unity Lister.

16 Bishop of Oxford since 1987, formerly Dean of King's College, London.

Chapter 7

1 In 1961 it merged with the World Council of Churches.

2 Kathleen Mary Bliss (1908-89). She deserves a full biography. At present there are short accounts of her life in Trevor Beeson, *Christian Reconciliation Rebels and Reformers* (London: SCM, 1999) and Ion Brea and D Heller (ed) *Ecumenical Pilgrims: Profiles of Pioneers in Christian Reconciliation* (Geneva: WCC Publications, 1995).

3   Rupert Bliss was ordained as a Congregational minister in 1943, but resigned a few years later. He eventually became an Anglican priest.

4   R Rouse and S C Neill (eds), *A History of the Ecumenical Movement 1517-1948* (London: SPCK, 1954).

5   The others were: the Christian approach to Jews, the significance of the laity in the Church, and Christian reconstruction after the war.

6   This figure was given in the Newsletter of the Society for Ministry of Women in the Church in January 1955, Fawcett Library, London.

7   At the fourth meeting in Uppsala in 1968 9% of the delegates were women; the proportion at Nairobi in 1975 was 22%, and at Vancouver in 1983 30%. Since then the proportion of women has further increased.

8   She actually attended at the instigation of the American Methodist Church.

9   Olive Wyon (1881-1966) came from a Congregational family and was well-known as the translator of the works of Emil Brunner. She had contributed papers to the 1937 Conference on Life and Work in Oxford. Her sister, Dorothy Wyon (1888-1970) was a Congregational minister.

10   *The Service and Status of Women*, p. 198.

11   *The Service and Status of Women*, p. 21.

12   *The Service and Status of Women*, p. 31.

13   In 1955 she contributed an important article to *The Ecumenical Review*, vol 7, no 2, pp. 151-60 on 'Considerations on the need for a theology of the place of women in the Church.'

14   Gwenyth Hubble (1906-72) was a Baptist minister whose whole ministry was spent in ecumenical work. Her last post was with the World Council of Churches Division on World Mission and Evangelism. See the *Baptist Union Directory 1973-4*, p. 291.

15   David M Paton (ed), *Breaking Barriers, Nairobi 1975*, (London, SPCK: 1976).

16   The United Reformed Church response to these recommendations is recounted in chapter three on 'Structures'.

17   Founded in 1875. Until 1954 all delegates had to be ordained, a practice which automatically excluded most women. In 1970 the World Alliance of Reformed Churches united with the International Congregational Council.

18   See *Living Letters: A Report of Visits to the Churches During the Ecumenical Decade – Churches in Solidarity with Women* (Geneva: WCC Publications, 1997) p. 44.

19   See Diane Kessler, *Together on the Way: Official Report of the Eighth Assembly of the World Council of Churches* (Geneva, World Council of Churches: 1999), pp. 242-52. The membership of the Assembly comprised 966 delegates, 599 men and 367 women. The United Reformed Church delegates were Anthony Burnham, Wilma Frew and Jenny Hale: Philip Woods was an official observer.

20   Irene Parker Crane was the author of an important historical work, *Dissenting Academies in England* (Cambridge: Cambridge University Press, 1914) as well as an able teacher and administrator.

21   See *Congregational YearBook 1970-71*, p. 427.

22   Letter 16 September 1995, DoD Archive. Rachel Storr (died 2002) was the daughter of a Canon of Westminster Abbey. She became a great friend of Elsie Chamberlain, who encouraged her to enter the Congregational ministry.

23   Allowing herself some poetic licence concerning the calendar, she liked to remind others that, according to Genesis 8:4, Noah's Ark came to rest on Mount Ararat on the 17th day of the

7th month. See *United Reformed Church Yearbook 1996*, p. 265. See also Ivy Rawkins Jeffers, *Between You and Me: Friendly Talks for Women's Meetings and Others* (Evesham: Arthur James, 1978), and *I'd Like to Tell You: More Friendly Talks* (Evesham: Arthur James, 1979).

24 *The Free Catholic* October 1920.

Chapter 8

1 This is a line from the poem 'Getting' de Spirit', by the Jamaican poet Una Marson, who is mentioned on page 109.

2 Io Smith, *An Ebony Cross; being a Black Christian in Britian Today* (London: Marshall Pickering, 1989), p.111.

3 Haideh Moghissi, 'Racism and Sexism in Academic Practice', in H Afshar and M Maynard (eds.) *The Dynamics of 'Race' and Genders: Some Feminist Interventions* (London: Taylor and Francis, 1994), p. 225.

4 Marjorie Lewis-Cooper (now Marjorie Lewis), from the United Church of Jamaica through the Council of World Mission to the United Reformed Church as Multi-Racial, Multi-Cultural Development Officer 1997-2000.

5 Catherine Hall, Feminism and Feminist History, chapter 1 of *White, Male and Middle Class: Explorations in Feminism and History* (London: Polity Press, 1992), p. 20.

6 Catherine Hall, p. 20.

7 Marjorie Lewis-Cooper used this phrase in one of her 'Letters of Reflection on Racism and Related Issues', to Anne Wilkinson-Hayes, a white British Baptist minister (London: United Reformed Church, 1998).

8 Genesis 16-21.

9 'Caught in the middle' is the title of the section about Caribbean Women by an anonymous writer in *'With Love and With Passion: Women's Life and Work in the Worldwide Church'*, pp. 38-39, edited by E Raiser and B Robra (Geneva: WCC 2001).

10 M Phillips and T Phillips, *Windrush: The Irresistible Rise of Multi-Racial Britain.* (London: Harper Collins, 1999), p. 6. An estimated 20,000 black people had settled in Britain, before *Windrush*, as a result of the Slave Trade.

11 WCC definition of racism, adopted at Uppsala in 1968: 'By racism we mean ethnocentric pride in one's own racial group and preference for the distinctive characteristics of that group; belief that these characteristics are fundamentally biological in nature and are thus transmitted to succeeding generations; strong negative feelings towards other groups who do not share these characteristics, coupled with the thrust to discriminate against and exclude the outgroup from full participation in the life of the community', pp. 152-53.

12 'The Elizabethan repatriation policy', in *The Black Handbook*, edited by E L Bute ad H J P Harmer. (London: Cassell, 1997), p. 81.

13 Both of these quotations appear in the chapter on 'Race prejudice and racism', in Peter Fryer, *Staying Power: The History of Black People in Britain* (London: Pluto Press, 1984), p. 152-3.

14 The Society for the Mitigation and Gradual Abolition of Slavery was formed in London in 1823.

15 Martha Gundry of Calne and Mary Rawson of Sheffield are two of the women leaders mentioned by Kenneth Corfield (p. 52).

16 Kenneth Corfield, 'Elizabeth Heyrick: Radical Quaker' in Gail Malmgreen, *Religion in the Lives of English Women,* (London: Croom Helm, 1986), p. 41.

[17] The Female Society for the Relief of British Negro Slaves was established by a group of evangelical Christian women in 1825 and it pledged itself to work closely with the Birmingham Anti-Slavery Society, formed by middle class men a year later.

[18] Kenneth Corfield, p. 41.

[19] Kenneth Corfield, p. 41.

[20] She wrote at least seven similar pamphlets; four in 1824 and three more by 1828. Others also advocated immediate abolition but she was one of the most vocal and insistent. Heyrick was not typical of women from her background, writing as she did over 20 pamphlets between 1815 and 1830 presenting radical views on a whole range of politcal, social and economic subjects: 'every subject that had the remotest relation to the cause of social and political liberty' (Corfield, p.52).

[21] Pamphlets were also used by groups engaged in other campaigns: e.g. Anti-Corn Law League, Ladies' National Association for the Repeal of the Contagious Diseases Act. Indeed comparisons between slavery and the sexual slavery of women were often made by the later.

[22] Dates for Mary Prince are given as c.1788-after 1833 in *Daughters of Africa*, edited by Margaret Busby (London: Jonathan Cape, 1992), p. 27.

[23] Her story is told in *The History of Mary Prince, a West Indian Slave, Related by Herself*, which was published in London and Edinburgh in 1831. She was born in Bermuda and was a slave there and in the Turks Islands and Antigua. Coming to London in 1828 with her owners, she escaped there after they refused to let her buy her freedom, although she had enough money to do so'; thus even this right was denied her.

[24] See also chapter 10.

[25] John Williamson, *The History of Congregationalism in Cardiff and District* (Cardiff: the Educational Publishing Company Ltd, 1920), p. 48.

[26] After Moody's death, the minister of the church he attended, David Vaughan, wrote a biography: *Negro victory: The Life Story of Harold Moody* (London, 1950). See also David Killingray, *Race, Faith and Politics: Harold Moody and the League of Coloured Peoples*, (London: Goldsmith's College, 1999).

[27] The Colonial Missionary Society was founded in 1836. In 1956 its name was changed to the Commonwealth Missionary Society. In 1966 it amalgamated with the London Missionary Society to form the Congregational Council for World Mission, which went on to become the Council for World Mission.

[28] The title of the magazine derived from a remark by Dr Aggrey that a harmony in music can only be achieved by using both the black and white keys of a piano, so the same applies to human beings.

[29] Delia Jarrett-Macauley, *The Life of Una Marson 1905-1965* (Manchester: Manchester University Press, 1998).

[30] Jarrett-Macauley, p. 90.

[31] The *Reina del Pacifico* (1948) and the *Georgic* (1949) are said to have brought 15 and 45 women respectively. Peter Fryer, quoted in Vivienne Francis, *With Hope in the Eyes* (London: Nia Press, 1998), p. 63.

[32] M Phillips and T Phillips, *Windrush: The Irresistible Rise of Multi-Racial Britain* (London: Harper Collins, 1999), p. 201.

[33] Phillips and Phillips, p. 149; interview with Carmel Jones.

[34] Phillips and Phillips, p. 201.

35 Phillips and Phillips, p. 339: Ros Howells came from Grenada in 1951 and settled in South London, working as a counsellor.

36 Io Smith, *An Ebony Cross; Being a Black Christian in Britain Today* (London: Marshall Pickering, 1989), p. 31.

37 *The Congregational Monthly*, September 1965, p. 15.

38 *Congregational Year Book 1965/6*, p. 86-87.

39 *Congregational Year Book 1968/9*, p. 92.

40 *Congregational Year Book 1972*, p. 37.

41 *The Congregational Monthly*, November 1963, p. 12.

42 *The Congregational Monthly*, November 1963, p. 13.

43 Council for World Mission was founded in 1977 through a merger of the London Missionary Society, the Commonwealth Missionary Society and the Presbyterian Board of Missions. It is now a community of 31 Protestant churches worldwide.

44 From an interview with Madge Saunders, conducted in Jamaica by Barbara Nelson, a journalist, who was working on Madge Saunders' biography. The interview now in the DoD Archive, p. 1.

45 Madge Saunders, pp. 1-2.

46 Madge Saunders, pp. 4-5.

47 Madge Saunders, The United Church in Mission, *The United Church Herald*, December 1968, p. 6.

48 The Girl's Guildry, which began in Scotland and came to Jamaica in 1923, was a Christian uniformed organisation for girls, which eventually became part of the Girls Brigade.

49 Madge Saunders, 'The Challenge of Service', in the *Tenth Anniversary Brochure of the United Church of Jamaica and Grand Cayman, 1 December 1965-1975*, p. 5.

50 From 'Revd Marjorie Prentice Saunders Sojourn as a Missionary' in *Souvenir Brochure: 25th Anniversary of the United Church of Jamaica and Grand Cayman*, p 25.

51 Madge Saunders, quoted in John Vincent, *Into the City* (London:Epworth, 1982), p. 37.

52 Madge Saunders, p. 6.

53 Madge Saunders, *Living in Britain* (London: The British Council of Church's Community and Race Relations Unit and the Friends Community Relations Committee, 1972).

54 From 'The Challenge of Service' by Madge Saunders, in the 10th Anniversary Brochure of the United Church of Jamaica and Grand Cayman, 1 December 1965-1975, p. 5.

55 Madge Saunders, p. 6.

56 Selem Fagan, member and Elder of St James, came to the UK from Jamaica in 1957.

57 Madge Saunders, p.7.

58 Madge Saunders, 'The Challenge of Service', in the 10th Anniversary Brochure of the United Church of Jamaica and Grand Cayman, 1st December 1965-1975, p. 6.

59 Diane Abbott was born in London in 1953 of Jamaican parents. She became the first black woman MP in the British House of Commons when she was elected for Hackney and Stoke Newington in 1987.

60 A Local Ecumenical Partnership on the Blackbird Leys estate, east Oxford.

61 Such incidents include the shooting of Cherry Groce in September 1985, when armed police entered her home, triggering the 1985 Brixton riot, and the death of Cynthia Jarrett from a heart attack a few weeks later when police raided her home. After this youth clashed with police in what became known as the Broadwater Farm riot.

62 Janet Lees for the DoD Archive.

63 Elizabeth Nash, 'Servicing or Caring?' in E Graham and M Halsey, *Women and Pastoral Care*, (London: SPCK, 1993), p. 103.

64 Tizeta (Tiny) Powell is a member and Elder of St James United Reformed Church.

65 The Revd Robert Gillespie was the minister at St James at this time.

66 Interview with Tizeta (Tiny) Powell for DoD project.

67 Elizabeth Nash, p. 101.

68 Margaret Busby, *Daughters of Africa: an International Anthology of Words and Writing by Women of African Descent from the Ancient Egyptians to the Present* (London: Jonathan Cape, 1992), page xxxix.

69 Elizabeth Nash, p.102.

70 Margaret Busby, p. xxxx.

71 Marjorie Lewis-Cooper in 'Crossing the Threshold from Racism to the Reign of God', *Articles*, issue 10, summer 2000, pp. 5-6.

72 Marjorie Lewis-Cooper, p. 6.

73 The larger, now St Andrew's United Reformed Church, also had a woman as minister at the time: Revd Fleur Houston.

74 Conversations with members of St James', by Revd Brenda Hill, in the DoD Archive.

75 From 'The Challenge of Service' by Madge Saunders, in the 10th Anniversary Brochure of the United Church of Jamaica and Grand Cayman, 1 December 1965-1975, p. 6.

76 Madge Dale, *African Caribbean Community Cultural Awareness* (Sheffield: Sheffield Libraries and Information Services, 1998).

77 Notes in this section are taken from Diaconate Minutes Book Number 4 of St James' Presbyterian Church of England, Sheffield, covering the period 1952-1970, and available at St James United Reformed Church, Scott Road, Sheffield. In the Presbyterian Church of England the Diaconate was responsible for practical matters of church maintenance, finance, etc.

78 1955: Minute Book 4, p. 42

79 1961: Minute Book 4, p. 120

80 1962: Minute Book 4, p. 126

81 1964: Minute Book 4, p. 148

82 1964: Minute Book 4, p. 172-173. Although the salary of a deaconess was paid from central funds the expenses were paid by the local church.

83 1964: Minute Book 4, p. 206

84 1965: Minute Book 4, p 212. The East London scheme was a 'home mission' of the PCE.

85 From 'The Challenge of Service' by Madge Saunders, in the 10th Anniversary Brochure of the United Church of Jamaica and Grand Cayman, 1 December 1965-1975, p. 6.

86 1966: Minute Book 4, p. 222

87 1966: Minute Book 4, p. 231

88 1966: Minute Book 4, p. 253

89 1967: Minute Book 4, p. 273

90 1968: Minute Book 4, p. 346

91 1969: Minute Book 4, p. 347-350

92 Madge Saunders, 'United in Mission', in the *United Church Herald*, December 1968, p. 6.

93 Madge Saunders, 'Multi-racial Pre-school Playground [sic] Sheffield', in the *United Church Herald*, March 1969, p. 2.

[94] 1967: Minute Book 4, p. 288

[95] 1967: Minute Book 4, p. 297

[96] 1969: Minute Book 4, pp. 361, 365 and 377-378

[97] Source: 1991 Population Census figures put the black population in Sheffield at 1.5%. In 1997 it was estimated at 10,000 people.

[98] There are at least 40 different languages spoken in the households of the Burngreave ward of the city of Sheffield. This project has been described in J Lees, G Smithies and C Chambers (2001) 'Let's Talk: A Speech and Language Promotion Programme for Sure Start'. Paper presented at the Royal College of Speech and Language Therapists Conference 'Communicating the Evidence', Birmingham, April 2001.

[99] 1968: Minute Book 4, p. 336

[100] Icilda Brown died in 1997 and Stewart Brown in 2002.

[101] The United Reformed Church Multi-Racial, Multi-Cultural Development Programme Provincial visit to the Yorkshire Province, 18-21 May 1998 (London: United Reformed Church), p. 2.

[102] Ibid, p. 7.

[103] Ibid, p. 25.

[104] Janet Llewellyn, personal communication.

[105] Marjorie Lewis-Cooper, *Articles*, 10, summer 200, p. 7.

[106] United Reformed Church Declaration on Racism (London: United Reformed Church, 1987).

[107] United Reformed Church Multi-Cultural, Multi-Racial Development Officer. Marjorie Lewis was born in Jamaica in 1956 and was later ordained in the United Church of Jamaica. The story of her ministry in her own words is told in *'We Cannot Dream Alone: A Story of Women in Development'*, edited by Ranjini Rebera, pp. 91-93 (Geneva, WWC Publications, 1990).

[108] See Honor Ford Smith, *Lionheart Gal: Life Stories of Jamaican Women* (London: Women's Press, 1986).

[109] Marlene Brown, was the first black woman to be ordained to the Ministry of Word and Sacrament in the United Reformed Church, in 1997, and was trained at Northern College, Manchester. She is no longer serving in the United Reformed Church.

Chapter 9

[1] Nancy J Ramsay, 'Truth, Power and Love: Challenges for Clergywomen across the Life Span', in *In Her Own Time*, ed. Jeanne Stevenson-Moessner (Minneapolis: Fortress Press, 2000), p. 270.

[2] Nancy J Ramsay, p. 270.

[3] Letter from Helen Rose letter, 31 December 1994, DoD Archive.

[4] Mary Osborn narrative, DoD Archive, pp. 1-2.

[5] Mary Osborn narrative, DoD Archive, p. 4.

[6] Mary Osborn narrative, DoD Archive, p. 3.

[7] Obituary in *United Reformed Church Year Book 2000*, p. 303.

[8] Obituary in *The Congregational Year Book 1968-9*, p. 436.

[9] Kathleen Hendry, *Don't Ask Me Why – Sixty Years a Woman Minister*, (London: URC, 1991) p. 4.

[10] Susannah Ellis married Robert Rankin in Papua whilst serving with the LMS.

[11] Laurel Gray, *Sinabada: Woman Among Warriors. A Biography of the Revd Sue Rankin*, (Melbourne: Joint Board of Christian Education, 1989), p. 6.

12 Doris Leyshon interview, 6 October 1996, DoD Archive.

13 Yvonne Tomes, 'Introducing two women ministers', in *Church Times*, 2 May 1975, p. 11.

14 Yvonne Tomes, 'Five of the fifty-five', in *Reform*, July 1975, p. 7.

15 Janet Wootton, 'Janet's Story' in *The Society for the Ministry of Women in the Church Newsletter* Autumn 1997, p. 19.

16 Joan Duncan narrative, DoD Archive, p. 1.

17 Joan Duncan narrative, DoD Archive, p. 2.

18 Janet Webber narrative, DoD Archive, p. 1.

19 Janet Webber narrative, DoD Archive, p. 1.

20 Laurel Gray, p. 9.

21 Laurel Gray, p. 10.

22 Laurel Gray, p. 11.

23 Laurel Gray, pp. 11-12.

24 Janet Webber narrative, DoD Archive, p. 3.

25 Janet Webber narrative, DoD Archive, p. 3.

26 Janet Webber narrative, DoD Archive, pp. 4-5.

27 Mary Evans narrative, DoD Archive, p. 3.

28 Gill Troop, 'Women's Work' in *Idea, the Magazine for Members of the Evangelical Alliance UK*, January – March 1999, p. 23. In 2002 Mia Hilborn transferred to the Church of England.

29 Janet Wootton, 'Janet's Story' in *The Society for the Ministry of Women in the Church Newsletter* Autumn 1997, p. 20.

30 David Lawrence, 'A sense of call' in *Reform*, November 1999, p. 22. General Assembly of the United Reformed Church decided in 2003 to close Yardley Hastings.

31 Nancy J Ramsay, 'Truth, Power and Love: Challenges for Clergywomen across the Life Span', in Jeanne Stevenson-Moessner, (ed.), *In Her Own Time*, (Minneapolis: Fortress Press, 2000), p. 274.

32 Lady Stansgate, Obituary in *Society for the Ministry of Women in the Church Newsletter* no. 29 July, 1969 p. 9.

33 Obituary in *United Reformed Church Year Book 1976* p. 302.

34 Kathleen Hendry, *Don't Ask Me Why – Sixty Years a Woman Minister*, (London: URC, 1991), p. 44.

35 Kathleen Hendry, p. 53.

36 Kathleen Hendry, p. 59.

37 Elsie Chamberlain always went by her maiden name rather than her husband's name, Garrington. Kathleen Hendry's autobiography notes that, unlike herself, Elsie Chamberlain was given permission by the Ccongregational Union to do this.

38 Janette Williams, *First Lady of the Pulpit, A Biography of Elsie Chamberlain*, (Sussex: The Book Guild, 1993), p. 38.

39 Beryl Bennett narrative, DoD Archive, pp. 2-3. Later on her ministry was recognised when eight churches nominated her as chairman of the Leicestershire and Rutland Congregational Union, a position to which she was elected – the only woman to hold this particular office.

40 Letter from Betty Williams, 18 July 1996, DoD Archive.

41 Letter from Jacky Smith, 13 October 1995, DoD Archive.

42 Kate McIlhagga, 'Voices in my head', in Lesley Orr Mac Donald (ed.), *In Good Company*, (Glasgow: Wild Goose Publications, 1999) p. 83.

43 Kate McIlhagga, p. 82.

44 Kate McIlhagga, p. 82.

45 Kate McIlhagga, p. 86.

46 Yvonne Tomes, 'Five of the fifty-five', *Reform*, July 1975, p. 6.

47 Letter from Jessie Clare, 6 March 1996, DoD Archive.

48 Arthur Macarthur, 'Ella Gordon (1909-1999)' in *The Journal, United Reformed Church History Society* Vol 6. No. 4, July 1999, p. 295.

49 Letter from Frances Chambers, 30 November 1995, DoD Archive.

50 Joan Duncan narrative, DoD Archive, p. 14.

51 Joan Duncan letter, 24 August 2003, DoD Archive.

52 Constance Coltman, 'What shall I do? Practical Problems', in *The Sunday at Home*, (The Religious Tract Society, London) February 1931 p. xiv.

53 Mary Evans narrative, DoD Archive, p. 4.

54 *Congregational Year Book 1972*, p. 336.

55 Alice Platts, 'Experiment in fellowship', in *The Congregational Monthly*, August 1965, p. 10.

56 Margaret Taylor letter, 14 September 1995, DoD Archive

57 Yvonne Tomes, 'Five of the fifty-five', in *Reform*, July 1975 p. 7.

58 Mary Wyatt letter, 13 January 1996, DoD Archive.

59 Arthur Macarthur, 'Ella Gordon (1909-1999)' in *The Journal, United Reformed Church History Society* Vol 6. No. 4, July 1999, p. 297.

60 SheilaThorpe interview, 28 June 2002, DoD Archive.

61 Ian Gregory, 'What do we owe to spinsters?' in *The Congregational Monthly*, August 1966, p. 8.

62 Janet Webber narrative, DoD Archive, p. 11.

63 MSF, the Manufacturing, Science and Finance trade union has since merged with the AUEW to form AMICUS.

64 Hazel Barkham narrative, DoD Archive, p. 3.

65 Arthur Macarthur, 'Ella Gordon (1909-1999)' in *The Journal, United Reformed Church History Society* Vol 6. No. 4, July 1999, p. 296.

66 Daphne Jones obituary, *United Reformed Church Year Book 1985-6*, p. 198.

67 Madge Saunders interview, DoD Archive, p. 5.

68 Catherine (Kate) Anne McIlhagga (1938-2002). See *United Reformed Church Year Book* 2003, p. 327.

69 Lesley Orr MacDonald (ed), *In Good Company* (Glasgow: Wild Goose Publications, 1999) p. 21.

70 Kate McIlhagga, 'Voices in my head', in *In Good Company*, p. 85.

71 Hazel Barkham narrative, DoD Archive, p. 2.

72 John Humphreys, Thanksgiving for Mary Evans, 23 June 1997.

73 Yvonne Tomes, 'Introducing two women ministers', *Church Times*, 2 May 1975, p. 11.

74 Constance Coltman 'The need for women confessors', in *The Free Catholic*, April 1921, Volume vi, No. 4, p. 67.

75 D M Northcroft, *Women Free Church Ministers*, (London: Edgar G.Dunstan & Co, 1929) p. 17.

76 Letter from Gillian Bobbett, 4 March 1996, DoD Archive.

77 Yvonne Tomes, 'Introducing two women ministers', *Church Times*, 2 May 1975, p. 11.

78 Letter from Betty Williams, 17 July 1996, DoD Archive.

79 Letter from Margaret Laurie, 16 October 1995, DoD Archive.

80 Yvonne Tomes, 'Five of the fifty-five', in *Reform*, July 1975, p. 7.

81 Letter from Frances Chambers, 30 September 1995, DoD Archive.

82   Letter from Sheila Sanderson, October 1995, DoD Archive.

83   Kirsty Thorpe narrative, DoD Archive.

84   *Illustrated News*, 30 November 1957, p. 24.

85   Janet Webber narrative, DoD archive, p. 7.

86   Janet Webber narrative, DoD archive, p. 12.

87   John Humphreys, Thanksgiving for Mary Evans, 23 June 1997.

88   Obituary in *Congregational Year Book 1979*, p. 256.

89   Obituary in *Congregational Year Book 1988-9*, p. 193.

90   Gwynith Chalmers letter, 14 April 1997, DoD Archive.

91   *The Congregational Monthly*, July 1968, p. 17.

92   Yvonne Tomes, 'Introducing two women ministers', *Church Times*, 2 May 1975, p. 11.

93   Mary Evans narrative, DoD Archive, p. 8.

94   Kate McIlhagga, 'Voices in my head', p. 97.

95   Rose Barrett, letter submitted to *Reform*, 1995.

96   Alan Pearce statement, 1995, DoD Archive.

97   Yvonne Tomes, 'Five of the fifty-five', in *Reform*, July 1975, p. 6.

98   Hazel Barkham narrative, DoD Archive, p. 1.

99   'On a wing and a prayer', *Reform*, November 1997, p. 17.

100 'On a wing and a prayer', *Reform*, November 1997, p. 15.

101 Her daughter's biography records that her name first appeared in the welfare section of the RAF list. Lord Stansgate, Secretary of State for Air, insisted the original lists were pulped and her name included amongst the chaplains.

102 Janette Williams, *First Lady of the Pulpit; A Biography of Elsie Chamberlain*, (Sussex: The Book Guild, 1993), p. 36.

103 Gwen Smithies narrative, DoD Archive, pp. 4-5.

104 Doris Leyshon interview, 6 October 1996.

105 Doris Leyshon interview, 6 October 1996.

106 *A Portrait of Trinity with Palm Grove 1863-1988*, p. 23

107 'Vive la Différence!', *Reform*, July/August 1996, p. 24.

108 'Vive la Différence!', p. 25.

109 Cheryl Dibeela, talk at Women in Ministries Network, Windermere Centre, January 2001

110 Letter from Margaret Knee letter, 2 March 1995,DoD Archive.

111 Letter from Janet Chisholm, 9 February 1995, DoD archive.

112 Obituary in *Mansfield College Magazine*, January 1957, p. 325.

113 '25 years with LMS', in *The Congregational Monthly*, March 1968, p. 21.

114 Yvonne Tomes, 'Five of the fifty-five', in *Reform*, July 1975, p. 8.

115 Kate McIlhagga, 'Voices in my head', p. 100.

116 Kathleen Hendry, p. iii.

Chapter 10

1   *The Christian Commonwealth*, 18 September 1917.

2   Elaine Kaye & Ross Mackenzie, *W E Orchard – A Study in Christian Exploration* (Oxford: Education Services, 1990) p. 68.

3   R Tudur Jones, *Congregationalism in England 1662-1962* (London: Independent Press, 1962) p. 419.

4   Constance Coltman took a London degree. Until 1920 women were excluded from all Oxford degrees. Nonconformists were also excluded from divinity degrees there until that date.

5   *The Christian World*, 4 October 1917.

6   *The Christian World*, 12 December 1917.

7   *CUEW General Purposes Committee Minutes*, 1 October 1917.

8   *British Weekly*, 4 October 1917.

9   *Minutes of Joint Meeting of General Purposes and Settlements & Removals*, 7 September 1909.

10   *CUEW Council Minutes*, 12 October 1909.

11   *British Weekly*, 21 October 1909.

12   *Congregational Year Book 1969-70*, pp. 429-430.

13   Ann D Gordon, Mari Jo Buhle and Nancy Dye Schrom 'The Problem of Women's History' in Berenice Carroll (ed.), *Liberating Women's History*, (University of Illinois Press, 1976) p. 75.

14   Adrian Hastings, *A History of English Christianity 1920-1990* (London: SCM Press, 1991) p. 44.

15   Adrian Hastings, pp. 610-11.

16   Constance Coltman 'Post-Reformation: The Free Churches', in Maude Royden *The Church and Woman* (London: James Clarke and Co, 1924) pp. 115-116.

17   Constance Coltman 'Post-Reformation: The Free Churches', p. 116.

18   D M Northcroft also wrote *Women at Work in the League of Nations*, *British Women MPs* and *Women Police*.

19   Maude Royden in D M Northcroft, *Women Free Church Ministers* (London: Dunstan & Co, 1929) p. 1.

20   *Commission of Inquiry* Report to Congregational Union of England and Wales Council May 1934, p. 131.

21   Letter of 24 October 1934 to General Purposes Committee chairman from Miss Doris Ingleson, secretary of the Women's Guild.

22   See chapter 3.

23   *Report of the Commission on the Ministry of Women* 1936, p. 6.

24   *Report of the Commission on the Ministry of Women* 1936, p. 9.

25   *Report of the Commission on the Ministry of Women* 1936, pp. 9–10.

26   This idea was never implemented. No college was specified.

27   Marion H Chaffey, *Towards Co-operation: A Record of the Service of the Women's Committee to the Congregational Union of England and Wales* (London: Independent Press, 1966), p. 7.

28   Report on the 'Outline of a Reunion Scheme' to CUEW Council March 1939.

29   Nathaniel Micklem, *Congregationalism and Episcopacy* (London: Independent Press, 1951) p. 19.

30   *World Council of Churches Summary of Facts about the Ordination of Women in the Member Churches of the World Council of Churches* (WCC Geneva, 1958) p. 23.

31   Erik Routley, The *Story of Congregationalism* (London: Independent Press, 1962) p. 99.

32   Erik Routley, *The Story of Congregationalism* (London: Independent Press, 1962) p. 99.

33   In 1947 St Paul's House requested an entry in the Congregational Year Book. The Special Committee of the CUEW granted Home Missionaries a salary of £230 per annum through the Home Churches Fund. See Minutes of the Special Committee, 6 November 1947.

34   Erik Routley, *Congregationalists and Unity* (London: Mowbray and Co, 1962) p. 55.

35   Erik Routley, p. 57.

36 R Tudur Jones, *Congregationalism in England 1662-1962* (London: Independent Press, 1962) pp. 408-9.

37 Another failure to include enough women on a group researching their role in the church, 30 years after the same thing happened in setting up the Commission on the Ministry of Women.

38 See chapter 2 on Statistics and Storytelling, for an account of Sallie Ffrench's experience.

39 *Report on the Co-operation of Men and Women in the CUEW,* September 1965, p. 4.

40 Kenneth Slack, *The United Reformed Church* (Exeter: Religious Education Press, 1978) pp. 36-7.

41 *Reflections - how the churches view their life and mission* (London: British Council of Churches/ Catholic Truth Society, 1986) p. 97.

42 The Baptist Union of Great Britain and Ireland contribution made no mention of women's ordination. The Congregational Federation referred to women alongside men, both in lay and ordained roles. The Salvation Army affirmed recognition of the equal place of women and men in all aspects of ministry and leadership.

43 Edward Lehman Jr, *Women Clergy in England – Sexism, Modern Consciousness and Church Viability* (Lewiston, New York/Queenston, Canada: Edwin Mellen Press, 1987) p. 14.

44 Edward Lehman Jr, p. 25.

45 Edward Lehman Jr, p. 188.

46 Kenneth D Brown, *A Social History of the Nonconformist Ministry in England and Wales 1800-1930* (Oxford: Clarendon Press, 1988) pp. 229-31.

47 Bernard Thorogood, *No Abiding City – Change and Changelessness in the Church* (London: SCM, 1989) p. 87.

48 Edmund Banyard, *Straws in the Wind* (London: URC, 1992) p. 34.

49 Keith Forecast, *Getting the Name Right,* address from the chair, United Reformed Church General Assembly 1 July 1989.

50 Kathleen Hendry, *Don't Ask Me Why – Sixty Years a Woman Minister* (London: URC, 1991) p. 74.

51 *The Christian World, May 1955,* quoted in Janette Williams *First Lady of the Pulpit – A Biography of Elsie Chamberlain* (Sussex: The Book Guild, 1993) p. 80.

52 Lavinia Byrne ed., *Women in the Church – An Educational Resource* (London: CCBI, 1994) p. 79.

53 Janet Wootton, 'The Ministry of Women in the Free Churches' in *Feminist Theology* (Sheffield Academic Press: no. 8 January 1995) p. 74.

54 Tracey Lewis ed., *From Streams to Oceans* (London: URC, 1997) p. 72.

55 David Cornick, *Under God's Good Hand* (London: URC, 1998) p. 188.

Chapter 11

1 Carlyle writing to his mother in Froude, 'Carlyle's Early Life', ii. pp. 218-219, quoted in Henry W Clark, *History of English Nonconformity,* (London: Chapman & Hall, 1913), Volume II p. 392.

2 A Dallimore, *The Life of Edward Irving, Forerunner of the Charismatic Movement* (Edinburgh: 1983)

3 Henry W Clark, *History of English Nonconformity* (London: Chapman & Hall, 1913), Volume II p. 392.

4 Rosemary Radford Ruether and Eleanor McLaughlin (eds.), *Women of Spirit: Female Leadership in the Jewish and Christian Traditions* (New York: Simon and Schuster, 1979), p. 19.

5 Elisabeth Schüssler Fiorenza, 'Women in the Early Christian Movement', in Carol P Christ and

Judith Plaskow (eds.), *Womanspirit Rising: A Feminist Reader in Religion* (San Francisco: Harper and Row, 1979), p. 92.

6 Jacqueline Field-Bibb, *Women Towards Priesthood – Ministerial Politics and Feminist Praxis* (Cambridge University Press, 1991), p.14.

7 David Shorney, "Women may preach but men must govern", Gender roles in the growth and development of the Bible Christian denomination' in R W Swanson, (ed.), *Gender and Christian Religion, Studies in Church History* XXXIV (Woodbridge, 1998).

8 Jacqueline Field-Bibb, *Women Towards Priesthood*, p. 21.

9 Jacqueline Field-Bibb, *Women Towards Priesthood*, p. 18.

10 Jacqueline Field-Bibb, p. 21.

11 Jacqueline Field-Bibb, p. 23.

12 James Munson, *The Nonconformists: In Search of a Lost Culture* (London: SPCK, 1991) p. 110.

13 Lois Deacon, *'So I Went my Way': William Mason and his Wife, Mary 1790-1873* (London: Epworth Press, 1951). p. 83

14 Monica Furlong (ed.), *Feminine in the Church* (London: SPCK, 1984), p. 6.

15 'Three Women with a View', *Reform*, April 1982, p. vi.

16 Michael Kinnaman and Brian E Cope, *The Ecumenical Movement* (Geneva/Grand Rapids: WCC/ Eerdmans, 1997), p. 425.

17 Monica Furlong (ed.), *Act of Synod – Act of Folly?* (London: SCM Press, 1998), p. 75.

18 *An Anglican-Methodist Covenant* (Methodist Publishing House/Church House Publishing, 2001), p. 50.

19 *An Anglican-Methodist Covenant*, p. 53.

20 B Nightingale, *Lancashire Nonconformity or Sketches, Historical and Descriptive of the Congregational and Old Presbyterian Churches in the County, Volume V* (Manchester: John Heywood, 1890).

21 B Nightingale, *Lancashire Nonconformity* pp.236-7.

22 See R O Latham, *Gladys Aylward* (London: Lutterworth Press, 1950).

23 Elizabeth Stuart, *Spitting at Dragons, Towards a Feminist Theology of Sainthood* (London: Mowbray, 1996), p.26.

24 Derek Watson, *Angel of Jesus, Muriel Paulden of Liverpool 8* (Wimborne: The Minster Press, 1994), p. 59.

25 Alice Platts, *Muriel Olympia Paulden M.A.* DoD archive

26 *United Reformed Church Year Book 1981*, p. 249.

27 Rosemary Radford Ruether & Eleanor McLaughlin (eds.), *Women of Spirit: Female Leadership in the Jewish and Christian Traditions* (New York: Simon and Schuster, 1979), p. 21.

28 Ruth A Tucker and Walter Liefeld, *Daughters of the Church – Women and Ministry from New Testament times to the Present* (Michigan: Zondervan, 1987), p. 281.

29 Norman Moon, *Education for Ministry, Bristol Baptist College 1679-1979* (Bristol Baptist College, 1979), p. 76.

30 *The Christian Commonwealth*, 18 September 1917, 'Another Woman Minister'.

31 *Report on the Co-operation of Men and Women in Church, Family and Society for the World Council of Churches from the Congregational Union of England and Wales* (London: CUEW, 1965) p. 3.

32 Figures based only on stipendiary ministry. Local Ecumenical Partnerships included where served by a United Reformed Church minister, where large in membership, or with a substantial proportion of URC membership. Churches listed in vacancy but inducting a woman minister during the year not included.

33 Christine Fowler, *Unsung, Unpaid, Women NSM's* (1995 unpublished paper),.

34 Figures from the 2001 *United Reformed Church Year Book* show an increase in the proportion of paid women ministers to 67% (158) stipendiary and 33% (77) non-stipendiary. However the proportion of male ministers who are paid had risen faster – 84% (496) stipendiary and 16% (92) non-stipendiary for the same period.

35 *Decade Link No.8* (WCC: Geneva, 1991), p. 1.

36 *The Christian World*, 11 January 1917, p. 9.

37 *The Christian World*, 29 March 1917, p. 3.

38 *The Christian World*, 21 June 1917, p. 3.

39 *The Christian Commonwealth*, 28 March 1917.

40 Angela Holdsworth, *Out of the Doll's House –The Story of Women in the Twentieth Century* (BBC Books, 1988), p. 67.

41 Alan and Margaret Webster, Obituary of the Revd Dr Florence Tim Oi Li *The Independent*, 29 February 1992.

42 Kathleen Bliss, *The Service and Status of Women in the Churches* (London: SCM, 1952), p. 154.

43 Kathleen Bliss, *The Service and Status*, p. 154.

44 Letter from Revd Jacky Smith, 13 October 1995, DoD Archive.

45 Martin Pugh, *Women and the Women's Movement in Britain 1914-1959* (London: Macmillan Press, 1992), p. 191.

46 Maurice Collins, *Nancy Astor – An Informal Biography* (Faber and Faber, 1960), p. 77.

47 Shirley Williams, letter to *The Guardian*, 10 October 1979, quoted by Silvia Rodgers 'Women's Space in a Men's House: the British House of Commons' in Shirley Ardener, (ed.), *Women and Space – Ground Rules and Social Maps* (Oxford: Berg, 1993), p. 50.

48 Shirley Ardener, *Women and Space – Ground Rules and Social Maps* (Oxford: Berg 1993), p. 12.

49 Mrs Frank Penny, 'Women's medical work in India', in *Ladies at Work. Papers on Paid Employments for Ladies.* (London: A D Innes & Co, 1893), p. 86.

50 Norman Fairclough, *Language and Power* (London: Longman, 1989), p. 195.

51 Sheila Collins 'Theology in the politics of Appalachian Women' in Carol P Christ and Judith Plaskow (eds.), Womanspirit Rising – A Feminist Reader in Religion (San Francisco: Harper & Row, 1979), p. 154.

Chapter 12

1 A contribution from Susan Durber to the Daughters of Dissent conference in Mansfield College, Oxford on 19 September 1998.

Appendix

1 Kirsten Nielsen, *Ruth: A Commentary* (London: SCM, 1997).
2 E. Isichei, *Victorian Quakers* (Oxford 1970), pp. 94-5; 107-9.

3 L King, *Memoir of David King* (n.d.), pp. 287-8, 305-6, 316-20.

4 *Christian Advocate* (1880), pp. 381-3; cf D.M. Thompson, *Let Sects and Parties Fall* (Birmingham 1980), pp. 72-3.

5 *Christian Advocate* (1885: Annual Meeting number), p. 35.

6 *Christian Advocate* (1882), pp. 443-8, 475-9, 523-9; (1883), pp. 371-82; (1884: Annual Meeting number), p. 26; (1887), pp. 465-70, 508-15; (1888), p. 383.

7 *Christian Advocate* (1882), pp. 379-80.

8 *Churches of Christ Year Book* (1889), pp. 12-35; T.J. Ainsworth, *Sydney Black* (London 1911), pp. 51-3.

9 *Ecclesiastical Observer* (1889), pp. 125, 135-6.

10 *Christian Advocate* (1889), pp. 497-506.

11 Resolution 2 of Annual Conference, 1910, *Year Book 1910,* p. 163.

12 *Year Book 1912,* p. 53.

13 A C Watters, *History of the British Churches of Christ* (Indianapolis 1948), pp. 96-9; Thompson, *Let Sects and Parties Fall,* pp. 96-8.

14 Resolution 12, *Year Book 1909,* p. 166.

15 *Year Book 1910,* pp. 78-9, 86 (italics mine).

16 *Year Book 1912,* pp. 81, 86-7.

17 *Year Book 1913,* pp. 84 (italics mine), 86.

18 *Year Book 1935,* pp 69-70; 1941, p 154; *Christian Advocate* (1940), pp 481-4.

19 *Year Book 1953,* p. 141; *Christian Advocate* (1978), p. 116.

20 The book followed a similar pattern to that by the Indian missionary, Anne Piggot, entitled *Pen Pictures from India* (1928), which had a frontispiece showing the author with Biblewomen in India.

21 *Christian Advocate* (1963), pp. 545-7.

Index

Copyright Acknowledgements

Sheila Collins 'Theology in the politics of Appalachian Women' in *Womanspirit Rising: A Feminist Reader in Religion,* edited by Carol P Christ & Judith Plaskow (San Francisco: Harper & Row, 1979). Permission sought.

Madge Saunders, quoted in John Vincent, *Into the City* (London: Epworth Press, 1982). Used by permission.

Rosemary Radford Reuther, 'The Preacher and the Priest: Two Typologies of Ministry and the Ordination of Women' in Constance F Parvey (ed), *Ordination of Women in Ecumenical Perspective* (Geneva: World Council of Churches, 1980). Permission sought.

World Council of Churches Summary of Facts about the Ordination of Women in the Member Churches of the World Council of Churches (WCC: Geneva 1958). Permission sought.

Decade Link No 8 (WCC: Geneva, 1991). Permission sought.

Dorothy Havergal Shaw, 'What we want is a woman minister', *Women Speaking,* January to March 1971. Used by permission.

Spitting at Dragons, Towards a Feminist Theology of Sainthood, Elizabeth Stuart (London: Mowbray 1996), Mowbray, a Continuum Imprint. Used by permission.

Rosemary Radford Ruether & Eleanor McLaughlin (eds), *Women of Spirit: Female Leadership in the Jewish and Christian Traditions* (New York: Simon and Schuster, 1979). Permission sought.

Extracts from *Sinabada: Woman Among Warriors, A Biography of the Rev Sue Rankin* by Laurel Gray (Melbourne: Joint Board of Christian Education, 1989). Permission sought.

Kenneth Corfield, 'Elizabeth Heyrick: Radical Quaker' in Gail Malmgreen, *Religion in the Lives of English Women* (London: Croom Helm, 1986). Used by permission.

Extracts from Yvonne Tomes, 'Introducing two women ministers', *Church Times,* 2 May 1975. Used by permission.

Lavinia Byrne (ed), *Women in the Church – An Educational Resource* (London: CCBI, 1994). Used by permission.

Kenneth D Brown, *A Social History of the Nonconformist Ministry in England and Wales 1800-1930* (Oxford: Clarendon Press, 1988). Used by permission of Oxford University Press.

Norman Fairclough, *Language and Power* (London: Longman, 1989). Used by permission of Pearson Education Ltd, Publishers.

List of Illustrations